D1611562

BARE PAGE

BARE PAGE

Unbearably Good!

The Junior Service League of Americus, Georgia

The Junior Service League of Americus, Georgia, Incorporated, is an organization dedicated to the betterment of the educational, social, economic, cultural and civic conditions of our community.

Each purchase of **Unbearably Good!** will benefit the community through the volunteer projects of the Junior Service League of Americus.

First Edition
First Printing: January 1987 ..... 10,000 copies
Second Printing: May 1988 ..... 10,000 copies

To order additional copies of **Unbearably Good!,** use the order form in the back of the book or write:

Unbearably Good!
Post Office Box 92
Americus, Georgia 31709

Library of Congress Catalogue Card Number 86-82894
ISBN: 0-9617759-0-4

FATHER&SON
ASSOCIATES, INC.
4840 Tower Road • Tallahassee, FL 32303
(904) 562-2712

Unbearably Good!
Cookbook Committee

Meda DuBose Krenson, Cookbook Chairman, 1986
Lana Shaw Hicks, Cookbook Co-chairman, 1986
Susan Hendricks Powell, League President, 1986

FOOD AND RECIPES
Carole Bailey Mott, Chairman
Gail Goen Hooks, Co-Chairman
Alice Levy Argo
Ginger Hill Austin
Carol Mercer Baxter
Sandra Whitaker Bowen
Gayle Roobin Bullington
Phyllis Horn Daniel
Susan Colley Hall
Lana Shaw Hicks
Beth New Johnson
Meda DuBose Krenson
Anne Marshall Peagler
Susan Hendricks Powell
Trish Graves Powell
Susan Needles Schlecht
Tammy Lashley Teaford
Marjorie Cornwell Webb

DESIGN AND FORMAT
Sally Vestal Edgemon, Chairman
Isabelle Heard Sullivan, Co-chairman
Jane Broadhurst Arnold
Karen Brown Austin
Lana Crumpton Bass
Georgia Sullivan Duke
Meda DuBose Krenson
Susan Hendricks Powell
Claire Pryor Titshaw

MARKETING AND SALES
Lisa Heaton Edgemon, Chairman
Kristan Stroner Powell, Co-chairman
Lisa Whitten Bowen
Joy Collins Carter
Kitty Carlan Fricks
Theresa Holcomb Heffernan
Gail Stevenson Horne
Judy Wilson Klein
Gail Faucett Knox
Meda DuBose Krenson
Cheney Hill Reinhart
Susan Hendricks Powell
Karen Dillard Sheffield
Pamela Loper Stepp
Sandy Brown Sudduth
Susan Turner Winston

PRODUCTION
Betty Lee Bell Scott, Chairman
Linda Banks Hagins, Co-chairman
Gail Hall Barksdale
Jean Sheffield Buchanan
Martha Ann Sewell Fennessey
Diane Gammage Fletcher
Meda DuBose Krenson
Melanie Snead Mathis
Cathy Culpepper Miller
Lynn Light Rivers
Joyce Hadley Rogers
Carol Reddish Shiver
Mary Lynn Stevenson Sullivan
Sheila Amann Williams

Cookbook Committee — 1985
Sally Vestal Edgemon, Chairman
Claire Pryor Titshaw, Co-chairman
Beth New Johnson, League President

Special thanks to:
Neill Kipp, computer programmer, for his patience and help.

Mary Beth Powell Rogers, our artist, for her creativity and enthusiasm.

Mrs. William Smith, Mrs. Walter Rylander, Mrs. Tommy Warren, and Mrs. Ron Bass, our Honorary Advisors, for their advice and expertise.

Our families, who have been so supportive and patient in the last two years.

CONTRIBUTORS

Unbearably Good! is a collection of 565 recipes that were selected from over 2,000 submitted. We wish to thank all of you who contributed your "all time favorites". Regrettably, due to similarities and lack of space, all could not be included in this book. After two years of thoroughly testing and tasting, we have tried to present the most unbearably good recipes, while still being diversified enough to make every cook happy.

Arlene Achterberg
Alabama Grill
Americus Country Club
Alice Levy Argo
Mrs. J. Thomas Argo
Mrs. Ervan Arial, Jr.
Jane Broadhurst Arnold
Mr. Ricky Arnold
Karen Brown Austin
Ginger Hill Austin
Mrs. Leonard Banks
Mrs. George W. Bagley, IV
Gail Hall Barksdale
Mrs. A.F. Bass
Mrs. Aron F. Bass, Jr.
Lana Crumpton Bass
Mrs. Ron Bass
Carol Mercer Baxter
Mrs. Luther Bell
Mrs. Robert Bell
Mrs. Carlton Benford
Mrs. Billy Blair
Lisa Whitten Bowen
Sandra Whitaker Bowen
Mrs. Randy Bowen
Mrs. James P. Bowen
Mrs. N.C. Brown
Ruth Bryars
Mrs. James R. Buchanan
Jean Sheffield Buchanan
Bud and Alley's,
  Seaside, Florida
Gayle Roobin Bullington
Mrs. George Burkett
Mrs. Frank Butler
Mrs. Frank Butler, Jr.
Mrs. J.W. Calhoun
Mrs. Robert Calhoun
Minnie Burnham Calkins
Mrs. Roger Campbell
Mrs. A.B. Carlan
Mrs. Robert Carmichael
Mrs. Walker Carter
Mrs. Hugh Carter, Jr.
Mrs. Hugh Carter, Sr.
Mrs. James E. Carter,
  (Rosalynn)
Joy Collins Carter
Mrs. J.C. Carter, Jr.

Mrs. Frank Castellow
Mary Chastain
The Cheeseboard,
  Americus, Georgia
Mrs. J.D. Clements
Martha Cobb
Mrs. Preston Cobb
Mrs. W.H. Cobb
Mrs. W.H. Cobb, Jr.
Martha Cody
Mrs. Ferd Cohen
Mrs. Jerome Cohen
Lottie Cohron
Mrs. Henry L. Collier
Mrs. William F. Collins
Mrs. Larry Comer
Mrs. Nell Council
Mrs. R.T. Crabb
Mrs. Charles Crisp
Sue Crum
Mrs. Leon Culpepper
Mr. Stephen Culpepper
Mrs. N.M. Cunningham
Mrs. C.W. Curry
Phyllis Horn Daniel
Mrs. B.R.B. Davis
Mrs. Elmo Davis
Mrs. Kenneth Davis
Mrs. Julian Dillard
Mrs. Jim Dolson, Jr.
Mrs. Edwin Rembert
  DuBose
Mrs. James Dudley
Mrs. Lewis Duke
Georgia Sullivan Duke
Mrs. Ricky Duke
Mrs. Bon Durham
Mr. Steve Durham
Doris Dykes
Lisa Heaton Edgemon
Sarah Vestal Edgemon
Mrs. Joe Ellis
Mrs. George Ellis
Mrs. George Ellis, Jr.
Mrs. W.H. Emmett
Mrs. Mark English
Mrs. Harry Entrekin
Mrs. Paul Eusner
Carole Hicks Farr

Mrs. Fred Faucette
Martha Ann Sewell
  Fennessey
Mrs. T.P. Fennessey
Mr. James R. Ferguson
Mrs. Luke Flatt
Diane Gammage Fletcher
Mrs. Leonard Fletcher
Rosalind Lipscomb Forrest
Catherine Fouche
Phyllis Freemon
Kitty Carlan Fricks
Mrs. Walker Fricks
Mrs. Mac Furlow
Mrs. Johnny Gaddis
Mrs. Dan Gammage
Mrs. T. Schley Gatewood, Jr.
Linda James Gayton
Mrs. Lee George
Mary Gilbert
Mrs. Johnny Gladden
Mrs. John Gladden
Mrs. Larry Glass
Mrs. Roy E. Goen
Mrs. Clarence Graddick
Mrs. Jeff Green
Lucille Greene
Mrs. Wilson Greene
Mrs. E.S. Hagins
Linda Banks Hagins
Irene Haive
Mrs. Charles Hall
Susan Colley Hall
Mrs. Carey Harbuck, Jr.
Mrs. Plez Hardin
Mrs. Bill Harris
Mrs. James Hawkins
Mrs. John P. Heard
Theresa Holcomb Heffernan
Mrs. Larry Heisler
Mrs. Charles Henderson
Mrs. Charles J. Hendricks
Mrs. Richard Hewitt
Mrs. L.C. Hicks, Jr.
Lana Shaw Hicks
Mrs. Byron Hill
Mrs. R.B. Hill
Mrs. Charles Hodges
Mrs. Robert Hodges

Mrs. Charles Hogg
Mrs. John S. Holt
Mrs. Thomas B. Hooks, Jr.
Gail Goen Hooks
Rep. George Hooks
Bonnie Hoos
Mrs. Fred Horn
Gail Stevenson Horne
Mrs. J.W.C. Horne, Jr.
Mrs. J.W. Horne, Sr.
Mrs. Sam Hunter
Mrs. Stewart Howell
Mrs. Woodrow James
Beth New Johnson
Debra Johnson
Phyllis Johnston
Mrs. E.L. Jones
Mrs. F.L. Jones
Mrs. Phil Jones, Sr.
Mrs. Robert Jones
Mrs. Charles King
Mrs. Hulme Kinnebrew, III
Mrs. E.H. Kinnebrew, Jr.
Judy Wilson Klein
Gail Faucett Knox
Meda DuBose Krenson
Mrs. Charles Lanier
Mrs. W.W. Larsen, Jr.
Mrs. Henry Lumpkin
Mr. W.H. McCall
Mrs. W.H. McCall
Mrs. Dennis McEntire
Mrs. S.H. McKee
Mr. Jerry McLurch
Thelma S. McMichael
Mrs. Marvin McNeill
Mrs. R.D. McNeill
Kay McWilliams
Mrs. Tony Maddox
Mrs. T.O. Marshall
Mrs. T.O. Marshall, Jr.
Mrs. Floyd Martin
Mrs. Guerry Mashburn
Mrs. Herbert Mason, Jr.
Mrs. Evan Mathis, Sr.
Melanie Snead Mathis
Mrs. Tom Matthews
Mrs. Sam Merritt
Cathy Culpepper Miller
Mr. John Morgan
Mrs. John Morgan
Mrs. Bill Morton
Carole Bailey Mott
Mrs. Jim Moyd
Mrs. J. Frank Myers
Mrs. Brantley New
Mrs. Horace Odum
Mrs. George Oliver

Mrs. Harris Oxford
Mrs. Hubert Parker
Mrs. Emory Parker
Mrs. Roy Parker
Anne Marshall Peagler
Mrs. Robert S. Perry
Frankie Lee Phillips
Mrs. J.B. Phinizy
Lorraine Pinkerton
Mrs. Robert Pond
Mrs. Ed Pope
Mrs. John M. Pope
Mrs. Ronald D. Potts
Mrs. John Powell
Kristan Stroner Powell
Trish Graves Powell
Susan Hendricks Powell
Mrs. Spencer Pryor
Mrs. David Purvis
Mrs. Earl Rainey
Mrs. James D. Ray
Mrs. Roy Don Reeves
Mrs. Charles Reeves, Jr.
Cheney Hill Reinhart
Mary A. Reinhart
Carolyn Kinnebrew Riccardi
Mrs. John Rivers
Mrs. Edward C. Roberts
Joyce Hadley Rogers
Mae Rogers
Mrs. Avrom Roobin
Mrs. Arthur Rylander
Mrs. Walter Rylander
Susan Needles Schlecht
Frances Hogg Scoggins
Betty Lee Bell Scott
Debbie Scott
Mr. Gordon Searcy
Jeni Seiler
Mrs. Frank Sheffield, Jr.
Mrs. John W. Sheffield
Mrs. John W. Sheffield, Jr.
Karen Dillard Sheffield
Mrs. Langdon C. Sheffield
Carol Reddish Shiver
Eva Claire Shiver
Mrs. Jack Short
Bettye Sims
Mrs. J.E. Slappey
Mrs. Leon Slappey
Mrs. Herschel Smith
Mrs. Herschel Smith, Jr.
Mrs. James W. Smith
Mrs. Stephen R. Smith
Susan Smith
Mrs. William E. Smith
Carolyn Sproull

Mrs. Steve Stanfield
Claire Smith Stapleton
Mrs. Albin Steiner
Mrs. Marcus Stephanides
Pamela Loper-Stepp
Angie Stevens
Mrs. John T. Stevenson, Sr.
Mrs. Henry Claiborne Stokes
Janiss Katherine Stone
Pam Stowers
Mrs. R.B. Strickland
Eleanor Stroner
Mrs. Gary Stroner
Mrs. Gene Stroner
Mrs. Roy Studstill
Sandy Brown Sudduth
Mrs. Will Sullivan, III
Mary Lynn Stevenson
 Sullivan
Isabelle Heard Sullivan
Mrs. Matt Sullivan
Mrs. Wally Summers
Mrs. Neill Taylor
Mrs. George Teaford
Tammy Lashley Teaford
Mrs. T. Edwin Tharpe
Mrs. Thomas Tharpe
Mrs. M.B. Thomas
Claire Pryor Titshaw
Judy Tott
Mrs. Allen Turner
Mr. Billy Tye
Mrs. Billy Tye
Jackie Tyer
Mrs. Hubert Veal
Mrs. James Edward Vestal
Libby Wade
Mrs. Bob Wall
Mrs. Chuck Wall
Mrs. Rowe Wall
Mrs. David Wansley
Mrs. Tommy Warren
Mr. Ard Watson
Mrs. Falba Webb
Marjie Cornwell Webb
Mrs. W.W. Webb
Mrs. Marshall Welch
Sheila Amann Williams
Shirley Williams
Marsha Wilson
Mrs. Frank A. Wilson, III
Susan Turner Winston
Mrs. M.H. Woods
Mrs. Tom Wylie
Mrs. William Wysochansky
Frances W. Young
Hallie Hendricks Young

6

This Bears Reading

 next to a recipe title indicates that it was selected as a favorite from the out-of-print **Americus Recipes**, published in 1957 and 1961 by the Junior Welfare League of Americus.

Brand names have not been used except where absolutely necessary.

BEAR IN MIND below a recipe gives variations, storage or cooking hints.

BEAR FLAIR below a recipe suggests different and interesting ways to garnish and/or present the finished dish.

On the back of each section divider page you will find:

BEARING GIFTS — One tradition we all enjoy is the gift of food. Something special that comes from the heart, it is a constant reminder of the giver as it is enjoyed. Therefore, we have suggested gift ideas for every section, with specific recipes to select for different occasions.

BEAR ESSENTIALS FOR ENTERTAINING — In today's busy world we can all use some helpful ideas for saving time while we impress our guests. For every section you will find new and attractive serving and presentation ideas.

At the end of the book, you will find *GRIN AND BEAR IT,* with helpful hints for:

WHEN YOUR CUPBOARD IS BARE — what you can substitute when you don't have time to run to the store.

WHEN GUESTS CATCH YOU BARE-HANDED — quick and easy ideas to whip up on the spur of the moment.

WHEN YOU CAN'T BEAR THE RESULTS — tips for salvaging cooking disasters.

TABLE OF CONTENTS

A BEAR TAIL

There once was a bear so charming
With a big smile so disarming.
His eyes did twinkle,
But his brow did wrinkle —
When he heard some news so alarming!

Some people said he was too cute?!
At first he thought — what a hoot.
But then he knew
He must convince a few
That his place in history had a firm root!

His reputation he felt was at stake —
What a terrible error to make.
What would Roosevelt say
As in his grave he lay?
"Why, Teddy's a classic for goodness sake!"

He's been around for years and years,
Making people smile and drying up tears.
He'd do anything he could
To be unbearably good,
And help sell cookbooks, have no fears!

— Meda Krenson

Appetizers

"BEARING GIFTS"

*KRAUT CHEESE BALL, page 42 ... when ready to shape into ball, divide into 6 individual balls. Place on small holiday plates. Wrap with clear wrap; add a bow and give with a stack of crackers and a copy of the recipe.

*BEAR CLAWS, page 11 ... tie "hobo-style" in a bandana. Great for football weekends and tailgate parties.

*SMOKEY THE BEAR (cheese ball), page 43 ... or use any of our terrific cheese balls and give with a cheeseboard and spreader.

*MARVELOUS MUSTARD SAUCE, page 44 ... save mustard jars, pour in sauce, add a cloth "top" and a ribbon.

*CHEESE DATE POCKETS, page 27 ... take these while still warm in a cloth-lined basket to a new neighbor. Plan to stay for coffee and a chat.

*SMOKED SAUSAGE ROLL, page 32 ... a great do-ahead gift. Make several and freeze. Give at Christmas in a mini market basket; add a jar of MARVELOUS MUSTARD SAUCE for the finishing touch.

*PADDINGTON BEAR'S CHEESE STRAWS, page 27 ... pack in an attractive tin and attach tin to a stuffed bear.

*CHEESEBOARD HERBED CREAM CHEESE, page 34 ... this is great for piping into fresh snowpeas (blanch snowpeas one minute in boiling water, then chill in ice water for one minute, drain and pat dry; then stuff the peas).

*ARTICHOKES AND CHILIES DIP, page 37 ... these ingredients can be purchased and placed in a 1-quart size electric crockpot along with the recipe.

"BARE ESSENTIALS FOR ENTERTAINING"

*When entertaining, always have something cooking when guests arrive, even if it's a pot of simmering herbs or spices. The fragrance greeting your guests adds an extra welcome.

*Red or green bell pepper, fresh pineapple, acorn squash or any winter squash can be hollowed and filled with a variety of dips or spreads. Various fruits make nice bases in which to place toothpicks.

*Use large sea shells or miniature flower pots with liners to hold dips and spreads for pool parties. Use a baby pool filled with ice and drinks and beach toy buckets and shovels as serving bowls and utensils for buffet.

*Create olive rose buds by removing pimiento from large green stuffed olive. Using knife, cut the olive into "fourths", but not all the way through, only enough to pipe in softened flavored cream cheese. Shape to resemble rose bud. Arrange in groups of 3 with parsley sprigs.

*Flowers can be used to hold dips and spreads in the same way that hollowed-out vegetables can; for instance, for cocktail buffet, cover an old-fashioned cake plate with grape or watercress leaves. Arrange stately hollyhocks atop the leaves then fill each blossom with a thick-consistency dip. Each person can pick up their individual serving as they go through the buffet line.

*Make pastry shells, using madeleine pans; bake and fill with a shrimp salad.

*To extend refrigerator life of parsley, wash in cold water, then place stems in warm water for a couple of hours; dry parsley and wrap in paper towel, put in ziploc bag.

Bear Claws

4	bacon slices, cooked crisp and crumbled	1	cup shredded cheddar cheese
1	green onion, with top, chopped		Dash red pepper
4	tablespoons mayonnaise	1	(9-inch) pastry shell

Preheat oven to 375°. Combine bacon, onion, mayonnaise, cheese and red pepper and mix well. Roll pastry into a 9x12-inch rectangle. Cut rectangle in half lengthwise. Spread each rectangle with cheese mixture. Starting on the long side, fold over 3 to 4 times, pressing lightly to seal edges. Turn seam side down, cut into 1-inch pieces. Make 2 cuts in center of each piece. Spread to create a claw effect. Bake on ungreased cookie sheet 10 to 15 minutes until golden brown.

Yield: 24 bear claws

BEAR IN MIND: *Ready-made refrigerated pastry in dairy section may be substituted. Must be pressed or rolled into rectangles.*

Fabulous Phyllo

8	ounces Brie cheese	1	(10-ounce) jar apricot preserves
¼	(1-pound) package phyllo sheets, thawed		
1	stick unsalted butter, melted		

Preheat oven to 400°. Cut cheese into bite-size pieces. Cut the phyllo into 3-inch squares. (Keep squares you are not working with covered with plastic wrap to prevent drying out.) Brush each square with melted butter. Layer 3 to 4 squares and put a cheese piece in center. Spoon on ½ teaspoon preserves. Fold squares in a pillow-shape. Continue until you "run out" of cheese and squares. Place on cookie sheet. Bake 5 to 8 minutes or until golden brown. Serve warm.

Yield: 5 dozen

BEAR IN MIND:
- (1) *These can be prepared a few days in advance, refrigerated and baked at serving time.*
- (2) *Look for phyllo sheets in freezer section of supermarket or ask your local grocer to order for special occasions.*

Brie en Croûte

1	(3-ounce) package cream cheese, softened	1	(4½-ounce) package Brie cheese (purchase the circle form, NOT the wedges)
½	stick butter, softened		
¾	cup all-purpose flour	½	teaspoon sesame seeds

Preheat oven to 400°. In bowl, combine cream cheese, butter and flour. Using pastry blender, blend until particles resemble "small peas". Shape into ball and divide in half. Wrap in foil or plastic wrap and chill at least 1 hour. On lightly-floured surface, roll out each half about ⅛-inch thick. Cut each half into 6-inch circle, reserving excess dough for trim. Place one circle of dough on ungreased baking sheet. Place Brie cheese in center of dough; top with remaining pastry circle. Pinch pastry edges together to seal. Roll out excess dough into decorative shapes and place on top and sides of croûte as desired. Sprinkle with sesame seeds. Bake 15 to 17 minutes or until golden brown. Let stand several minutes before cutting into wedges. Serve warm.

Yield: 16 to 18 servings

BEAR IN MIND: *This needs to be served warm for optimum flavor.*

Zesty Parmesan Crisps

8	to 10 slices white or wheat bread, crusts removed	1½	cups grated Parmesan cheese
1¼	teaspoons chili powder	2	sticks melted butter

Cut each slice of bread into 8 strips (easier to do when slightly frozen). Place on baking sheet and toast 5 minutes. Meanwhile, in shallow dish, combine chili powder and Parmesan cheese. In another dish, pour the melted butter. Roll each stick first in butter, then in cheese mixture. Refrigerate overnight or freeze. When ready to serve, place on baking sheet and bake at 400° for 4 minutes (5 to 6 minutes if frozen) or until golden brown. Drain on paper towels.

Yield: 6 to 7 dozen sticks

Asparagus Toasties

2	sticks butter	1	cup grated sharp cheddar cheese
2	tablespoons minced onion		
1	tablespoon lemon juice	½	stick butter, melted
¼	teaspoon garlic juice, or 1 garlic clove, pressed	24	black olive slices
		24	pimiento slices
24	slices white bread		
1	(15-ounce) can asparagus spears, drained		

Preheat oven to 350°. Combine 2 sticks butter, onion, lemon juice and garlic juice; set aside. Trim crusts from bread. Using rolling pin, press each slice to ⅛-inch thickness. Spread each piece of bread with butter mixture, about 2 teaspoons per slice. Place asparagus spear on each slice, sprinkle cheddar cheese over spear and roll up tightly. Secure with wooden tooth pick. Brush rolls with melted butter and place on ungreased baking sheet. Bake 35 minutes. Remove pick and top each roll with a black olive slice and a pimiento slice. Serve warm.

Yield: 24 "toasties"

Ham Delights

1	pound ham	1	stick margarine, softened
5	ounces Swiss cheese	1	teaspoon Worcester- shire sauce
1	medium onion, cubed		
3	tablespoons prepared mustard	2	packages small dinner rolls (approximately 24 rolls per package)
3	tablespoons poppy seed		

Preheat oven to 400°. Place ham, cheese and onion in bowl of food processor with steel blade. Process until finely chopped. Add mustard, poppy seed, margarine and Worcestershire to ham mixture. Mix by hand. Take rolls out of package as a whole unit. Slice off top layer halfway down. Spread with mixture and replace top. Place on cookie sheet, cover with foil and bake 15 to 20 minutes.

Yield: 48 small sandwiches

Chicken Salad Mini-Cream Puffs

Mini-Cream Puffs:

½   stick margarine
½   cup water
½   cup all-purpose flour
⅛   teaspoon salt
2   large eggs, room temperature

Chicken Salad Filling:

2   cups finely chopped cooked chicken
½   cup finely minced celery
1   apple, finely chopped (unpeeled)
2   tablespoons finely diced pimiento
5   tablespoons mayonnaise
5   tablespoons sour cream
1   teaspoon fresh lemon juice
1   teaspoon sugar
½   teaspoon salt
½   teaspoon freshly ground pepper
1   tablespoon finely chopped green onion

For Cream Puffs:
Preheat oven to 425°. Lightly oil 2 cookie sheets. In 1-quart saucepan over high heat, bring margarine and water to a boil. As soon as margarine is melted, add flour and salt all at once, stirring constantly with wooden spoon until dough forms into shape of a ball. Remove from heat and cool about 5 minutes. Add eggs, one at a time, beating well after each egg, until dough comes back to a "round mass". Drop by scant teaspoon onto cookie sheet. Bake 10 minutes at 425°; lower temperature to 375° and bake another 10 to 15 minutes or until puffs are golden brown and no moisture is evident. Cool completely on wire rack. Cut off top third of cream puffs (can leave slightly attached, if desired). Scoop out any mixture that may be in center. Fill with chicken salad.

For Chicken Salad:
Preheat oven to 400°. Combine chicken, celery, apple and pimiento in bowl. In separate bowl combine mayonnaise, sour cream, lemon juice, sugar, salt, pepper and green onion. Pour over chicken mixture, toss gently and fill cream puffs. Bake 5 to 7 minutes before serving.

Yield: about 40 (1-inch) cream puffs

BEAR IN MIND:
> *(1) Bake the puffs as quickly as you mix them up because the dough will "deflate" if allowed to "sit around" too long and the cream puffs will collapse. Also, if you take out of the oven before they are dry in the center, they will collapse.*
> *(2) The cream puff shells freeze well after baking and before filling with chicken salad.*

Cheddar Cheese Puffs

1	recipe Mini-Cream Puff	¼	cup chopped pimiento-stuffed green olives
¾	cup spreadable cheddar cheese	1	tablespoon minced chives
1	tablespoon mayonnaise		

Prepare Mini-Cream Puffs according to previous recipe. Whip cheese and mayonnaise until fluffy. Add olives and chives and mix well. Cut off tops of puffs and scoop out moist centers. Place about 1 teaspoon of mixture in each puff. Replace tops and refrigerate until serving time.

Yield: 25 puffs

Mushroom Roll-Ups

2	(8-ounce) cans refrigerated crescent dinner rolls	1	teaspoon seasoned salt
1	(8-ounce) package cream cheese, softened	1	egg, slightly beaten
1	(4-ounce) can mushroom pieces, drained and chopped	1	to 2 tablespoons poppy seeds

Preheat oven to 375°. Open both cans of crescent rolls. Unroll dough, but do not tear dough into triangles. Separate dough into 8 rectangles. Pinch "seams" together. Mix well cream cheese, mushrooms and salt, then spread equally on each rectangle of dough. Roll each rectangle starting with longest side in jelly-roll fashion. Pinch ends to seal. Cut each rolled rectangle into 1-inch slices and place seamside down on ungreased baking pan. Beat egg well and brush each piece with egg then sprinkle with poppy seed. Bake 10 to 12 minutes. Serve hot.

Yield: 4 dozen roll-ups

BEAR IN MIND: *These can be prepared in advance up to the "brush with egg" stage, and refrigerated several hours until ready to bake.*

Miniature Pizzas

Sauce:

1	(3-ounce) can Italian tomato paste
1	garlic clove, pressed
¼	teaspoon Worcestershire sauce
¼	cup water
¼	teaspoon oregano
1	teaspoon salt
½	teaspoon pepper

Pastry:

½	teaspoon salt
2	cups all-purpose flour
¼	cup cold milk
¼	cup oil

Topping:

1	cup grated sharp cheddar or grated Mozzerella cheese
6	to 8 bacon slices, cooked and crumbled

Combine all ingredients of sauce. Preheat oven to 450°. Add salt to flour; add milk and oil. Roll until ⅛ inch thick. Cut into 2½-inch rounds, remove centers from half the rounds with 2-inch biscuit cutter to make rings. Set rings on top of rounds. Fill centers with cheese, one teaspoon pizza sauce and crumbled bacon on top. Bake on cookie sheet 12 minutes.

Yield: 3 dozen pizzas

Hot Ripe Olive Hors d'Oeuvres

1	cup chopped ripe olives
½	cup finely chopped onion
1½	cups grated cheddar cheese
¼	teaspoon salt
½	cup mayonnaise
6	bacon slices, cooked crisp and crumbled
1	teaspoon curry powder
22	slices very thin-sliced bread

Mix together olives, onions, cheese, salt, mayonnaise, bacon and curry powder. (Makes thick mixture.) Trim crust from bread and cut each slice into 4 squares. Toast on one side under the broiler. Spread mixture on untoasted side. Freeze until ready to use, or place on cookie sheet and broil a few minutes until lightly browned. Serve immediately.

Yield: 88 hors d'oeuvres

BEAR IN MIND: *This is great cold! Spread on bread and roll up jelly roll fashion, then slice in ½-inch pinwheel slices.*

Buttercups

4	hard-cooked eggs
2	tablespoons chopped radish
1	tablespoon chopped green onion
2	tablespoons mayonnaise
1	tablespoon Italian salad dressing
¼	teaspoon salt
¼	teaspoon freshly ground pepper
¼	teaspoon Worcestershire sauce
1	loaf unsliced whole wheat bread
30	thin radish slices and sprigs of parsley

Shell eggs, chop fine and combine with radish, onion, mayonnaise, salad dressing, salt, pepper and Worcestershire. Chill. Cut loaf bread into 1-inch thick slices. Cut into rounds with small biscuit cutter. Hollow out rounds with kitchen shears, leaving ¼-inch sides and bottoms. To serve, brush inside of bread cups with mayonnaise or butter; fill cups with egg salad. Quarter thin radish slices. Arrange on egg salad "buttercups" and add sprigs of parsley.

Yield: 30 sandwiches

BEAR IN MIND:

(1) Nice to use with other party sandwiches for an open house or bridge.

(2) If preparing the day before, brush with butter instead of mayonnaise, fill with egg salad and store in airtight container in refrigerator.

🐾 Deviled Egg Sandwiches

12	hard-cooked eggs, put through food chopper
6	bacon slices, cooked crisp and crumbled very fine
1	cup finely chopped celery
½	cup chopped sweet mixed pickles
1	teaspoon prepared mustard
	Salt to taste
	Dash red pepper
	Mayonnaise to make spreading consistency

Combine all ingredients and spread on bread.

Yield: 16 sandwiches

🐾 Rich Rum Sandwiches

1	pint whipping cream	2	tablespoons mayonnaise
1	tablespoon sugar	4	tablespoons rum
1	cup chopped dates	24	slices thin-sliced white
¼	cup chopped pecans		bread, crust removed

Whip cream with sugar until stiff. Fold in remaining ingredients and spread between thin bread slices. Cut in "quarters".

Yield: 48 triangles

Shrimp Toast

1½	pounds fresh shrimp, peeled and deveined	¼	teaspoon crushed rosemary
1	(8-ounce) can water chestnuts, drained	1	egg, beaten
½	cup chopped green onion tops	15	slices or more of white or whole wheat bread, crusts removed
1	teaspoon salt		Fine dry bread crumbs
1	(0.035-ounce) package artificial sweetener	¾	cup oil, add more when needed

In food processor, using steel blade, grind shrimp, water chestnuts and green onions to form a paste. Add salt, sweetener, rosemary and egg. Mix well. Spread mixture on bread. Sprinkle lightly with bread crumbs. Cut each slice into 4 triangles. Heat oil (1 inch deep) in frying pan. Fry each triangle shrimp-side down first, then brown on other side, about 2 minutes on each side. Drain on paper towel. Serve warm.

Yield: 60 triangles

BEAR IN MIND: *May be frozen after cooking. When ready to serve, defrost and reheat in 400° oven 5 to 7 minutes. Watch closely, they brown quickly!*

Shrimp Wraps

2	pounds fresh jumbo shrimp, peeled and deveined
2	cups lemon juice
1	tablespoon garlic juice

1	pound bacon, each slice cut in thirds
3	eggs
1½	cups all-purpose flour
	Salt and pepper to taste

Place fresh shrimp in medium-size bowl. Pour lemon and garlic juice over shrimp. Cover and chill 2 to 4 hours. Remove shrimp from marinade. Wrap slice of bacon around each shrimp, stretching it; secure with toothpick. Beat eggs in small bowl. Combine flour, salt and pepper in another small bowl. Dip each shrimp into egg, then into flour mixture. Fry on medium-high heat until golden brown.

Yield: 6 servings

Shrimp Mousse

1	(10¾-ounce) can tomato soup or cream of mushroom soup or cream of shrimp soup
1	(8-ounce) package cream cheese
2	packages unflavored gelatin
½	cup cold water

¼	cup chopped bell pepper, optional
½	cup chopped onion
½	cup chopped celery
¼	teaspoon dry mustard
1	cup mayonnaise
2	(4½-ounce) cans small shrimp, save a few to garnish if desired

Lightly oil a 4-cup mold (shell or fish mold is great!) In a saucepan, heat soup and beat in cheese until smooth. Sprinkle gelatin in cold water. Add to soup mixture and cool. Add remaining ingredients and blend well. Pour into mold and chill overnight. Serve with crackers.

Yield: serves 45 easily with other hors d'oeuvres

BEAR FLAIR: Put in individual molds or tins and serve on lettuce leaves for luncheon. Garnish with tiny whole, cooked shrimp and fresh dill or parsley.

Shrimp Stuffed Celery

1 (4½-ounce) can shrimp, drained and mashed
2 tablespoons chopped chives
2 teaspoons lemon juice
2 dashes hot pepper sauce
¼ cup mayonnaise
¼ teaspoon salt
1 bunch celery

Mix shrimp, chives, lemon juice, pepper sauce, mayonnaise and salt. Stuff celery stalks that have been cut into 2-inch pieces.

Yield: 8 to 10 servings

BEAR IN MIND: *Rinse canned shrimp before using and let marinate in a little lemon juice at least one hour to improve flavor.*

Creamy Marinated Shrimp

2 to 3 pounds fresh shrimp, peeled and deveined
1 cup mayonnaise
1 cup sour cream
1 (0.6 ounce) package dry Italian dressing mix

In large saucepan, boil shrimp until they turn pink. Drain. Stop cooking by placing shrimp under cold water. Mix mayonnaise, sour cream and dressing mix. Pour over shrimp. Cover and chill at least 2 hours. Serve with picks or cocktail forks.

Yield: 12 to 16 servings

BEAR IN MIND: *Overcooking will cause shrimp to be tough.*

Barbecued Shrimp

2 pounds fresh shrimp, peeled and deveined
1 cup corn oil
2 tablespoons Worcestershire sauce
1 garlic clove, pressed
1 teaspoon dry mustard
2 tablespoons minced parsley
Juice of 2 lemons

Combine all ingredients and marinate at least 2 hours in refrigerator. Put shrimp on skewers and cook over charcoal. (They cook very quickly.)

Yield: 8 servings

Shrimp Sea Island

5 pounds fresh shrimp, peeled, deveined and cooked	1½ cups cider vinegar
10 mild white onions, thinly sliced	1 (3½-ounce) jar capers, with juice
2 cups virgin olive oil	Salt, sugar, hot pepper sauce and Worcestershire sauce to taste

Layer shrimp and onions in a deep casserole. Combine remaining ingredients to make dressing. Pour dressing over shrimp and onions. Cover and chill 12 hours before serving. Stir occasionally. Lift out of dressing and arrange on large platter. Garnish with parsley.

Yield: 10 to 12 servings

BEAR FLAIR:

(1) Can also wrap each shrimp in smoked turkey slice and pick onto beautiful head of savoy cabbage.

(2) May add 2 (14-ounce) cans artichoke hearts and/or 1½ pounds fresh button mushrooms.

(3) Prepare an ice ring by placing greenery and seashells in the bottom of a 5 to 6-cup ring mold. Fill with water and freeze. Unmold onto serving platter and fill with shrimp. Garnish with parsley.

Little Crabmeat Canapés

1 (5-ounce) jar Old English Cheese Spread	1 (7-ounce) can crabmeat, rinsed and cartilage removed
1 stick butter	
½ teaspoon garlic powder	6 English muffins
½ teaspoon celery salt	Paprika to taste

Mix all ingredients except muffins and paprika. Set aside. Separate muffins into 12 halves. Spread mixture generously on each half. Cut each half into 4 triangles. Place on cookie sheet and freeze. Transfer to plastic bags for storage when frozen.

When ready to serve, place on cookie sheet, sprinkle with paprika, and broil 5 minutes.

Yield: 48 pieces

BEAR IN MIND: *Cutting is easier when muffin halves are allowed to freeze slightly. Cut and return to freezer.*

Salmon Cucumber Rounds

1	(3-ounce) package cream cheese, softened	¼	cup green onions, thinly sliced
2	tablespoons sour cream	2	tablespoons fresh dill, chopped
1	(3¼-ounce) can salmon, drained	1	tablespoon lemon juice
3	ounces smoked salmon, finely chopped	¼	teaspoon pepper
½	cup bread crumbs	3	to 4 medium cucumbers, unpared

Combine all ingredients except cucumbers in small bowl and blend thoroughly. Score cucumbers with the tines of a fork until they have a striped effect. Cut points off each end and scoop out pulp and seeds. Drain on paper towels at least 30 minutes. Fill hollow cylinder with salmon mixture. Place each filled cucumber on waxed paper and wrap securely. Chill several hours or overnight. About 1 hour before serving, cut cucumbers in ¼-inch slices and arrange on serving plate. Keep chilled until serving time.

Yield: about 48 rounds

BEAR FLAIR: *Garnish with fresh dill or parsley placed on center of each.*

Belgian Endive Hors d'Oeuvres

2	short heads Belgian endive	⅛	teaspoon finely minced garlic
1	(3-ounce) package cream cheese, softened	⅛	teaspoon chopped fresh marjoram
2	tablespoons unsalted butter, softened	⅛	teaspoon chopped fresh dill
2	teaspoons finely chopped chives		

Wipe endive with damp cloth. Never soak in water. Cut bottom off, leaving 2 to 3-inch leaves. Mix cream cheese, butter, chives, garlic, marjoram and dill in blender or food processor. Using a spatula, spread about 1 teaspoon of cheese mixture near the base of each endive leaf. Garnish with a sprig of dill toward top of leaf. Can arrange the "spears" of endive around a spiral-zested lemon with chive flowers.

Yield: 25 appetizers

BEAR IN MIND:

(1) Can add finely grated raw carrots and onion for color and flavor.
(2) Add well-drained marinated shrimp.
(3) Packaged Boursin or Rondale cheese can be used instead of "home-made" cheese mixture.
(4) Store endive in cool, dark place. If not using immediately, place in brown bag and put in crisper section of refrigerator.

Mini-Spinach Pies

1	(10-ounce) package frozen spinach	2	tablespoons chopped green onion
6	eggs, beaten	1	tablespoon snipped fresh parsley
1	(3-ounce) package cream cheese, softened		Salt and pepper to taste
¼	cup grated sharp cheddar cheese	16	miniature pastry shells, thawed

Preheat oven to 425°. Cook spinach according to package directions. Drain well. Combine eggs, cream cheese and cheddar cheese. Mix well. Stir in spinach, onion, parsley, salt and pepper. Pour into pastry shells. Bake 8 to 10 minutes or until set. Remove and let stand 8 to 10 minutes before serving.

Yield: 16 pies

BEAR IN MIND:

(1) You can use 2 frozen spinach soufflés cooked until almost done. Then add onions, cream cheese, cheddar cheese, parsley, salt and pepper. Pour into pastry shells and bake.
(2) Can also use 4 regular pastry shells thawed and rolled into circle to cover pie plate. This makes a nice brunch pie.

Marinated Vegetables

2	heads cauliflower, cut in medium-size pieces	3	squash, sliced
3	green peppers, cut in medium-size pieces	2	cucumbers, sliced
2	pounds carrots, cut in strips	½	cup salad oil
1	bunch celery, cut in strips	½	cup olive oil
1	pound mushrooms, stem ends removed	3	cups tarragon vinegar
1	bunch broccoli, divided into flowerets, stems cut in medium-size pieces	½	to ¾ cup sugar
		3	garlic cloves, minced
		1	tablespoon prepared mustard
		1	tablespoon salt
		2	teaspoons tarragon leaves Pepper to taste

Combine all vegetables. Combine remaining ingredients and pour over vegetables. Cover and chill at least 12 hours. Vegetables should be stirred occasionally.

Yield: 30 servings

BEAR IN MIND: *Any fresh vegetable that is good raw may be used.*

Stuffed Mushroom Caps

20	fresh mushrooms, medium-size	1	(8-ounce) package cream cheese, cut into 8 small pieces
3	ounces pepperoni, sliced ¼-inch thick		

Wash mushrooms and drain on paper towels. Remove stems from mushrooms and put in food processor with steel blade. Add pepperoni and cream cheese. Process until mixture is smooth. Spoon mixture into mushroom caps. Broil 3 to 5 minutes. Serve warm.

Yield: 20 mushroom caps

BEAR FLAIR: *For an extra special effect, you can put the pepperoni cream cheese mixture into a decorating bag with a large star tip and pipe mixture into mushroom caps. Place on baking sheet and put in freezer 5 to 10 minutes before baking to help mixture hold shape.*

Ethereal Mushrooms

2	sticks butter	½	teaspoon garlic powder
2	cups burgundy wine	1	cup boiling water
2	teaspoons Worcester-shire sauce	2	beef bouillon cubes
½	teaspoon dill seed	2	chicken bouillon cubes
½	teaspoon pepper	2	pounds fresh mushrooms

Combine all ingredients except mushrooms in large Dutch oven. Bring to a slow boil over medium heat. Add mushrooms. Reduce to simmer. Cover and cook 5 to 6 hours. Remove lid. Mushrooms will be very dark. Cook another 3 to 4 hours. Serve as an appetizer in a chafing dish with toothpicks or warm in ramekins as a side dish.

Yield: 10 servings

BEAR IN MIND: Freeze in small quantities (1½ to 2 cups) and thaw as needed. Good for Christmas gifts.

Spicy Stuffed Mushrooms Jambalaya

1	pound large fresh mushrooms	2	cups finely crushed butter-flavored cracker crumbs
2	tablespoons butter	3	tablespoons grated Parmesan cheese
½	cup finely chopped yellow onion	1¾	tablespoons chopped parsley
½	cup finely diced pepperoni	½	teaspoon seasoned salt
¼	cup finely chopped bell pepper	¼	teaspoon oregano
¼	teaspoon finely minced garlic	⅛	teaspoon pepper
		1	cup chicken broth

Preheat oven to 350°. Clean mushrooms with brush. Remove mushroom stems and chop finely. Place in skillet butter, onion, pepperoni, bell pepper, garlic and mushroom stems. Cook mixture 10 minutes, until tender but not brown. Add cracker crumbs, cheese, parsley, salt, oregano and pepper. Mix well; stir in broth. Spoon stuffing into mushroom caps, rounding the tops. Place mushrooms in shallow pan with about ¼ inch water. Bake 25 minutes. Serve immediately.

Yield: 12 servings

Pesto-Stuffed Mushroom Caps

1	**pound fresh mushrooms**
3	**tablespoons butter, melted**
½	**cup fresh pesto sauce**
	(see recipe on page 44)

Pimiento for garnish

Preheat oven to 350°. Clean mushrooms and remove stems. Place butter in shallow baking dish. Add mushrooms and toss. Arrange mushrooms cap side down. Spoon pesto into caps. Cover with foil and bake 15 to 20 minutes. Top each with strip of pimiento.

Yield: approximately 18 stuffed mushrooms

Cheese Wafers

2	**sticks butter, softened**
16	**ounces New York sharp cheddar cheese, grated**
3	**cups sifted all-purpose flour**

1	**teaspoon cayenne pepper**
1	**teaspoon salt**
	Pecan halves

Cream butter and grated cheese. Add flour, red pepper and salt; mix well. Use hands, if needed, to mix dough and ensure even mixing. Divide dough into 3 equal parts. Shape each into a log about 1½ inches in diameter and wrap in waxed paper. Chill about 30 minutes. (Can freeze at this stage.) Preheat oven to 350°. Slice logs into ⅛-inch thick wafers. Place on ungreased cookie sheet and press pecan half into each wafer. Bake 10 to 15 minutes.

Yield: 3 dozen wafers

BEAR IN MIND:
(1) Add ¾ cup chopped cashew nuts to dough before shaping. Omit pecan half.
(2) If you really want your "claws" to show, use 2 teaspoons cayenne pepper!
(3) Dough may be processed through pastry tube to make cheese straws. Omit nuts.

Paddington Bear's Cheese Straws

so very easy

1 (5-ounce) jar Old English Cheese Spread
2½ cups sifted all-purpose flour
2¼ sticks margarine, softened

1 tablespoon Worcestershire sauce
1 teaspoon cayenne pepper

Preheat oven to 275°. Knead all ingredients together in large bowl. Chill if desired. Put in cookie press. Press onto ungreased cookie sheet. Pre-cut at 2-inch intervals. Bake 8 minutes. Turn oven off; leave in oven 2 minutes.

Yield: 3 dozen

Cheese Date Pockets

extra nice not-too-sweet pickup

1 stick butter
1 cup grated sharp cheddar cheese
1⅓ cups sifted all-purpose flour
¼ teaspoon salt
2 tablespoons water

1 (6¼-ounce) package chopped dates
½ cup brown sugar, firmly packed
¼ cup water

Cream butter and cheese well. Add flour, salt and water; mix well. Roll dough into ball and chill several hours.

Date filling: Combine dates, brown sugar and water in saucepan. Cook over medium heat, stirring until thickened. Cool. Preheat oven to 375°. Roll dough thin on a floured board. Cut into 2-inch circles. Place 1 teaspoon filling on half of each circle. Fold and seal edges. Bake on ungreased baking sheet about 10 minutes. Cool slightly and remove from pan.

Yield: 35 to 40 pieces

French Fried Cheese Balls

1¼	cups grated Swiss cheese	1	teaspoon finely grated onion
1	tablespoon all-purpose flour	3	egg whites
¼	teaspoon salt	¾	cup finely crushed corn flakes
½	teaspoon Worcestershire sauce		Oil for deep frying

Combine cheese, flour, salt, Worcestershire sauce and onion. Beat egg whites until stiff peaks form. Fold into cheese mixture. (This mixture will be soft.) Shape into walnut-size balls, roll in crushed cereal and fry in deep oil just until golden brown. Drain well. Serve hot.

Yield: 18 to 20 cheese balls

BEAR IN MIND: *These are wonderful dipped in Marvelous Mustard Sauce, page 44.*

Toasty Potato Skins

6	medium-size baking potatoes, baked and cooled	4	tablespoons butter
2½	teaspoons Worcestershire sauce	2	teaspoons minced garlic
			Salt and freshly ground pepper to taste

Cut potatoes in half lengthwise, then cut each half lengthwise into thirds. With spoon scoop out centers, leaving about ¼-inch shell. (Reserve centers for another use.) Place skins on jelly roll pan and let dry at least 1 hour. Meanwhile, in small saucepan melt Worcestershire sauce and butter. Add garlic and sauté 1 minute. Strain. Preheat oven to 500°. Brush potato skins on both sides with flavored butter. Sprinkle with salt and pepper. Bake 10 minutes or until crisp, turning once. Serve immediately.

Yield: 6 servings

BEAR FLAIR: *Serve with chopped chives, sour cream, minced red onion, guacamole, bacon and shredded cheddar cheese.*

Bear Nibbles

2	(12-ounce) boxes oyster-style crackers
¾	cup Wesson Oil (do not substitute another brand)
1	teaspoon garlic salt
1	teaspoon dried dill weed
1	(0.7-ounce) package dry ranch dressing mix (original recipe)
1	teaspoon lemon pepper

Pour crackers into large container with tight seal. Combine remaining ingredients. Mix well. Pour mixture over crackers and stir, mixing evenly. Put lid on container and toss vigorously to mix. Shake the container every 20 to 30 minutes for 3 hours. Be sure the container you use is large enough for the contents to toss freely and mix thoroughly.

Yield: 20 to 30 servings (8 to 10 cups)

BEAR IN MIND: Mixture keeps 2 to 3 weeks in airtight container. Great do-ahead!

Crystallized Orange Nuts

a different snack or appetizer

¼	cup orange juice
1	cup sugar

Grated rind of one orange
2 cups pecans

Grease cookie sheet. Mix orange juice, sugar and orange rind in 2-quart microwave baking dish. Stir in pecans. Microwave 6 minutes on MEDIUM-HIGH. Stir well, cook on MEDIUM-HIGH 8 minutes longer. Spread nuts on cookie sheet. Allow to cool.

Yield: 2 cups pecans

Fancy Franks

1	(12-ounce) bottle chili sauce	½	teaspoon ground ginger
3	tablespoons brown sugar	⅛	teaspoon dry mustard
2	tablespoons minced onion	1	pound frankfurters, cut
½	cup bourbon		diagonally into ¾-inch slices

Combine all ingredients, except frankfurters, in microwave-proof bowl. Cover with plastic wrap and microwave on HIGH 1½ to 2½ minutes. Stir in cut frankfurters and cover. Microwave on HIGH 4 to 5 minutes. Stir once. Serve from a chafing dish.

Yield: Approximately 50 pieces

BEAR IN MIND: *May substitute cocktail sausages for frankfurters.*

Cocktail Eye of Round

5	to 6-pound eye of round roast	½	cup bourbon
1	(8-ounce) bottle Italian dressing	2	tablespoons Worcestershire sauce
1	teaspoon salt		Salt and coarsely ground pepper to taste

Marinate roast overnight in mixture of Italian dressing, salt, bourbon and Worcestershire. Rotate roast several times to insure meat is equally marinated. When ready to cook, preheat oven to 325°. Drain off marinade. Dry roast with paper towel. Coat roast heavily with pepper and lightly with salt. Place in roasting pan and cook uncovered until desired doneness. (About 2 hours for a 5 to 6-pound roast to achieve medium-rare.)

Yield: 30 to 40 servings

BEAR FLAIR:
(1) Serve with horseradish on party rye.
(2) Cut extra thin slices, overlap slices and secure to head of cabbage with marinated mushroom caps and/or shrimp on toothpicks.

Sour Cream Sausage Balls

unusual, easy, and never any left!

1	pound "hot" ground sausage	½	cup sherry
1	(9-ounce) jar Major Gray's Chutney, finely chopped	½	pint sour cream

Roll sausage into bite-size balls. Cook in skillet. Remove sausage and pour off grease. In saucepan combine chutney, sherry and sour cream. Simmer 5 minutes; add sausage. Heat thoroughly. Transfer to chafing or serving dish. Serve warm with tooth picks.

Yield: 35 to 40 balls

Barbecued Sausage Balls

1	pound bulk pork sausage	½	cup ketchup
1	egg, slightly beaten	2	tablespoons brown sugar
⅓	cup fine dry bread crumbs	1	tablespoon vinegar
½	teaspoon sage	1	tablespoon soy sauce

Preheat oven to 350°. Mix sausage, egg, bread crumbs and sage; shape into bite-size balls. In ungreased skillet, brown balls slowly on all sides, about 15 minutes. Pour off excess fat and place balls in 2-quart casserole. Combine remaining ingredients and pour over meat. Cover and bake 30 minutes. Stir occasionally to coat meat balls.

Yield: 9 servings

Mara's Chicken Wings

4	pounds chicken wings, separated into three parts using 2 main parts	1	(5-ounce) bottle soy sauce
		1	(1-pound) box brown sugar

Preheat oven to 300°. Place wings in pan in single layer. Mix soy sauce with sugar. Pour over wings. Cover. Bake 3 hours. Turn once. Serve from chafing dish.

Yield: 12 servings

Smoked Sausage Roll

1 **(1-pound) package whole hog sausage**	**Hickory chips, soaked**

Using a covered charcoal grill, set the rack 10 inches above coals. When the fire is hot, remove the plastic case from sausage and place sausage on the grill on the end away from the fire. Add wet hickory pieces to the hot charcoal fire. The smoking of the wet hickory gives the sausage added flavor. After 1 hour turn the sausage roll and continue smoking 1 more hour, adding hickory to the fire as needed. The sausage can be served when smoked or frozen for later use.

Yield: 8 to 10 servings

Famous Crab Dish

1	**(8-ounce) package cream cheese, softened**	4	**drops hot pepper sauce (or to taste)**
4	**green onions, with tops, finely chopped**	2	**teaspoons lemon juice**
1	**tablespoon Worcestershire sauce**	1	**(6-ounce) can fancy white crabmeat, rinsed and cartilage removed**
1	**cup ketchup**	¾	**cup finely chopped parsley**
1	**tablespoon horseradish**		**Crackers**

Spread cream cheese into a 10-inch circle. Cover with green onions. Sprinkle with Worcestershire and pat or press onions and Worcestershire into cream cheese. Mix ketchup, horseradish and hot pepper sauce. Spread over green onions. Sprinkle lemon juice on crabmeat and toss. Cover ketchup with crabmeat and sprinkle with parsley. Serve with crackers.

Yield: 8 to 10 generous servings

BEAR IN MIND: *Cream cheese can be spread into any shape. At Christmas, shape into tree or wreath. Since parsley is added last, it creates a lovely green festive touch!*

Fancy Chicken Log

2 (8-ounce) packages cream cheese, softened
1 tablespoon bottled steak sauce
½ teaspoon curry powder
1½ cups minced cooked chicken
⅓ cup finely chopped celery
½ cup chopped parsley, divided
¼ cup chopped almonds, toasted
Butter-flavored crackers

In a mixing bowl, beat well cream cheese, steak sauce and curry powder. Fold in chicken, celery and 2 tablespoons parsley. Shape into a 9-inch log and wrap with plastic wrap. Chill 4 hours. To serve, roll in remaining parsley and almonds. Serve on crackers.

Yield: 10 to 12 servings or more

Cocktail Party Loaf

2 (8-ounce) packages cream cheese, softened
4 ounces sharp cheddar cheese, grated
1 (2-ounce) wedge Roquefort cheese
1 teaspoon garlic salt
½ teaspoon curry powder
1 teaspoon paprika
2 tablespoons Worcestershire sauce
1 tablespoon mayonnaise
1 tablespoon lemon juice
1 (7-ounce) can lobster, crabmeat or shrimp
Whipping cream, if needed, to blend

Oil a cold 1-quart mold (small loaf shape). All ingredients must be room temperature. Mix all ingredients, adding cream if necessary to blend. Fill mold with mixture. Chill overnight. Unmold. Serve with crackers.

Yield: 20 servings

BEAR IN MIND: *When ready to unmold, loosen from sides of mold with a knife. Turn upside down onto platter, place a very hot towel over mold and shake gently.*

Brandied Country Pâté

1	pound chicken livers	1	teaspoon rosemary
6	tablespoons butter	½	teaspoon freshly ground
2	eggs		pepper
1	onion, cut in wedges	1	pound mild ground sausage
2	garlic cloves, coarsely	¼	cup all-purpose flour
	chopped	10	to 12 bacon slices
½	cup brandy		Red currant jelly for
½	teaspoon allspice		garnish
1	teaspoon salt		Crackers

Preheat oven to 350°. In skillet, lightly sauté chicken livers in butter. Put them through the fine blade of food processor with eggs, onion and garlic. Combine this mixture with brandy, allspice, salt, rosemary, pepper, sausage and flour. Line bottom and sides of 5x9-inch loaf pan with bacon slices. Pour pâté mixture into pan and cover with aluminum foil. Bake 1½ to 2 hours or until liquid in pan and fat are clear. Cool 15 minutes. Pour off fat. Recover with foil. Weight pâté with a brick and cool completely in refrigerator (allow 6 hours). To serve, unmold and remove excess fat. Garnish with red currant jelly. Serve with crackers.

Yield: 40 to 50 servings

BEAR FLAIR: *To spotlight your pâté, surround it with galax leaves.*

Cheeseboard Herbed Cream Cheese

1	(8-ounce) package cream	¼	teaspoon salt
	cheese, softened	1	teaspoon chopped fresh
½	stick butter, softened		dill weed
½	teaspoon minced garlic	1	teaspoon chopped fresh
¼	teaspoon freshly ground		parsley
	pepper		Crackers

Blend cream cheese and butter until fluffy. Beat in garlic, pepper, salt, dill and parsley. Pour into desired mold. Chill at least 2 hours. Unmold and serve with crackers.

Yield: 6 to 8 servings or more if serving more than one appetizer.

BEAR IN MIND: *This freezes well.*

"Plains Special" Cheese Ring

by Mrs. Jimmy Carter

16 ounces cheddar cheese, grated

1 cup mayonnaise

1 cup chopped pecans

1 small onion, grated
Pepper to taste
Dash cayenne pepper
Strawberry preserves

Mix all ingredients except strawberry preserves. Form into desired shape and chill. If molded into a circle, spoon preserves into center of ring. If not, serve on the side.

Yield: 10 servings

BEAR IN MIND:

   (1) Good also as cheese spread, without preserves.
   (2) Substitute Monterey Jack cheese for cheddar; substitute pepper jelly for strawberry preserves.

Tea Eggs

4 eggs

1 tablespoon sesame salt

2 tablespoons dark soy sauce

1 whole star anise

3 teaspoons smoky tea (like Earl Grey)
Sesame salt to garnish

Put eggs in cold water. Bring to a boil over high heat. Reduce heat and simmer 20 minutes. Drain water. Cool in cold water. Drain. Tap shells with back of spoon until completely cracked. Return eggs to pan, cover with cold water, 1 tablespoon sesame salt, soy sauce, anise and tea. Bring to a boil, reduce heat and simmer very slowly 2 to 3 hours. Turn off heat and leave eggs in liquid 8 hours. Tea eggs are then drained and left in their shells until ready to use. Keep well-wrapped in the refrigerator (up to 1 week). To serve, carefully peel the eggs. Whites of eggs will be marbled with dark lines. Cut into halves or quarters. Serve with sesame salt.

Yield: 4 to 8 servings

"Save a Few" Cheese Spread

1 (8-ounce) package cream cheese, softened
2 tablespoons skim milk
½ cup low calorie Thousand Island dressing
1 (4¼-ounce) jar pimientos, drained and chopped
2 teaspoons lemon juice
Dash Worcestershire sauce
½ to 1 whole bell pepper, chopped, optional
½ small onion, chopped

Combine cheese, milk and dressing. Add pimientos, lemon juice, Worcestershire, bell pepper and onion. Mix well. Mold in desired shape. Chill.

Yield: 10 servings

BEAR IN MIND: *You can save a few calories by using skim milk and low calorie dressing. Don't fool yourself, there's plenty of calories in the cream cheese! Use Neufchâtel cheese for even fewer calories.*

Caviar Egg Mold

4 hard-cooked eggs, riced
5⅓ tablespoons butter, softened
¼ to ⅓ cup Homemade Mayonnaise, page 131
⅓ cup chopped green onions
2 tablespoons lemon juice
Salt and red pepper to taste
½ cup sour cream
1 (2-ounce) jar black caviar, well-drained

Grease 2-cup mold. Combine eggs, butter, mayonnaise, green onion, lemon juice, salt and red pepper. Pack in mold and chill several hours. To serve, unmold, frost with sour cream and spoon caviar on top. Serve with unsalted crackers.

Yield: 8 to 10 servings

BEAR IN MIND: *Drain caviar at least 15 minutes. The sour cream won't turn grey. At Christmas, use red caviar.*

Best Pimiento Cheese

16 ounces sharp cheddar
cheese, grated
2 tablespoons lemon juice
1 medium onion, chopped

1 (2-ounce) jar diced
pimientos, drained
½ cup mayonnaise

Mix well together all ingredients. Use as spread for crackers or sandwiches.

Yield: 2½ cups

BEAR IN MIND:

(1) Lemon juice gives this a great flavor and spreading texture.
(2) Add ½ cup finely chopped toasted pecans, for a variation.

Artichokes and Chilies Dip

1 (14-ounce) can artichoke
hearts, drained and
chopped
1 (4-ounce) can green
chilies, seeded and
chopped

1 cup grated Parmesan
cheese
1 cup mayonnaise
Dash hot pepper sauce

Preheat oven to 350°. Combine all ingredients and pour into an 8-inch square baking dish or a small decorative baking dish. Bake 20 minutes. Serve with plain tortilla chips or bread sticks.

Yield: 12 servings

BEAR IN MIND: You can also spread on tortilla chips and broil a few minutes.

Hot Mushroom Dip

½ stick butter
(do not use margarine)
1 garlic clove, pressed
3 (4-ounce) cans sliced
mushrooms, drained

2 tablespoons chopped
fresh parsley
½ teaspoon salt
⅛ teaspoon pepper
½ pint sour cream

Melt butter and add garlic. Add mushrooms, parsley, salt, pepper and fold in sour cream. Heat gently. Serve in chafing dish.

Yield: 12 servings

Crunchy Bacon Chip Dip

½   (8-ounce) package cream
    cheese, softened
½   cup chopped cooked bacon
2   teaspoons ketchup
2   teaspoons prepared
    mustard

⅛   teaspoon ginger
¼   cup sour cream
    Crackers or fresh
    vegetables

Beat cream cheese with mixer until smooth. Add bacon, ketchup, mustard, ginger and sour cream. Mix until thoroughly blended. Chill. Serve with crackers or fresh vegetables.

Yield: about 1 cup

BEAR IN MIND: *Flavor is enhanced if prepared a day ahead.*

Sombrero Dip

men say olé!

1   pound lean ground beef
1   medium onion, chopped
½   cup ketchup
3   tablespoons chili powder
½   teaspoon salt
1   (16-ounce) can red kidney
    beans with liquid

1   cup grated cheddar cheese
    Sour cream, optional
    Black olives, sliced,
    optional
    Corn chips

Brown meat in skillet and drain fat. Add onion, ketchup, chili powder and salt. Place kidney beans in blender or food processor with liquid. Process until beans are mashed slightly (don't liquify). Add beans to beef mixture and mix thoroughly. Top with grated cheddar cheese. Dollops of sour cream and black olives may be added if desired. Serve warm with corn chips.

Yield: 3 cups

BEAR IN MIND: *For casual affairs, use a 1-quart crockpot to keep dip warm while serving.*

Hot Crabmeat Dip

1	(8-ounce) package cream cheese, softened	1	(6½-ounce) can crabmeat, drained and cartilage removed
½	teaspoon horseradish		Dash salt and pepper
1	tablespoon chopped onion		Crackers
1	tablespoon lemon juice		
¼	cup milk		

Preheat oven to 350°. Mix well all ingredients. Pour into oven-proof serving dish and bake 20 to 30 minutes or until bubbly. Serve with crackers.

Yield: 15 to 18 servings

 # For the Chafing Dish

16	ounces sharp New York cheddar cheese, grated	1	cup Thin Cream Sauce (refer to page 164)
16	ounces Swiss cheese, grated		Sherry to taste
2	tablespoons caraway seeds		Melba toast

Mix cheeses, caraway seeds and cream sauce over low heat until melted. Do not allow mixture to get too hot, just warm. Transfer to chafing dish and add sherry to taste. Wine will curdle cheese mixture if it gets too hot. Serve with melba toast.

Yield: 5 to 6 cups

Spinach Dip

1	(10-ounce) package frozen chopped spinach, thawed and well-drained	1	(0.4-ounce) package dry ranch dressing mix
½	pint sour cream		Dash dill weed
1	cup mayonnaise		Crackers or corn chips for dipping

Mix ingredients. Serve with crackers or chips.

Yield: 2 cups

BEAR IN MIND: *Scoop out round bread loaf, leaving 1-inch outer edge of bread. Fill with dip. If fresh spinach is available, add a small whole leaf on the edge of dip for garnish.*

Creamy Artichokes and Shrimp

4½	tablespoons butter	1½	pounds fresh shrimp, peeled, deveined and cooked
4½	tablespoons all-purpose flour		
½	cup milk	2	(14-ounce) cans artichoke hearts, drained and cut in chunks
¾	cup whipping cream		
	Salt and pepper to taste		
¼	cup dry vermouth	¼	cup grated Parmesan cheese
1	tablespoon Worcestershire sauce		Crackers

In large saucepan, melt butter and stir in flour. Blend well. Gradually add milk and cream stirring constantly with wire whisk. Cook over medium heat until smooth and thickened. Add salt, pepper, vermouth and Worcestershire sauce. Add shrimp, artichoke hearts and Parmesan cheese. Heat thoroughly and place in chafing dish. Serve with crackers.

Yield: 6 to 7 cups

Almond Pinecones

elegant at Christmas parties

1½	cups whole almonds	1	tablespoon chopped green onion
1	(8-ounce) package cream cheese, softened		
½	cup mayonnaise	½	teaspoon dill weed
8	bacon slices, cooked and crumbled	¼	teaspoon pepper
			Crackers

Preheat oven to 300°. Place almonds on cookie sheet in a single layer and bake 15 minutes to brown slightly. Mix cream cheese and mayonnaise. Add bacon, onion, dill weed and pepper. Mix well. Cover and chill at least 4 hours. Form mixture into shape of 2 pinecones on serving platter. Beginning at narrow end, press almonds into "pinecones" at a slight angle in rows until cheese is covered. Garnish with small white or sand pine cone sprigs tied with Christmas bow at the top of each "pinecone". Serve with crackers.

Yield: 20 servings

Fancy Cheese Ball

1 (8-ounce) package cream cheese, softened	2 tablespoons chopped green olives
8 ounces Roquefort cheese, softened	2 tablespoons chopped pecans
8 ounces Cheddar cheese, softened	2 tablespoons chopped fresh parsley
½ cup green onion with tops, chopped	2 tablespoons cooked, crumbled bacon
¾ teaspoon garlic salt	2 tablespoons chopped black olives
2 tablespoons paprika	
2 tablespoons chopped bell pepper	2 tablespoons chopped pimiento

Combine all cheeses, onions and garlic salt. Mix well and shape into a large ball. Mark ball with a knife into 8 sections (like a beach ball). Fill each section with one of the garnishes: paprika, bell pepper, green olives, pecans, parsley, bacon, black olives and pimiento.

Yield: 40 to 50 servings with other hors d'oeurvres

BEAR IN MIND:
    (1) Use red caviar and parsley at Christmas.
    (2) Use red and black caviar for a Georgia Bulldog Party.
    (3) Substitute your own school colors.

Onion Cheese Ball

1 (8-ounce) package cream cheese	½ cup finely chopped green onion
1 (0.7-ounce) package dry ranch dressing mix	Bacon bits to garnish

Combine cream cheese, dressing mix and onion. Form into ball and roll in bacon bits.

Yield: 10 to 12 servings

BEAR FLAIR: *Serve at room temperature with crackers or fruit of your choice.*

BEAR IN MIND: *Roll in crushed peppercorns instead of bacon bits.*

Kraut Cheese Ball

¼ cup mayonnaise	1 (10-ounce) can sauerkraut, well-drained
1 hard-cooked egg, chopped	
3 tablespoons diced pimiento	1 (4-ounce) can green chilies, well-drained
1 tablespoon sugar	
½ teaspoon salt	4 cups shredded sharp cheddar cheese
¼ teaspoon freshly ground pepper	
1 teaspoon Worcestershire sauce	

Frosting:

1 (8-ounce) package cream cheese	1 to 2 tablespoons milk
2 tablespoons chopped green onion	½ teaspoon salt
	½ teaspoon Worcestershire sauce
2 tablespoons chopped bell pepper, optional	Dash of hot pepper sauce

Put mayonnaise, egg, pimiento, sugar, salt, pepper and Worcestershire sauce in food processor. "Pulse" 4 to 5 times. Add sauerkraut and chilies and pulse until well-blended. Add shredded cheese a cup at a time, blending after each cup. Mound onto a dish or tray. Shape. Chill a few minutes while you mix together frosting ingredients. "Frost" cheese ball with cream cheese mixture. Garnish with pimiento and onion "flowers". Chill at least 4 hours or overnight.

Yield: serves 40 to 50 people with other appetizers

BEAR IN MIND: *This keeps up to a week in refrigerator.*

Chutney Cheese Ball

a nice sweet touch for cocktail party

½ cup raisins	1 cup slivered almonds
½ cup sherry	1 tablespoon curry powder
2 (8-ounce) packages cream cheese, softened	¼ teaspoon dry mustard
	3 tablespoons mayonnaise
½ cup chutney	Gingersnap crackers

Soak raisins in sherry overnight. Drain raisins and combine with all other ingredients. Chill until firm enough to handle. Form into 2 balls. Serve with gingersnaps. May freeze.

Yield: 2 balls

Smokey the Bear

1   (7¾-ounce) can red
     salmon, drained and
     cartilage removed
1   (8-ounce) package cream
     cheese, softened
2   tablespoons chopped bell
     pepper

1   tablespoon chopped
     fresh parsley
¼   teaspoon liquid smoke
¾   cup sliced almonds,
     toasted, divided

In medium-size bowl combine salmon, cream cheese, bell pepper, parsley and liquid smoke. Chop ¼ cup almonds; reserve remaining sliced almonds for garnish. Add chopped almonds to salmon mixture and mix well. Cover and chill until firm (at least 1 hour). Form mixture into a ball on waxed paper. Arrange remaining almonds on top in flower-like design. Cover and chill.

Yield: 15 to 20 servings, served with other appetizers

Pineapple Cheese Ball

2   cups chopped pecans,
     divided
2   (8-ounce) packages cream
     cheese, softened
1   (8½-ounce) can crushed
     pineapple, drained

¼   cup chopped bell pepper
2   tablespoons finely
     chopped onion
1   tablespoon seasoned salt

Reserve 1 cup of pecans. Blend remaining ingredients and shape into a ball. Chill. Roll cheese ball in remaining pecans.

Yield: 12 to 15 servings

BEAR FLAIR: *Form cheese mixture into shape of half a pineapple. Score diagonally both ways and press an almond in each diamond. Cut a crown out of bell pepper to complete the pineapple.*

Marvelous Mustard Sauce

½	cup tomato soup, undiluted	2	eggs, well-beaten
½	cup prepared mustard	½	cup sugar
2	tablespoons vinegar	2	tablespoons butter

Mix soup, mustard, vinegar, eggs and sugar in small saucepan over medium heat. Cook, stirring constantly with whisk, until mixture is thick. Add butter.

Yield: 2 cups sauce

BEAR FLAIR: *Serve hot with little wieners or sausage wrapped in crescent rolls, fried chicken fingers or Fried Cheese Balls, page 28. It's good with almost anything!*

BEAR IN MIND:
(1) Keeps several weeks in refrigerator. Freezes well, too.
(2) Try different types of mustards and vinegars.

Pesto Sauce

¼	cup pignolia nuts (pine nuts)	2	to 3 ounces Parmesan cheese, freshly grated
3	garlic cloves, pressed	2	to 3 ounces Romano cheese, freshly grated
½	teaspoon ground sea salt	½	cup olive oil (use the best you can find)
½	teaspoon freshly ground black pepper		
2	cups firmly packed fresh basil leaves		

Chop the nuts and garlic with salt and pepper until very fine. On the same chopping block, gradually add the basil, chopping until very fine. Put in bowl, add grated cheeses and then very slowly add the oil, drop by drop at first, until smooth. Then stir in the remaining oil.

Yield: About 1½ cups sauce

BEAR FLAIR:
(1) Sprinkle with toasted whole pine nuts and fresh basil leaves.
(2) This is potent stuff—a little goes a long way. Serve on hot pasta, toss and enjoy. Very good in cold pasta salad also. Try it on broiled fish and in soups and vegetables.

BEAR IN MIND: *Can do in food processor with steel blade. Just be sure basil leaves are completely dry after washing them.*

Beverages

"BEARING GIFTS"

*HOMEMADE IRISH CREAM LIQUEUR, page 48 ... put in a pretty wine or dressing bottle. Add fresh greenery to bow and keep gift chilled until ready to bestow.

*BAVARIAN MINT COFFEE MIX, page 54, or **HOT CHOCOLATE MIX,** page 54, or **CAPPUCCINO MIX,** page 54 ... give in a decorative jar with the recipe.

*KOALA KAHLUA, page 49 ... neat gifts in miniature bottles with a tiny bear attached to a colorful ribbon.

*MULLED WINE, page 50 ... bottle and present with 2 handsome mugs, along with recipe.

*WHISPERS, page 48 ... wrap 2 champagne glasses, a copy of recipe, and miniature bottles of brandy and crème de cacao.

*GOLDILOCKS SPECIAL, page 53 ... give an ice ring mold and tuck in recipe for punch, or even better, a copy of **Unbearably Good!** cookbook.

*ICED TEA SURPRISE, page 52 ... give a china pitcher in the bride's pattern, or a classic crystal one, and put recipe inside pitcher.

*ORANGE BLUSH, page 52 ... a set of goblets with the recipe included would be a welcomed gift.

*ICE CREAM COFFEE PUNCH, page 48 ... give a punch bowl and ladle and a small jar of instant coffee with the recipe card.

"BEAR ESSENTIALS FOR ENTERTAINING"

*When entertaining buffet-style, buy small size bottles of wine or champagne; attach a plastic wine or champagne glass to each bottle with a ribbon or fabric strip; pile in large basket lined with plastic and filled with ice. Let each guest help himself.

*Using a sturdy-stemmed flower, such as a daisy, remove lower leaves, then skewer lemon, orange or lime slices. Place in drink for garnish.

*Freeze an orange blossom or two in each ice cube freezer tray with some Goldilocks Special; as cube melts, flower floats in glass or cup.

*After dinner for demitasse, add whipped cream and liqueurs; serve with petite chocolates.

*"Frost" glasses for beer or champagne by placing in freezer for one hour. Pretty and keeps beverages chilled longer.

*Cinnamon stick or vanilla bean added to coffee maker basket with coffee will give subtle flavor and wonderful aroma.

*Coffee served in mugs with a cinnamon stick stirrer adds a festive, fun flair!

*For small parties, use a glass trifle dish or large salad bowl to serve punch.

*For outdoor, casual party or barbecue, ice down drinks in a wheelbarrow.

*For special iced tea, freeze in cubes some of our MINT JULEP SYRUP, page 168. Add to each glass one thawed cube. Especially lovely in the winter months when fresh mint is dormant.

Bear Hug

4 tablespoons chocolate ice cream
2 tablespoons coffee-flavored liqueur
2 tablespoons almond-flavored liqueur

4 tablespoons whipping cream
Nutmeg or instant coffee for garnish

Place ice cream in blender. Add other ingredients and blend until smooth. Serve in cordial glasses. Sprinkle with nutmeg or instant coffee.

Yield: 2 servings

BEAR IN MIND: *As a dessert, spoon 3 scoops ice cream into each champagne glass. Blend remaining ingredients and spoon over ice cream. Garnish with nutmeg or coffee.*

Dreamcicle

6 scoops vanilla ice cream
6 ounces fresh orange juice

4 ounces almond-flavored liqueur

Place all ingredients in blender. Blend until smooth.

Yield: 4 servings

BEAR FLAIR: *Elegant when served in stemmed glasses.*

Brandy Alexander

6 scoops Dutch chocolate ice cream
2½ ounces crème de cacao

4 ounces brandy
Dash nutmeg

Place all ingredients except nutmeg in a blender. Blend until smooth. Pour into stemmed glasses and sprinkle with nutmeg.

Yield: 6 servings

BEAR IN MIND: *If dieting, you may use 3 scoops ice cream and ice cubes instead of 6 scoops ice cream.*

Ice Cream Coffee Punch

9	teaspoons instant coffee	1	quart milk
1½	cups hot water	½	pint whipping cream,
6	tablespoons honey		whipped
1	quart vanilla ice cream, softened	13	ounces rum

Dissolve coffee in hot water. Mix coffee with honey and chill several hours. Add softened ice cream and milk to coffee-honey mixture. Blend, but leave ice cream in lumps. Fold in whipped cream. Add rum and stir gently.

Yield: 12 servings

BEAR FLAIR: *This is pretty served in a punch bowl perhaps at an afternoon tea!*

BEAR IN MIND: *Part of this recipe must be done in advance and chilled. Great for preparing in advance.*

Whispers

Great as a dessert!

1	quart coffee ice cream (or more if thicker consistency desired)	5	(1-ounce) jiggers brandy
		5	(1½-ounce) jiggers dark crème de cacao

Mix all ingredients in blender. Serve in champagne glasses.

Yield: 6 servings

Homemade Irish Cream Liqueur

1¼	cups Irish whiskey	4	tablespoons chocolate syrup
1	(14-ounce) can sweetened condensed milk	2	teaspoons instant coffee
1	cup whipping cream	1	teaspoon vanilla extract
4	eggs	½	teaspoon almond extract

In blender combine all ingredients. Blend until smooth. Refrigerate in tightly-covered jar, up to one month. Stir well before serving.

Yield: 5 cups

BEAR IN MIND: *Sinfully rich and so much like the real one! A wonderful gift idea.*

Koala Kahlua

1	(2-ounce) jar instant coffee	4	cups boiling water
4	cups sugar	4	cups vodka
		1	vanilla bean, slashed

Mix coffee, sugar and boiling water. Cool. Pour into ½ gallon bottle. Add vodka and vanilla bean. Cover and set aside in cool, dark, dry place for 30 days.

Yield: ½ gallon

Frozen Whiskey Sours

1	(6-ounce) can frozen orange juice concentrate	6	ounces bourbon
1	(6-ounce) can frozen limeade concentrate	½	cup water
			Ice

Mix all ingredients in blender. Blend on purée or frappé until well mixed.

Yield: 4 to 6 servings

BEAR IN MIND: *Can be frozen. Stir before serving.*

Frozen Margaritas

⅛	cup salt	¼	cup orange-flavored liqueur
2	to 4 lime wedges		Drop green food coloring
1	(6-ounce) can frozen limeade concentrate, thawed and undiluted		Crushed ice
¾	cup tequila		Lime slices

Place salt in a saucer. Rub rims of 4 cocktail glasses with wedge of lime. Dip each glass rim in salt and set aside. Combine limeade, tequila, liqueur and food coloring in blender. Blend well. Add crushed ice to fill blender ¾ full. Blend well. Pour mixture into prepared glasses and garnish with lime slices.

Yield: 4 servings

Sangria

½ cup sugar, more or less depending on taste
2 ounces brandy
1 quart red wine
½ orange, sliced

½ lemon, sliced
½ apple, sliced
24 ounces club soda
Ice cubes, to chill

Dissolve sugar in brandy by stirring. Add red wine, stir again. Add fruit slices. When ready to serve, add club soda and ice cubes.

Yield: 6 to 8 servings

Cranberry Wine

6 cups cranberry juice
3 cups red wine
¼ cup sugar

1 orange, sliced
1 lemon, sliced

In a tall pitcher combine cranberry juice, wine and sugar. Stir well. Add fruit. Chill several hours. Garnish with sliced fruit.

Yield: 12 servings

BEAR IN MIND: *For a lighter tasting drink, you may add club soda or gingerale.*

Mulled Wine

8 tablespoons sugar
¼ cup water
10 whole cloves
6 orange slices

6 lemon slices
4 cinnamon sticks
6 cups dry red wine

Combine all ingredients, except wine, in 2-quart saucepan. Heat slowly, stirring occasionally, until sugar is dissolved. Stir in wine and continue heating until just below boiling point. Strain into heated mugs. Serve.

Yield: 6 servings

Irish Coffee

1½ ounces Irish whiskey	2 tablespoons whipped
1 teaspoon sugar	cream
1 cup brewed coffee	

Stir Irish whiskey and sugar together in a coffee cup. Pour hot coffee over mixture in cup. Do not stir. Top with whipped cream. Serve immediately.

Yield: 1 serving

Hot Apple Cider Punch

1 gallon apple cider	2 cinnamon sticks
1 quart ginger ale	1½ teaspoons whole cloves
¾ cup red hot (cinnamon) candy	1 medium orange, sliced

Pour apple cider and ginger ale into large electric percolator. Place candy, cinnamon sticks, cloves and orange slices in coffee basket. Perk.

Yield: 20 servings

Hot Buttered Rum

1 (1-pound) box powdered sugar	2 teaspoons cinnamon
1 (1-pound) box brown sugar	2 teaspoons nutmeg
4 sticks butter, softened	1 quart vanilla ice cream, softened
	1½ ounces light rum per cup

Cream sugars, butter and spices. Fold in softened ice cream. Store in freezer until firm. When serving, add 2 tablespoons of ice cream mixture to serving cup, next add 1½ ounces rum. Fill cup with boiling water. Serve.

Yield: Approximately 30 cups

BEAR IN MIND:
  (1) A wonderful wintertime drink—always ready in the freezer.
  (2) For a deeper color and different taste use dark rum and dark brown sugar.

Cantaloupe Luscious

3½ cups cubed cantaloupe, chilled	⅓ cup sugar
	2 tablespoons lemon juice
3 cups pineapple juice, chilled	2 tablespoons lime juice
	Cantaloupe balls and
2 cups orange juice, chilled	orange slices for garnish

Place cantaloupe in blender and process until smooth; pour into pitcher or punch bowl. Stir in pineapple juice and orange juice. Add sugar, lemon juice and lime juice and stir until sugar dissolves.

Yield: about 7½ cups

BEAR FLAIR: *Float cantaloupe balls and orange slices in punch.*

Iced Tea Surprise

2 tablespoons instant tea	1 (12-ounce) can apricot nectar
4 cups water	
½ cup sugar	2 cups orange juice
1 (12-ounce) can un-sweetened pineapple juice	1 cup lemon juice

Dissolve tea in water in large pitcher. Stir in sugar until dissolved; then add pineapple juice, apricot nectar, orange juice and lemon juice. Stir well. Pour over ice in tall glasses.

Yield: 10 (1-cup) servings

BEAR FLAIR: *Trim rim of each glass with a wedge of orange or lemon.*

Orange Blush

1 (6-ounce) can frozen orange juice concentrate, thawed	4 tablespoons sugar
	16 ounces club soda
	Mint for garnish
1 cup cranberry juice	

Combine orange juice concentrate, cranberry juice and sugar. Chill. Just before serving, stir in club soda. Pour over crushed ice in goblets.

Yield: 6 servings

BEAR FLAIR: *Add sprigs of fresh mint or lemon balm to each goblet. For extra zip, add vodka.*

Goldilocks Special

1	(12-ounce) can frozen orange juice concentrate, thawed	4	cups apricot nectar Juice of 1 lemon
1	(12-ounce) can frozen lemonade concentrate, thawed	2	cups unsweetened grape-fruit juice
1	(46-ounce) can un-sweetened pineapple juice	⅔ 1	cup sugar liter gingerale, chilled Fruit slices and mint leaves for garnish

Combine orange juice, lemonade, pineapple juice, apricot nectar, lemon juice, grapefruit juice and sugar in punch bowl, stir until dissolved and chill. When ready to serve, add gingerale.

Yield: 4½ quarts

BEAR FLAIR: Make an ice ring using mint leaves, fruit slices of your choice and enough of the punch mixture (excluding gingerale) to fill the ring mold and freeze. (As the ring melts, the punch isn't diluted.)

Strawberry Punch

1	(6-ounce) package straw-berry-flavored gelatin	¾	cup lemon juice
2	cups sugar	1	(46-ounce) can un-sweetened pineapple juice
2	cups hot water	1	liter gingerale, chilled

Dissolve gelatin and sugar in hot water. Stir in lemon juice and pine-apple juice. Pour in gallon jug and fill almost to top with water. Chill several hours. Add gingerale at serving time.

Yield: 32 (½-cup) servings

BEAR IN MIND:

(1) May substitute 1 (6-ounce) package cherry or lime-flavored gela-tin. Remove from freezer 4 hours before serving to thaw. Add gin-gerale and serve.

(2) This punch freezes beautifully. However, be sure not to add the gingerale before freezing.

Bavarian Mint Coffee Mix

¼   cup powdered non-dairy
     coffee creamer
⅓   cup sugar

¼   cup instant coffee
2   hard candy peppermints,
     broken

Combine all ingredients in blender, then store in an airtight container. Use 1 tablespoon of mix to each 6 ounces boiling water. Stir well.

Yield: 1 cup mix or 16 (6-ounce) servings

BEAR IN MIND: *Garnish with whipped cream for parties.*

Cappuccino Mix

1   (8-quart) box instant
     nonfat dry milk
1   (8-ounce) jar instant
     coffee
1   (16-ounce) jar powdered
     non-dairy coffee creamer

1   (1-pound) box powdered
     sugar
1   (16-ounce) box instant
     chocolate mix

Mix all ingredients and store in an airtight container. To serve, add 4 tablespoons of mix to 1 cup of hot water.

Yield: 48 (8-ounce) servings

BEAR FLAIR: *Try adding a liqueur or brandy and top with whipped cream.*

Hot Chocolate Mix

1   (1-pound) box instant
     chocolate mix
1   (11-ounce) jar powdered
     non-dairy coffee creamer

1   (8-quart) box instant
     nonfat dry milk
½   (1-pound) box powdered
     sugar

Mix ingredients together and store in an airtight container. To make 1 cup of hot chocolate, mix ⅓ cup of hot chocolate mix with ⅔ cup hot water.

Yield: 4 quarts mix or 48 (8-ounce) servings

Bridge and Brunch

"BEARING GIFTS"

*GLAZED BACON, page 57 ... cut bacon into lengths that will fit in half-pint jar. Prepare and pack bacon into jar. Add a decorative, hand-stitched top, if desired. Makes terrific bridge prize.

*UNBEARABLY GOOD! cookbook ... for a bridge prize, nothing would be more appreciated than this book with a prepared favorite dish from the book.

*QUICHE AND TELL, page 69 ... bake one for your bridge party and another for a prize for the winner to share with her family as a meal or a snack.

*LINDA'S BRUNCH SPECIAL, page 73, or **SHRIMP & EGGS,** page 74 ... a delicious gift for someone who "needs a break today".

*COLD SPICED FRUIT, page 57 ... purchase oversized brandy snifter; add the prepared fruit, a bow and a few sprigs of fresh mint or lemon balm.

*AVOCADO FRUIT BASKET, page 58 ... be sure to coat cut edges of avocado with lemon juice to prevent browning. This makes a lovely, thoughtful gift for a friend.

*BAKED STUFFED PEACHES, page 59 ... a delightful, yet easy to prepare gift for those hot summer months.

*HEALTHY STRAWBERRIES, page 60 ... the new neighbor, new mother, or recuperating friend will savor every mouthful. Be sure to use the Bear Flair idea with recipe so there will be no dishes to wash or return.

*HOT BUTTERED RUM, page 51 ... give in freezer container with directions; add a set of mugs to compliment their kitchen or den.

*BLOODY MARY MIX, page 78 ... pour into empty Worcestershire or vinegar bottles for storage in refrigerator for a week.

"BEAR ESSENTIALS FOR ENTERTAINING"

*Put grape or galax leaves under **CRISPY APPLE TARTS,** page 66, for super presentation.

*Wreathe a plate of delectable pastries with Boston fern fronds for a colorful look.

*When sautéeing apples, cut apples crosswise, using a scalloped cookie cutter (about size of apple) to eliminate peeling. Then cut core section out using small scallop cookie cutter; then sauté in butter, add sugar, then flambé and stir in whipping cream.

*Carve "baskets" from lemons, oranges or grapefruit by cutting, leaving handle and scooping out pulp. Fill with jams or jelly for pretty service.

*For outdoor bridge or brunch, use plastic-coated wire trays to carry plate of food, glass, napkin and utensils to table.

*Line a 10 or 11-inch terra cotta shallow saucer with a pretty red plaid cloth and put a 9-inch quiche inside saucer for unusual serving.

*Use new washed terra cotta saucers for serving fresh fruit and a terra cotta container for a fresh floral arrangement.

*Terra cotta tiles look delicate when covered with crocheted doilies for use as placemats. Cover the table first with a white cloth and use white candles in terra cotta containers.

*Fresh violet blossoms look lovely strewn over a fresh fruit compote.

Glazed Bacon

½	pound sliced bacon	3	tablespoons red or white wine
¾	cup light brown sugar, firmly packed		
1½	tablespoons Dijon-style mustard		

Preheat oven to 350°. Place bacon in large baking dish. Bake 10 to 12 minutes. Bacon should be almost crisp. Drain off fat. Combine brown sugar, mustard and wine. Make into a paste. Spread half of mixture over bacon in dish. Return to oven 10 minutes. Turn bacon and cover with remaining mixture. Bake until bacon is golden brown. Remove bacon from oven and place on waxed paper. Serve hot or cold.

Yield: 6 to 8 servings

BEAR IN MIND: *Bacon can be broken into smaller pieces and served as an appetizer. As a variation, try wrapping bacon around apple slices (before it gets crisp) and then glaze.*

Cold Spiced Fruit

1	to 2 unpeeled oranges, sliced and seeded	1	(29-ounce) can pears
1	(20-ounce) can pineapple chunks	1	cup sugar
		½	cup vinegar
1	(16-ounce) can sliced peaches	3	sticks cinnamon
		5	whole cloves
1	(16-ounce) can apricot halves	1	(3-ounce) package cherry-flavored gelatin

Cut orange slices in half. Place in saucepan and cover with water. Simmer until tender. Drain well and set aside. Drain fruit, reserving half of all fruit juices. Combine reserved juices, sugar, vinegar, cinnamon, cloves and gelatin. Simmer 30 minutes. Combine fruits in a bowl and pour hot juice mixture over fruit. Chill 24 hours.

Yield: 15 servings

BEAR FLAIR: *Serve in champagne glass or brandy snifter.*

Cheesy Apple Annie

1	(20-ounce) can sliced apples, drained	1	cup all-purpose flour
1	stick butter	8	ounces processed cheese, cubed
¾	cup sugar	¼	cup milk

Preheat oven to 350°. Place apples in greased 1½-quart casserole. Combine butter, sugar, flour, cheese and milk in saucepan. Cook and stir over medium heat until cheese melts and ingredients are well blended. Spread over apples. Bake uncovered 30 to 40 minutes until top is lightly browned.

Yield: 6 to 8 servings

BEAR IN MIND: *(1) A great picnic covered dish. Can go anywhere! (2) Use 2 cups sliced golden delicious apples instead of 20-ounce canned. Also good with fresh fall pears.*

Avocado Fruit Basket

Dressing:

⅓	cup sugar	1	tablespoon prepared mustard
1½	teaspoons salt		
1	teaspoon lemon pepper	1	teaspoon grated onion
1½	teaspoons celery seed	1	cup salad oil
¼	cup vinegar	1	teaspoon paprika
¼	cup lemon juice		Poppy seeds to taste

Fruit:

2	avocados, peeled and cut in half	1	(11-ounce) can mandarin oranges, drained
1	grapefruit, peeled and sliced	2	dozen blueberries and/or raspberries
8	to 10 strawberries, halved		Romaine lettuce leaves
8	to 10 white grapes, halved		

For dressing: Mix sugar, salt, lemon pepper and celery seed. Add vinegar, lemon juice, mustard and onion. Mix well. Stirring constantly, slowly add oil, paprika and poppy seeds. When well-mixed, pour into container and store in refrigerator. Yields approximately 2 cups dressing.

For fruit: Cut avocados in half and place grapefruit, strawberries, grapes, oranges, and blueberries in avocado halves. When ready to serve, pour dressing over fruit-filled boats. Serve avocado halves on romaine lettuce.

Yield: 4 servings

Mandarin Pineapple Bake

1	(16-ounce) can crushed pineapple, with juice	¾	cup sugar
1	(11-ounce) can mandarin oranges, drained	4	tablespoons cornstarch
3	eggs, well-beaten	2	tablespoons butter
			Cinnamon to taste

Preheat oven to 350°. Combine pineapple, mandarin orange slices, eggs, sugar and cornstarch. Place in medium-size casserole, dot with butter and sprinkle with cinnamon. Bake 50 minutes.

Yield: 8 servings

BEAR FLAIR: *Delicious with ham, pork or fried chicken.*

Baked Stuffed Peaches

6	large, firm freestone peaches	1	tablespoon chopped, candied orange peel or grated orange peel
½	cup macaroon crumbs		
½	cup finely chopped almonds	⅓	cup sherry or Marsala wine
4	tablespoons sugar, divided		

Preheat oven to 350°. Lightly coat 7x11-inch baking dish with cooking spray. Wash peaches, pare and cut in half. Remove pit and a small portion of pulp around cavity. Combine macaroon crumbs, almonds, 2 tablespoons sugar and orange peel. Fill peach halves with mixture. Put two halves together and fasten with toothpicks. Place in dish and pour wine over peaches. Sprinkle with remaining sugar. Bake about 15 minutes. Serve hot or cold.

Yield: 6 servings

BEAR IN MIND: *Delicious served with a scoop of vanilla ice cream. Also try our Vanilla Sugar, page 267, to substitute for granulated sugar.*

Healthy Strawberries

2	pints strawberries, cut up (set aside 6 to 8 strawberries for garnish)
2	apples, peeled, cored and chopped
1	pint blueberries
2	cups plain yogurt
2	tablespoons honey
½	teaspoon vanilla extract
	Rind of 1 orange or lemon, finely grated (optional)
6	to 8 tablespoons granola
	Mint leaves for garnish

Divide cut up strawberries among dessert dishes. Spread apples and blueberries over strawberries. Mix yogurt, honey, vanilla extract and orange or lemon rind and pour over fruit immediately before serving. Sprinkle each with 1 tablespoon granola and garnish with whole berries and mint leaves.

Yield: 6 to 8 servings

BEAR FLAIR: *Serve in scallop-edged cantaloupe halves. Add fresh edible flower garnish with mint leaves, such as rose, violet or pansy.*

Beer Cheese Fondue

1	small garlic clove
¾	cup beer
2	cups shredded Swiss cheese
1	cup shredded sharp cheddar cheese
1	tablespoon all-purpose flour
	Dash hot pepper sauce
	Bagels, cut in cubes

Rub inside of fondue pot with cut garlic clove and discard. Add beer and heat slowly. Place both cheeses in bowl and coat with flour. Gradually add cheese to beer. Stir until smooth. Do not boil. Add pepper sauce. Use bagels for dipping.

Yield: 6 to 8 servings

BEAR IN MIND: *If fondue gets too thick, thin with warm beer.*

Cheese Blintzes

1 cup dry cottage cheese (see directions below)	2 (8-ounce) cans refrigerated crescent dinner rolls
1 egg	2 tablespoons butter, melted
1 (3-ounce) package cream cheese	Sour cream to garnish
1 tablespoon sugar	Preserves (any flavor) to garnish
½ teaspoon vanilla	

Preheat oven to 375°. Wrap cottage cheese in cheese cloth and squeeze out liquid before measuring. Prepare filling by mixing together egg, cottage cheese, cream cheese, sugar and vanilla. Separate crescent rolls and form rectangles by joining 2 triangles together. Cut each rectangle in half, forming 16 squares. Place 1 tablespoon filling on one side of each square. Fold over and seal with fork. Brush with melted butter. Bake on cookie sheet 12 to 15 minutes. Serve warm with sour cream and preserves on top.

Yield: 16 blintzes

BEAR IN MIND: May use fresh berries instead of preserves.

Baked Cheese Ring

1 cup water	1 cup all-purpose flour
1 stick butter or margarine	4 eggs
½ teaspoon salt	3 ounces Monterey Jack or Gruyère cheese, grated
Dash pepper	
1 small onion, grated	

Preheat oven to 375°. Grease 14x20-inch cookie sheet. In saucepan, combine water, butter, salt, pepper and onion; bring to a boil. Add flour all at once. Beat over low heat until mixture leaves sides of pan. Add eggs one at a time, beating after each. Continue beating until mixture has satiny sheen and does not separate. Stir in cheese. Spoon out mixture onto cookie sheet, forming a ring 8 to 10 inches in diameter. Bake 30 to 40 minutes.

Yield: 16 to 20 servings

BEAR FLAIR: Place a scooped-out red bell pepper filled with pepper jelly in middle of cheese ring. (Cut small slice off bottom of bell pepper if it wobbles.)

Beary Cranberry Muffins

1	cup fresh raw cranberries, cut in half	1	egg
¾	cup sugar, divided	¼	cup buttermilk
2	cups all-purpose flour	¼	cup oil
¾	teaspoon baking soda		Whipped topping and fresh
¼	teaspoon salt		cranberries for garnish

Preheat oven to 400°. Grease regular size muffin tins. Set aside. In medium bowl, combine cut cranberries with ½ cup sugar. Set aside. Combine remaining ¼ cup sugar with flour, soda, and salt in a large bowl. Combine the egg, buttermilk, and oil and pour into center of dry ingredients. Stir with a fork just until dry ingredients are moistened. Gently fold in the cranberries. Spoon batter into muffin tins, filling each ⅔ full. Bake 20 minutes, or until toothpick inserted in center comes out clean.

Yield: 18 (2½-inch) muffins

BEAR FLAIR: *Garnish with whipped topping and fresh cranberries.*

Luau Muffins

1	stick butter, room temperature	½	teaspoon baking soda
1	cup sugar	1	teaspoon baking powder
1	teaspoon vanilla extract	1	(8-ounce) can unsweetened
2	eggs		crushed pineapple,
2	bananas, mashed		undrained
2	cups all-purpose flour	½	cup shredded coconut

Preheat oven to 350°. Grease regular size muffin tins or use paper muffin liners. Cream butter, sugar and vanilla. Add eggs and bananas. Beat well. Sift together flour, soda and baking powder. Stir flour mixture into creamed mixture, a spoonful at a time. Fold in pineapple and coconut. Fill tins half full. Bake 20 to 25 minutes.

Yield: 16 to 18 (2½-inch) muffins

BEAR IN MIND: *May be baked in miniature muffin tins 17 to 18 minutes. Can also be baked in sheet cake pan 25 to 30 minutes.*

Lemony Date Nut Bread

1	box 2-layer lemon cake mix	½	cup finely chopped pecans
1	cup sour cream	3	tablespoons sugar
¾	stick butter, softened	1	teaspoon cinnamon
¼	cup water	2	tablespoons butter, melted
3	eggs		
1	(8-ounce) package dates, finely chopped		

Preheat oven to 350°. Grease and flour 2 (5x9-inch) loaf pans. Combine cake mix, sour cream, butter, water and eggs. Beat with electric mixer approximately 3 minutes. Stir in dates and nuts. Pour into pans. Bake 40 to 50 minutes. Cool. Combine sugar and cinnamon. Brush tops of cakes with melted butter. Sprinkle with sugar and cinnamon mixture. Garnish with fresh lemon twists.

Yield: 2 loaves

BEAR IN MIND: *Great for Bridge. Make the day before if you like. You may add vanilla extract to batter, if desired.*

Brunch Cake

1	stick butter	½	teaspoon baking soda
1	(8-ounce) package cream cheese	1	teaspoon baking powder
1¼	cups sugar	¼	teaspoon salt
2	eggs	¼	cup milk
1	teaspoon vanilla extract	¾	cup sugar
2	cups cake flour	1	stick butter, softened
		1	cup cake flour

Preheat oven to 350°. Grease 9x13-inch pan. Cream butter, cream cheese and sugar. Add eggs and vanilla. Beat well. Combine flour, baking soda, baking powder and salt. Add alternately with milk until smooth. Combine remaining ingredients until crumbly and spread over batter in pan. Bake 30 to 35 minutes.

Yield: 9x13-inch coffee cake

Blueberry Sweet Rolls

3¼	to 3½ cups all-purpose flour, divided	1	egg
		6	tablespoons butter
1	package dry yeast	½	cup sugar
2	(5-ounce) cans evaporated milk	2	teaspoons cinnamon
		1	teaspoon grated lemon peel
6	tablespoons butter	2	to 3 cups blueberries
¼	cup sugar	1	cup sifted powdered sugar
1	teaspoon salt	2	to 3 tablespoons milk

In large mixing bowl, combine 1½ cups flour and yeast. In saucepan heat milk, the first 6 tablespoons butter, ¼ cup sugar, and salt, just until warm, stirring while butter melts. Add to flour and yeast in bowl, add egg. Beat at low speed 30 seconds, scraping bowl constantly. Beat at high speed 3 minutes. By hand, stir in enough of remaining flour to make a moderately stiff dough. This dough will be fairly moist and sticky, but this is typical. Put dough in greased bowl. Cover with cloth and let rise in warm place until dough is doubled in size, about 1½ hours.

Punch dough down, turn onto well-floured surface, divide in half and let "rest" 10 minutes. Roll each half into an 8x14-inch rectangle. Melt second 6 tablespoons butter and brush on rectangles. Combine ½ cup sugar, cinnamon, and lemon peel and sprinkle on both rectangles. Scatter blueberries evenly on rectangles and press in lightly.

Roll up each rectangle jelly roll-fashion, starting at widest side; cut each roll into 12 equally sized pieces. Place on lightly greased cookie sheet or large casserole pans (place each slice ½ to 1-inch apart). Cover with lightweight cloth and let rise until doubled in size, about 30 to 45 minutes. Bake in 375° oven 20 to 25 minutes.

Remove rolls from oven. Mix powdered sugar and milk. Glaze rolls.

Yield: 24 sweet rolls

BEAR FLAIR:
(1) Garnish tray with fresh blueberry foliage, if available.
(2) You can also sprinkle grated lemon peel over the glaze.

BEAR IN MIND:
(1) If using frozen blueberries, make sure they are thawed at room temperature and well drained. (You can also roll them in a small amount of flour.)
(2) Use double strand of sewing thread (14 to 16 inches long) to slip under each rectangle after you roll it and "cross-over" the ends at the same place, cutting the slices evenly and easily. (A knife makes too much of a mess.)

Sinful Sour Cream Coffee Cake

2	sticks butter, no substitutes	1	teaspoon baking powder
2	cups sugar	½	teaspoon salt
2	eggs	1	cup pecans, chopped
1	cup sour cream	⅓	cup sugar
1	teaspoon vanilla extract	2	teaspoons cinnamon
2	cups all-purpose flour, unsifted		

Preheat oven to 325°. Grease and flour a springform pan (10-inch size). Cream butter and sugar until light and fluffy. Add eggs, one at a time, beating well after each. Fold in sour cream and vanilla. Mix flour, baking powder, and salt, then fold into batter. Spread about half the batter into pan. Combine pecans, sugar and cinnamon. Sprinkle ¾ of sugar mixture over batter in pan. Add the remaining batter and top with rest of the sugar mixture. Bake until wooden toothpick inserted in center comes out almost clean, about 1½ hours. Cool about 10 minutes on wire rack. Remove outer ring of springform pan. Cool completely.

Yield: 8 to 12 slices, depending on size of slice

BEAR IN MIND: *You can substitute ground almonds for pecans and almond extract for vanilla.*

Peach Blossom Crescents

½	cup peach preserves	12	raisins
2	tablespoons finely chopped pecans		Powdered sugar to dust
1	(8-ounce) can refrigerated crescent dinner rolls		

Preheat oven to 350°. Combine preserves and pecans. Unroll crescent dinner roll dough into 2 rectangles. Overlap long sides of rectangles ½ inch. Press edges and perforations in dough to seal. Roll to form a 9x12-inch rectangle. Cut dough into 12 (3-inch) squares. Put squares on an ungreased cookie sheet. Spoon a heaping teaspoon of preserve mixture on each square. Fold four corners of each square to center. Pinch firmly to seal. Bake 12 to 18 minutes, until lightly browned. Immediately press a raisin into center of each "blossom". Dust with powdered sugar.

Yield: 1 dozen "blossoms"

Sunshine Coffee Cake

2	sticks butter, softened	1	teaspoon vanilla extract
1	cup sugar	⅓	cup granulated sugar
2	eggs	¼	cup brown sugar,
2	cups all-purpose flour		firmly packed
1	teaspoon baking powder	1	tablespoon cinnamon
1	teaspoon baking soda	1	cup chopped pecans
¼	teaspoon salt	½	cup orange juice
1	cup sour cream	3	tablespoons sugar

Preheat oven to 325°. Grease 9x13-inch pan. In mixing bowl, cream butter and sugar; add eggs, one at a time, beating well after each. Sift together flour, baking powder, baking soda, salt; add alternately with sour cream, beating on lowest speed of mixer, beginning and ending with flour. Stir in vanilla extract. Pour into pan. Top this mixture with combined ⅓ cup sugar, brown sugar, and cinnamon. Sprinkle nuts on top. Bake 45 minutes or until cooked and brown on top. Cool in pan 10 minutes. Mix orange juice and 3 tablespoons sugar and pour over cake. Coffee cake gets more moist every day.

Yield: 9x13-inch coffee cake

Crispy Apple Tarts

3	large golden delicious apples	⅛	teaspoon cardamom
⅓	cup chopped raisins	⅛	teaspoon salt
¼	cup vanilla wafer crumbs	8	ounces frozen phyllo dough, about 12 sheets, thawed
2	tablespoons sugar		
2	teaspoons fresh orange juice	1¼	sticks unsalted butter, melted
½	teaspoon grated orange rind	½	cup vanilla wafer crumbs
½	teaspoon cinnamon		Powdered sugar for garnish

Preheat oven to 375°. Peel, core, chop apples to measure 3 cups. Mix apples with raisins, wafer crumbs, sugar, orange juice, rind, cinnamon, cardamom and salt. Set aside.

Work with one sheet of phyllo dough at a time. Keep remaining sheets covered with plastic wrap so it won't dry out and become impossible to deal with. Place first sheet of phyllo on a larger sheet of waxed paper.

Brush phyllo with cooled, melted butter. Sprinkle with vanilla wafer crumbs (about 1 tablespoon). Continue layering phyllo sheets, brushing with butter, sprinkling with crumbs.

When 6 sheets have been stacked, cut with knife into 3-inch squares. Repeat this step until all phyllo sheets have been used or your energy runs low. Place each 3-inch square in buttered miniature muffin tins and fill with apple mixture. Bake 15 to 20 minutes. Sprinkle with powdered sugar. Serve warm for peak flavor.

Yield: About 6 dozen miniature apple tarts

BEAR IN MIND: *Can also be prepared up to baking time, then refrigerate 2 days, then bake and devour! Freezes well, too.*

Strudel Special

4	sticks butter, softened	1	cup sugar
2	(3-ounce) packages cream cheese, softened	2	teaspoons cinnamon
		1	(10-ounce) jar preserves
2	eggs, beaten slightly	1	cup pecans, chopped
5	cups all-purpose flour		

Preheat oven to 400°. Cream butter and cream cheese. Add beaten eggs. Mix in flour, 1 cup at a time, thoroughly by hand. Knead dough on floured surface until a smooth compact ball is formed. Wrap dough in waxed paper and chill.

Next day, divide dough into 4 equal portions. Put 3 rolls in refrigerator while rolling out the other portion into a 13x15-inch rectangle. Stretch dough a little at a time as you roll. Combine sugar and cinnamon. Spread rolled dough with one-fourth of the preserves and sprinkle with ¼ cup pecans, then one-fourth the sugar mixture. Roll up jelly roll fashion. Pinch the ends so filling won't seep out during baking. Take another portion (or roll) out of refrigerator and repeat the rolling, filling process.

Place all four rolls on lightly greased baking sheet and bake about 25 minutes or until done. Cut in small pieces while hot.

Yield: 60 (½-inch thick) slices

BEAR IN MIND:
(1) Chill rolling pin and pastry cloth or marble rolling board to make rolling strudel dough easier for you.
(2) Can prepare, freeze and bake when ready to use.

Strawberry Crunchies

Easy and everyone loves them!

1	(10-ounce) can refrigerated biscuits	1	egg, beaten
½	cup sugar	½	stick butter, melted
½	teaspoon cinnamon	10	teaspoons strawberry preserves

Preheat oven to 375°. Separate dough into 10 biscuits. Combine sugar and cinnamon in small bowl. Dip both sides of each biscuit into beaten egg, then in melted butter and finally into sugar mixture. Place on ungreased cookie sheet. With thumb, make deep indentation in center of each biscuit and fill with one teaspoon of strawberry preserves. Bake 15 minutes or until golden brown. Serve warm.

Yield: 10 biscuits

Classic Cheese Soufflé

2	cups grated sharp cheddar cheese, divided	¼	teaspoon cayenne pepper
4	tablespoons butter	¼	teaspoon dry mustard
3	tablespoons all-purpose flour	¼	teaspoon nutmeg
1½	cups half and half	6	egg yolks
1	teaspoon salt	8	egg whites
		¼	teaspoon cream of tartar

Butter 2-quart soufflé dish and sprinkle lightly with ¼ cup grated cheese. Melt butter in saucepan over low heat. Add flour, stirring with wooden spoon until blended. Slowly add half and half, stirring constantly. Cook until mixture thickens, but do not let boil. Add salt, cayenne, mustard, nutmeg, and remaining cheese and blend. Beat egg yolks two at a time and add to mixture, blending after each addition. Remove from heat and place in large bowl. Add cream of tartar to egg whites and beat until stiff. Fold egg whites into cheese sauce and turn into soufflé dish. Sprinkle top with remaining grated cheese. Set soufflé dish in pan of hot water (not boiling) and place in cold oven. Bake at 325° 40 to 50 minutes. (Top should have a delicate brown crust.) Serve immediately!

Yield: 8 servings

BEAR IN MIND: *Cut 3 to 4-inch wide tin foil collar for soufflé dish. Butter lightly and tape to dish. Bake soufflé and remove foil. This makes your soufflé rise higher.*

Quiche and Tell

1½ cups whipping cream	1 (6-ounce) can large pitted
½ cup buttermilk	ripe olives, drained and
4 eggs, slightly beaten	sliced
½ teaspoon salt	1 (9-inch) pastry shell,
Dash pepper	unbaked
¼ pound bacon, cooked	Green onion tops and
and crumbled	whole pitted ripe olives
2 cups shredded Swiss	for garnish
cheese	
2 tablespoons chopped	
green onions	

Preheat oven to 375°. In saucepan heat cream and buttermilk; whisk in eggs and seasonings. Stir in bacon, cheese, onions and olives. Pour mixture into pastry shell. Bake 30 to 35 minutes or until mixture is set and golden brown.

Yield: 6 to 8 servings

BEAR FLAIR: *Push green onion tops into pitted olives and garnish each slice.*

Seafood Lorraine

1 (6-ounce) package	¼ cup chopped green
frozen king crabmeat,	onions
thawed and cleaned	½ cup mayonnaise
¾ cup fresh shrimp,	1 tablespoon all-purpose
peeled, deveined and	flour
cooked	½ cup dry white wine
4 ounces Swiss cheese,	2 eggs, slightly beaten
shredded	1 (9-inch) deep dish
¼ cup chopped celery	pastry shell, unbaked

Preheat oven to 350°. In large bowl combine crab, shrimp, cheese, celery and onions. Pour into pastry shell. In smaller bowl mix mayonnaise, flour, wine and eggs. Pour over seafood mixture in pie shell. Bake 35 to 40 minutes. Serve warm.

Yield: 6 to 8 servings

BEAR FLAIR: *Garnish with fresh lovage sprigs (an herb that has combined flavor of celery and parsley).*

Olive and Bacon Quiche

2	(9-inch) unbaked pastry shells	2	tablespoons chopped onion
8	bacon slices, cooked and crumbled	1	(4-ounce) can sliced mushrooms, drained
2½	tablespoons chopped pimiento-stuffed olives	2	cups shredded Swiss cheese
2	tablespoons chopped bell pepper	5	eggs, beaten
		2	cups half and half
		¼	teaspoon dry mustard

Preheat oven to 400°. Prick bottom and sides of pastry with fork. Bake 3 minutes; remove from oven and gently prick again with fork. Bake 5 minutes longer. Cool. Reset oven to 350°. Sprinkle crumbled bacon, olives, bell pepper and onion evenly into pastry shells. Top with mushrooms and cheese. Set aside. Mix well the beaten eggs, half and half and mustard. Pour mixture into pastry shell. Let stand 10 minutes. Bake 45 to 50 minutes or until set. Let stand 10 minutes before serving.

Yield: 16 slices or 32 or more appetizer servings, depending on size of slices.

Swiss Cheese Pie

1	cup butter-flavored cracker crumbs	¾	cup sour cream
4	tablespoons butter, melted	½	teaspoon salt
			Pepper to taste
6	bacon slices, cooked and crumbled	8	ounces Swiss cheese, shredded
1	cup chopped onion	½	cup shredded sharp cheddar cheese
2	eggs, beaten		

Preheat oven to 375°. Combine crumbs and butter in 8-inch pie plate, forming a crust. Combine crumbled bacon, onion, eggs, sour cream, salt and pepper, then stir in Swiss cheese. Pour very gently into crust. Sprinkle with cheddar cheese. Bake 30 minutes.

Yield: 6 to 8 servings

Sausage and Cheese Squares

1	(8-ounce) can refrigerated crescent rolls	4	eggs, slightly beaten
½	pound ground sausage	¾	cup milk
2	cups grated Monterey Jack or Swiss cheese	¼	teaspoon salt
		¼	teaspoon pepper
3	tablespoons chopped bell pepper	¼	teaspoon oregano

Preheat oven to 425°. Separate crescent rolls and press into ungreased 9x13-inch baking dish. Seal perforations. In skillet, sauté sausage. Drain and crumble. Sprinkle sausage over crescent roll dough. Add cheese, covering sausage. Top cheese with bell pepper. Mix remaining ingredients. Pour over sausage mixture. Bake 20 to 25 minutes or until golden brown. Cut into squares.

Yield: 6 to 8 servings

Artichoke and Ham Casserole

4	tablespoons butter	12	thin slices ham
4	tablespoons flour		Buttered bread crumbs for topping
2	cups milk		Grated Parmesan cheese to taste
1	cup grated Swiss cheese Paprika to taste Salt and pepper to taste		
2	(14-ounce) cans artichoke hearts, drained		

Preheat oven to 350°. Melt butter in saucepan, stir in flour, then milk. Heat, stirring constantly until thickened. Add cheese, paprika, salt and pepper, stirring until melted. Cut artichokes in half and wrap 2 halves in a slice of ham. Arrange in shallow casserole with sides touching. Pour sauce over ham. Combine bread crumbs and Parmesan cheese and sprinkle over sauce. Bake 30 minutes.

Yield: 6 servings

BEAR FLAIR:
(1) When serving buffet-style, cut ham in smaller pieces and wrap around a quarter of an artichoke heart. It will be easier to serve and eat.
(2) A shiny red colander filled with fresh green artichokes creates a unique centerpiece. Add touches of fresh greenery.

Florentine Eggs

8	hard-cooked eggs	2	teaspoons lemon juice
1	(10-ounce) package frozen chopped spinach, cooked and drained	2	tablespoons butter, melted Salt and pepper to taste
½	tablespoon grated onion	2	cups medium White Sauce, page 164
1	teaspoon Worcester-shire sauce		Buttered bread crumbs for topping

Preheat oven to 350°. Slice eggs in half lengthwise. Remove and mash yolks. Combine yolks, spinach, onion, Worcestershire, lemon juice, butter, salt and pepper. Mix well and fill egg whites. Place eggs in 8-inch square baking dish. Pour white sauce over eggs and top with buttered bread crumbs. Bake until bubbly.

Yield: 8 to 10 servings

BEAR FLAIR: Can be baked in individual 4-inch Sourdough Rolls, basic recipe page 95. Serve on plate lined with fresh spinach leaves.

BEAR IN MIND: Add dash of cayenne pepper to white sauce for an extra kick.

Eggs Cajun

tasty and different

1	(15-ounce) can tomatoes	6	hard-cooked eggs, sliced
1	small onion, chopped	1	cup thick White Sauce, page 164
1	bell pepper, chopped		Buttered bread crumbs for topping
2	celery stalks, chopped Salt and pepper to taste		

Preheat oven to 350°. Grease 1-quart baking dish. In saucepan, mix together tomatoes, onion, bell pepper, celery, salt and pepper. Cook 20 minutes on low heat until tender. Set aside. Prepare white sauce. Layer eggs in baking dish. Cover eggs with white sauce, then the tomato sauce. Top with buttered bread crumbs. Bake 30 minutes.

Yield: 6 to 8 servings

BEAR IN MIND: Great for preparing the night before your bridge party or brunch.

Brunch Eggs Sonora

6	(6-inch) flour tortillas	1	cup guacamole dip or mashed avocado
1	dozen eggs, scrambled		
1	cup grated cheddar cheese	¼	cup sliced pitted ripe olives
6	to 10 bacon slices, cooked and crumbled		
		6	tablespoons sour cream
1	medium onion, finely chopped	1	(8-ounce) jar taco sauce
1	(4-ounce) can chopped green chilies, drained		

Preheat oven to 350°. Lightly grease 11x14-inch cookie sheet. Wrap tortillas together in foil. Bake 15 minutes. Remove tortillas from oven and arrange them on cookie sheet. Layer eggs, cheese, bacon, onion, chilies, guacamole and olives, divided evenly on each warm tortilla. Return tortillas to oven and warm 5 to 10 minutes longer. Top each tortilla with a tablespoon of sour cream. Serve with taco sauce.

Yield: 6 servings

BEAR FLAIR: *For your family, make to order with different toppings for varying tastes.*

Linda's Brunch Special
wonderful and easy

8	eggs	8	ounces sharp cheddar cheese, grated
4	cups milk		
1½	teaspoons dry mustard	1	(8-ounce) can sliced mushrooms, drained
1	teaspoon salt		
1	teaspoon pepper	5	bacon slices, cooked and crumbled
1	(6-ounce) box croutons		

Preheat oven to 350°. Grease 9x13-inch baking dish. Beat together eggs, milk, mustard, salt and pepper until well-blended. Add croutons, cheese and mushrooms. Mix well. Pour into baking dish. Bake 50 to 60 minutes. Sprinkle with bacon.

Yield: 10 to 12 servings

Shrimp and Eggs
men love this

½	stick butter	¼	teaspoon dry mustard
¼	cup all-purpose flour	½	teaspoon instant minced onion
½	teaspoon salt		
2	cups milk	6	hard-cooked eggs, sliced
1½	cups shredded sharp cheddar cheese	1	pound fresh shrimp, peeled, deveined and cooked
1	tablespoon Worcestershire sauce		Bread crumbs for topping

Preheat oven to 350°. Grease 9x11-inch baking dish. Melt butter in saucepan over low heat. Stir in flour and salt. Gradually add milk, stirring until smooth. Add cheese, stirring until melted. Stir in Worcestershire sauce, mustard and onion. Set aside. Arrange slices of eggs on bottom of baking dish. Layer shrimp over eggs. Pour cheese sauce over shrimp and top with bread crumbs. Bake 25 minutes or until bubbly.

Yield: 4 to 6 servings

BEAR FLAIR: *This is a hardy brunch dish. Can also be used as an entrée, served over rice.*

Eggs Blackstone

2	English muffins, split and toasted	4	eggs, poached
		¾	cup mayonnaise
1	(10-ounce) package frozen chopped spinach, thawed	2	tablespoons lemon juice
		8	pitted ripe olives, sliced

Prepare English muffins. Cook spinach, drain well and divide among English muffins. Top each muffin with a poached egg. Mix mayonnaise and lemon juice; spread on each egg. Garnish with olives.

Yield: 4 servings

BEAR IN MIND: *If you don't have an egg poacher, fill an oiled skillet with boiling water; reduce heat to simmering. Break an egg in saucer and slip one at a time into the water. Slide egg toward side of pan to keep yolk in center. Cook below simmering 3 to 5 minutes.*

Deviled Eggs in Shrimp Sauce

8	hard-cooked eggs, sliced lengthwise
4	tablespoons mayonnaise
¼	teaspoon curry powder
2	(10½-ounce) cans cream of shrimp soup

Preheat oven to 350°. Remove egg yolks. Mash and mix yolks with mayonnaise and curry powder. Fill egg whites with yolk mixture and place in 8-inch square dish. Heat soup in saucepan and pour over eggs. Bake 20 minutes or until bubbly.

Yield: 6 to 8 servings

BEAR FLAIR: Just before serving, arrange fresh sprigs of dill on each egg.

Sour Cream-Shirred Eggs

1	cup sour cream, divided
4	eggs
	Salt and pepper to taste
2	teaspoons chopped fresh parsley, divided
2	teaspoons chopped fresh chives, divided
2	tablespoons unsalted butter, melted
¼	cup dry bread crumbs
8	toast points or English muffins
	Fresh parsley sprigs to garnish

Preheat oven to 450°. Spoon ¼ cup sour cream into each of 4 (5 or 6-ounce) custard cups. Make indentation in sour cream in each cup, using back of spoon. Break an egg into each indentation. Salt and pepper eggs to taste. Sprinkle ½ teaspoon parsley and ½ teaspoon chives on each egg. Melt butter in small skillet. Stir in bread crumbs and sauté in butter 2 to 3 minutes. Divide crumbs and butter evenly over 4 eggs. Bake 10 to 15 minutes. Spoon each egg with sour cream over 2 toast points. Serve immediately. (These have a marvelous aroma while baking, you'll find it hard to wait!)

Yield: 4 servings

BEAR FLAIR: Arrange parsley sprigs in center of each egg. Asparagus spears, bacon-wrapped broiled salmon and blueberry muffins would "top-off" this dining experience.

BEAR IN MIND: For oven-poached eggs, substitute 1 cup plain lowfat yogurt for sour cream and proceed as directed. Tangy and low in calories! However, drain eggs well after baking, before serving on crisp toast points.

Delicate Grits

4 cups milk	½ stick butter
1 stick butter	Freshly grated nutmeg
1 cup uncooked grits	for garnish
1 cup grated Swiss cheese	⅓ cup grated Parmesan
Salt and pepper to taste	cheese

Preheat oven to 375°. Grease 2-quart casserole. Bring milk and butter to a slow boil and stir in grits slowly. Stir often, until mixture thickens. Put in large bowl, beat with electric mixer until grits become creamy, about 5 minutes. Add grated Swiss cheese, salt and pepper. Mix well. Pour mixture into casserole. Dot with butter and grate nutmeg on top. Sprinkle with Parmesan cheese. Bake 35 to 40 minutes.

Yield: 6 to 8 servings

Nassau Grits

12 ounces bacon, cut in 1-inch pieces	½ teaspoon basil
	½ teaspoon oregano
1 bell pepper, finely chopped	½ teaspoon salt
	½ teaspoon garlic powder
2 small onions, finely chopped	½ teaspoon pepper
	½ teaspoon Worcester-
1 cup uncooked grits	shire sauce
2 (15-ounce) cans tomatoes, undrained	½ teaspoon hot pepper sauce

Fry bacon pieces in Dutch oven. Remove bacon, cool, crumble, and set aside. Sauté bell pepper and onions in bacon drippings. Drain and discard drippings. In same pan with onions and peppers, cook grits according to package directions. Cut up tomatoes; add tomatoes and their liquid to grits. Add remaining ingredients and bacon. Simmer 30 minutes.

Yield: 6 to 8 servings

BEAR IN MIND: *This recipe originally came from the Bahama Islands where it was served with fish. Since, it has been adapted to a breakfast brunch dish at Christmas time with scrambled eggs and trimmings!*

Grits Roulade

⅔	cup milk	2	cups fresh mushrooms, sliced
⅓	cup plain yogurt		
⅓	cup quick cooking grits	4	tablespoons butter, divided
4	ounces cheddar cheese, grated		
		3	tablespoons all-purpose flour
4	egg yolks		
	Salt and pepper to taste	2	cups milk
6	egg whites		

Preheat oven to 350°. Oil jelly roll pan, then oil waxed paper and line pan. Combine milk and yogurt in saucepan, heat to boiling, then add grits and cook according to package directions. Add cheese, egg yolks one at a time, then salt and pepper. Whisk egg whites until they stand in firm peaks. Fold in a spoonful of the egg whites, then add the rest. Do not overfold. Spread the entire mixture into the jelly roll pan. Bake 15 minutes or until toothpick inserted comes out clean.

While baking, prepare mushroom filling. Sauté mushrooms lightly in 1 tablespoon butter until tender. Set aside. Melt remaining butter and add flour. Stir in milk and cook until thickened. Add mushrooms and blend thoroughly. Remove grits from oven and turn pan upside down onto another piece of waxed paper. Remove pan and peel off waxed paper. Spread mushroom filling over grits. Roll up like a jelly roll.

Yield: 4 to 6 servings

BEAR IN MIND:
(1) Swiss and Parmesan cheese can be mixed and substituted for cheddar cheese in the grits mixture.
(2) The filling can be made of sour cream and mushrooms. You may also add ham.

Brunch Punch

1¼	ounces brandy (or bourbon)	1	teaspoon powdered sugar
⅓	cup half and half	⅛	teaspoon vanilla extract
			Dash nutmeg

Combine brandy, half and half, powdered sugar and vanilla in blender. Blend 10 to 30 seconds. Pour into ice-filled glass. Sprinkle with nutmeg.

Yield: 1 serving

Bloody Mary

1 (32-ounce) can tomato juice	1 teaspoon seasoned salt
½ cup canned beef broth	2 dashes hot pepper sauce
Juice of 3 lemons	Dash garlic powder
1 tablespoon Worcestershire sauce	Vodka to mix
	Lemon twists to garnish
½ teaspoon salt	Celery stalks to garnish
½ teaspoon pepper	

Combine tomato juice, beef broth, lemon juice, Worcestershire sauce, salt, pepper, seasoned salt, hot pepper sauce and garlic powder. Mix well. In a tall glass with ice, use 6 ounces of mix with 1½ ounces of vodka. Add a twist of lemon and garnish with celery stalk.

Yield: 8 servings

BEAR IN MIND: *The mix without vodka will keep 7 days in the refrigerator.*

Mock Julius

3 ounces frozen orange juice concentrate, thawed	1 tablespoon sugar
	½ teaspoon vanilla extract
1 cup milk	6 to 8 ice cubes

Put orange juice, milk, sugar, vanilla and ice in blender. Blend thoroughly until smooth. (You may need to start and stop blender several times, and stir with a wooden spoon to push ice cubes to bottom.)

Yield: 4 servings

BEAR IN MIND:
Reduce calories by substituting 1 cup skim milk, or ½ cup milk and ½ cup water, and a sugar substitute.

Breads

"BEARING GIFTS"

*WHOLE WHEAT BREAD, page 92 ... put in a basket with a bottle of wine and a crock filled with Monterey Jack cheese and your gift is instant picnic material!

*EASY YEAST ROLLS, page 93 ... bake in miniature muffin tins; place in napkin-lined basket and add a small container of **BETTER BUTTER**, page 83.

*SOURDOUGH STARTER, page 94 ... put in junior-size baby food jar; add recipe for ***SOURDOUGH CHEESE & CHIVES ROLLS,** page 95.

*SOURDOUGH BEAR BREAD, page 96 ... prepare bears, add a plaid ribbon where a necktie would be. Wrap in clear wrap and give with one of your homemade preserves or a honeyed butter.

*BEER BREAD, page 90 ... bake in miniature loaf pans. Slice and overlap in a circle around a hollowed-out winter squash filled with strawberry butter.

*FRENCH HARD ROLLS, page 84 ... are relatively easy and absolutely delectable with a cold pasta salad in the summer.

*FRUIT RAGE COFFEE CAKE, page 85 ... bake in muffin tins; pack in a basket. Take along some **SAUCY APPLE SENSATION,** page 314, to top it off!

*SINFUL SOUR CREAM COFFEE CAKE, page 65 ... bake cake in purchased gift springform pan — an unforgettable gift.

*BABY BROCCOLI MUFFINS, page 83 ... give recipe on card and a couple of miniature muffin tins.

*BROWN IN THE ROUND, page 87 ... give unsliced loaves nestled in a basket with the recipe for bread and a sweetened cream cheese spread and a jar of pepper jelly.

*PUMPKIN BREAD, page 87, or **SQUASH BREAD,** page 88 ... bake in miniature loaf pans. Tie with a burlap ribbon and place on top of fresh fruit basket. Perfect at Thanksgiving.

*THE BEST BANANA MUFFINS, page 82 ... wrap a produce basket with a pretty striped fabric (pink the edges with pinking shears if you are in a hurry). Tie a bow to handle, using fabric.

"BEAR ESSENTIALS FOR ENTERTAINING"

*Use scented geranium leaves to garnish stick of butter or use a row of leaves to form a frilly green doily for a pound cake. You can also bury fresh leaves of scented geranium to flavor sugar; leave in at least 24 hours, discard leaves and use sugar for tea or cooking cakes.

*Add some of your favorite preserves or jelly to softened butter, whip until blended. Serve with English muffins or bagels for a neighborhood coffee.

*When preparing sandwiches a few hours in advance, dampen a paper towel (squeeze out excess moisture); layer sandwiches with damp towel and waxed paper; cover with foil and chill until serving time.

*Combine small amount of **PESTO SAUCE,** page 44, with butter or mayonnaise; spread on French bread slices. Broil in oven. Great with **MARINATED TOMATOES,** page 122.

*Dip both sides of 2 slices of French or Italian bread in ¼ cup dairy eggnog and 1 tablespoon orange-flavored liqueur; cook in 2 tablespoons butter over medium heat until golden brown. Dust with powdered sugar; add grated orange rind and freshly grated nutmeg; serve warm with honey or syrup.

Aunt Estha's Mayonnaise Biscuits

1	**cup self-rising flour**	**2**	**tablespoons mayonnaise**
½	**cup milk**		

Preheat oven to 450°. Lightly grease muffin tins. Mix ingredients in bowl with a fork just until moistened. Drop by teaspoonful into muffin tins. Bake for 20 to 25 minutes. Some add an egg, but Aunt Estha says with self-rising flour, you don't need an egg.

Yield: 12 biscuits

BEAR IN MIND: Add 1 teaspoon finely chopped chives to dough when mixing. Or for a peppery flavor, add 1 teaspoon finely chopped nasturium leaves.

Stir and Roll Biscuits

2	**cups self-rising flour**	**⅓**	**cup vegetable oil**
	Pinch salt	**⅔**	**cup buttermilk**
¼	**teaspoon baking soda**		

Preheat oven to 450°. Put flour, salt, and soda in mixing bowl. Combine oil and buttermilk in liquid measuring cup. Pour liquid ingredients into dry ingredients and stir quickly with a fork until dough clings together. Turn out onto lightly floured surface, knead lightly. Roll out and cut with biscuit cutter. Place on ungreased baking sheet and bake about 10 minutes.

Yield: 16 to 20 biscuits

BEAR IN MIND:

(1) If you don't have a biscuit cutter, use a glass or an empty tin can.
(2) Add minced green onion to dough for ham biscuits; add grated orange rind to dough for biscuits with orange marmalade.

🐾 Cheese Biscuits

8	ounces New York sharp cheddar cheese, grated
1	stick butter
2	cups all-purpose flour
½	teaspoon Worcestershire sauce
	Salt and red pepper to taste

Preheat oven to 350°. Mix all ingredients well; roll thin. Cut with small biscuit cutter and then cut centers out with small thimble! Bake with oven door cracked.

Yield: 4 to 5 dozen

BEAR IN MIND: *Chopped nuts may be added for variation.*

The Best Banana Muffins

½	cup shortening
1½	cups sugar
2	eggs, well beaten
2	cups all-purpose flour
¾	teaspoon baking soda
1	teaspoon baking powder
2	teaspoons salt
½	cup buttermilk
1	cup mashed bananas
1½	teaspoons vanilla extract
½	cup chopped pecans
4	tablespoons margarine, melted
1	teaspoon cinnamon
2	tablespoons sugar

Preheat oven to 375°. Butter regular size muffin tins. Cream shortening, sugar and eggs. Sift the flour, baking soda, baking powder and salt. Add alternately the flour and buttermilk, beginning and ending with the flour. Stir in bananas, vanilla and pecans. Fill muffin tins ¾ full. Bake 15 to 20 minutes. While still warm, dip tops of muffins in melted butter, then in cinnamon/sugar mixture.

Yield: 24 (2½-inch) muffins

Baby Broccoli Muffins

1	(10-ounce) package frozen chopped broccoli	4	eggs, beaten
1	(7½-ounce) box corn muffin mix	1	stick margarine, melted
		¾	cup cottage cheese
		1	large onion, chopped

Preheat oven to 425°. Grease miniature muffin tins. Cook broccoli according to package directions. Drain well. Mix corn muffin mix, eggs, melted margarine, cottage cheese, onion, and drained broccoli until blended. Put in miniature muffin tins and bake 10-12 minutes.

Yield: About 5 to 6 dozen muffins

BEAR FLAIR: *Dollop with sour cream and a tiny fresh broccoli floweret. Marvelous.*

BEAR IN MIND: *These freeze very nicely.*

Better Butter

2	sticks unsalted butter, softened	2	tablespoons chopped fresh dill weed
2	tablespoons chopped parsley	1	tablespoon chopped fresh chives

Process the butter and herbs in food processor, using steel blade, until well-blended. Press into molds or shape by hand or butter paddles. Chill at least 4 hours for flavors to blend.

Yield: 1 cup butter

BEAR FLAIR:
   (1) *Scoop out a small cabbage head and fill with better butter. Add a sprig of fresh dill or parsley on top.*
   (2) *Great on baked potatoes, French bread, broiled fish and anything your heart desires.*

French Hard Rolls

Easy mixer method!

3	to 3¼ cups all-purpose flour, divided	1	tablespoon sugar
1	package dry yeast	2	tablespoons shortening
1	cup water	1½	teaspoons salt
		2	egg whites

In large mixing bowl, combine 1¼ cups flour and yeast. In saucepan, heat water, sugar, shortening and salt just until warm; stirring occasionally to melt shortening. Add water mixture to dry ingredients in mixer bowl; add egg whites. Beat at low speed of mixer 30 seconds, scraping sides of bowl carefully. Beat 3 minutes at high speed. By hand or spoon, stir in enough of the remaining flour to make a moderately soft dough. Turn onto floured surface; knead 8 to 10 minutes. Place dough in well-greased bowl, turn to coat surface. Cover bowl with damp cloth. Let rise in warm place until doubled, about 50 to 60 minutes.

Punch dough down with fist. Let rest 10 minutes. Divide dough into 20 balls. Shape into an oval and place on lightly greased cookie sheet. With sharp knife, make a ⅛-inch deep slit down top of each roll. Cover with slightly damp cloth and let rise in warm place until doubled in size, 30 to 40 minutes.

Place large shallow pan on bottom rack of 450° oven. Pour boiling water into pan. Bake rolls on rack above water 10 to 12 minutes until golden brown.

Yield: 20 rolls

BEAR IN MIND: *These rolls are not extremely crusty or hard; they are great with a cold pasta salad.*

Fruit Rage Coffee Cake

½	cup brown sugar, firmly packed	¾	cup sugar
2	tablespoons butter, softened	¾	stick butter, melted
½	teaspoon cinnamon	1½	cups all-purpose flour
15	fig-filled bar cookies, crumbled	1½	teaspoons baking powder
2	eggs	½	teaspoon salt
		½	cup milk
		1	teaspoon vanilla extract

Preheat oven to 350°. Grease and flour an 8-inch square pan. Combine brown sugar, butter, cinnamon and crumbled cookies; mix well and set aside. Beat eggs in a large bowl until frothy; add sugar and melted butter. Beat well. Combine flour, baking powder and salt. Gradually add flour mixture to egg mixture alternately with milk; blending well. Stir in vanilla. Pour half of batter into pan; top with half of fig mixture. Pour remaining batter over fig layer. Sprinkle remaining fig mixture on top. Bake in 350° oven 40 to 45 minutes.

Yield: 8-inch square coffee cake or 12 (2½-inch) muffins

BEAR IN MIND:
(1) If you prefer muffins, the batter and filling will be ⅞ of muffin tin. It will not rise and spill out of muffin tins as you fear it might.
(2) Use any other fruit flavor bar cookies such as apple, cherry or blueberry.

Orange Nut Bread

2	cups all-purpose flour	1	teaspoon grated orange rind
1	teaspoon baking soda		
¾	teaspoon salt	¼	teaspoon grated lemon rind
½	cup sugar		
1	egg, well beaten	¼	cup shortening, melted
¾	cup orange juice	¾	cup chopped pecans
2	tablespoons lemon juice		

Preheat oven to 350°. Grease 5x9-inch loaf pan; line with wax paper. Combine flour, soda, salt and sugar. Sift. Combine egg, orange juice, lemon juice, grated rinds, and shortening. Stir only until well mixed. Add pecans. Pour into pan. Cover and let stand 20 minutes. Bake 1 hour.

Yield: 1 (5x9-inch) loaf

Blueberry Sour Cream Coffee Cake

2	sticks butter	1	cup fresh or
1	cup sugar		frozen blueberries
2	eggs	¼	cup brown sugar,
1	cup sour cream		firmly packed
1	teaspoon baking soda	2	tablespoons sugar
1	teaspoon almond extract	1	tablespoon cinnamon
2	cups all-purpose flour	2	tablespoons milk
1	teaspoon baking powder	1	cup powdered sugar, sifted
½	teaspoon salt	½	teaspoon vanilla extract

Preheat oven to 350°. Grease or spray 10-inch tube or Bundt pan. Cream butter and sugar. Add eggs, one at a time, beating well after each egg. Then stir in sour cream, to which baking soda has been mixed in. Add almond extract. Sift flour, baking powder and salt. Stir dry ingredients into batter. Pour half to two-thirds batter into pan. Sprinkle one cup blueberries over batter. Combine brown sugar, sugar and cinnamon and sprinkle over blueberries. Pour remaining batter over blueberries and sugar. Bake 40 to 45 minutes.

While coffeecake is cooling, prepare glaze mixture; add milk slowly to powdered sugar and beat well and stir in vanilla. Remove cake from pan after 20 minutes of cooling. Drizzle cake with glaze.

Yield: 10-inch tube cake

BEAR IN MIND: *If using frozen blueberries, make sure they are thawed and well-drained and at room temperature before sprinkling over batter.*

Poppy Seed Bread

2	cups sugar	1	teaspoon baking soda
4	eggs	2	ounces poppy seeds
1½	cups oil	1	cup milk
3	cups all-purpose flour	1	teaspoon vanilla extract
1	teaspoon salt		

Preheat oven to 325°. Grease and flour 6 (3x6x2-inch) loaf pans. Combine sugar and eggs; beat well. Add oil and mix to blend. Combine flour, salt, soda and poppy seeds. Add flour mixture, alternately with milk to sugar and eggs. Beat in vanilla. Pour equally into pans. Bake 20 minutes or until toothpick inserted in center comes out clean.

Yield: 6 miniature loaves

Brown in the Round

1	cup raisins	3	cups all-purpose flour
2	cups water	2	teaspoons baking soda
1	cup sugar	½	teaspoon salt
2	eggs	½	cup chopped nuts
2	tablespoons shortening		

Preheat oven to 325°. Thoroughly grease and flour 4 (16-ounce) cans. Boil raisins in water in small saucepan 5 minutes. Process in blender to finely distribute raisins in liquid. Mix sugar, eggs and shortening in mixing bowl until well blended, then add raisin mixture. Beat well. Add combined mixture of flour, soda, salt and nuts. Pour into cans. Cans should be about half full. Bake 40 to 45 minutes. Cool in cans about 10 minutes. Turn out of cans onto cooling rack. Slice and serve.

Yield: 4 round loaves, 3-inch diameter x 4-inches long

BEAR FLAIR: *Especially good with cream cheese spread and hot pepper jelly.*

BEAR IN MIND: *Freezes well. Great gifts at Christmas.*

Pumpkin Bread

1½	cups sugar	½	teaspoon cinnamon
1⅔	cups all-purpose flour	½	cup vegetable oil
¼	teaspoon baking powder	½	cup water
1	teaspoon baking soda	1	cup mashed pumpkin
¾	teaspoon salt	2	eggs
½	teaspoon cloves	½	cup chopped pecans
½	teaspoon nutmeg		

Preheat oven to 350°. Butter and flour 2 (5x9-inch) loaf pans. Sift together sugar, flour, baking powder, baking soda, salt, cloves, nutmeg and cinnamon. Stir in remaining ingredients. Pour the batter into pans and bake 1 hour.

Yield: 2 (5x9-inch) loaves

BEAR IN MIND:
(1) Add miniature chocolate chips in batter for a different "bear twist."
(2) Can bake 35 to 40 minutes in 6 miniature loaf pans.
(3) Make several batches in October and put in freezer for super gifts for favorite people.

Squash Bread

1	cup cooked, mashed yellow squash	1	cup all-purpose flour
1	cup granulated sugar	1	teaspoon baking soda
½	cup brown sugar, firmly packed	½	teaspoon salt
		½	teaspoon cinnamon
2	eggs	¾	teaspoon nutmeg
½	cup oil	¼	teaspoon ginger
¼	cup water	1	cup golden raisins
1	cup whole wheat flour	½	cup chopped pecans

Preheat oven to 350°. Thoroughly grease and flour 5x7-inch loaf pan. In medium mixing bowl, combine squash, sugars, eggs, oil and water. In large bowl stir together flours, baking soda, salt, cinnamon, nutmeg and ginger. Add squash mixture to dry ingredients. Mix well. Stir in raisins and pecans. Turn batter into pan. Bake 70 to 75 minutes until done. Remove from pan after 10 minutes to cool. Cool on rack.

Yield: 1 (5x7-inch) loaf

Apple Dumplings

1	cup sugar	1	(8-ounce) can refrigerated crescent dinner rolls
1	cup water	1	(20-ounce) can apple pie filling
1	stick butter, divided		
½	teaspoon cinnamon		Cinnamon, sugar and nutmeg to sprinkle
½	teaspoon nutmeg		

Preheat oven to 350°. In medium saucepan combine sugar, water, 5½ tablespoons butter, cinnamon and nutmeg. Bring to a boil; set aside. Separate dinner rolls and roll thin. Spoon 2 tablespoons of pie filling into middle of each piece of dough. Fold over and seal edges. Place in shallow baking dish. Sprinkle with a little cinnamon, sugar and nutmeg. Dot with remaining butter. Pour sugar mixture over dumplings. Bake 30 minutes or until brown, basting often.

Yield: 8 dumplings

BEAR IN MIND: *Keep these ingredients "on hand" for a quick and easy treat.*

Back-to-School Breakfast Treats

½	pound bacon, cooked crisp	1	cup all-purpose flour
1	stick butter	¼	teaspoon baking soda
½	cup sugar	2½	cups corn flakes
¼	cup dark brown sugar, firmly packed	¾	cup raisins
		½	teaspoon vanilla extract
1	egg	½	teaspoon cinnamon

Preheat oven to 350°. Cream butter and both sugars until light and fluffy. Add egg and beat well. Combine flour and soda. Stir into butter mixture. Crumble bacon and add to batter. Add corn flakes, raisins, vanilla and cinnamon. Mix well. Place rounded tablespoons of mixture 2 inches apart on ungreased cookie sheet. Bake about 12 minutes or until golden brown. Remove from cookie sheet and cool.

Yield: 2 dozen cookies

BEAR IN MIND: *Allow to cool completely and store in refrigerator for quick and easy school-morning breakfasts. Also perfect for trips or camping.*

Seasoned Parmesan Pull-Aparts

3	tablespoons butter or margarine	1	teaspoon poppy seed
1	tablespoon instant minced onion	1	(10-ounce) can refrigerated biscuits
2	teaspoons dill weed or seed	⅓	cup grated Parmesan cheese

Preheat oven to 400°. Melt butter in 8 or 9-inch cake pan (in oven). Tilt pan to coat bottom with butter. Sprinkle onion, dill and poppy seed evenly over melted butter. Separate dough into 10 biscuits, then cut each one into 4 pieces. Place biscuit pieces and cheese in plastic bag; shake evenly to coat. Arrange the coated biscuit pieces evenly in prepared pan. Sprinkle any remaining cheese in the bag over biscuits in the pan. Bake 15 to 18 minutes, or until golden brown. Turn out onto serving plate and serve warm.

Yield: 10 biscuits

Circle of Cheese Pastry

2½   cups all-purpose flour
2   sticks margarine, softened
1   cup sour cream
1   teaspoon seasoned salt

3   cups shredded sharp
     cheddar cheese
½   teaspoon paprika
     Sliced olives, optional

Preheat oven to 350°. Blend together flour, margarine and sour cream. Chill at least 30 minutes. Roll dough into approximately a 12x20-inch rectangle and sprinkle with seasoned salt, cheese and paprika. (At this time you may add sliced olives, scattered over the cheese.) Roll up jelly roll fashion, beginning at longest side and form into a circle. With kitchen shears, cut three-fourths of the way through the dough on the top side. Be sure the seam side of the ring of dough is on the bottom of the lightly greased pan. Bake 30 to 35 minutes.

Yield: 12 large servings or 24 small servings

BEAR IN MIND:
  *(1) For variety, sprinkle with toasted pecans or bacon before rolling
       jelly roll fashion.*
  (2) Can be prepared the day before and baked before serving.

Beer Bread

hearty, crunchy, "easy-to-do" bread

3   cups self-rising flour
3   tablespoons sugar
1   (10½-ounce) can warm
     beer

3   teaspoons butter,
     melted, divided

Preheat oven to 400°. Grease 5x9-inch loaf pan. In mixing bowl, mix flour, sugar and beer. Place into pan. Butter top with 1½ teaspoons butter. Bake 60 to 70 minutes. Butter top again while hot. Keeps well.

Yield: 5x9-inch loaf

Angel Biscuits with Variations

2 packages dry yeast	1 teaspoon baking soda
¼ cup warm water	1 cup shortening
5 cups self-rising flour	2 cups buttermilk
⅓ cup sugar	

Preheat oven to 450°. Dissolve yeast in warm water. Set aside 5 to 10 minutes. Combine flour, sugar and baking soda; work in shortening using pastry blender or two knives until mixture resembles "small peas" in size and shape. Stir in yeast water and room temperature buttermilk. Roll out on heavily floured board. Cut as desired. Let rise one hour and bake until golden brown. Unused dough keeps a week in refrigerator.

Yield: 5 to 6 dozen biscuits

Variation #1—Onion Bread:

Use ⅓ of the above dough. Add ⅓ cup chopped onion and ½ teaspoon garlic salt; mix. Roll out on floured board and cut strips 1x3-inch, roll in melted butter and place 8 to 12 pieces in a buttered loaf pan. Top with sesame or poppy seeds and more garlic salt. Bake at 425° until golden brown. Biscuits pull apart easily for serving.

Variation #2—Cinnamon Rolls:

Use ⅓ of the above dough for 12 to 15 rolls. Roll out dough on floured board and spread ½ stick melted butter easily over it. Sprinkle with mixture of cinnamon and sugar (about 1 teaspoon cinnamon to ¼ cup sugar, mixed together). Roll up jellyroll fashion and slice with a string, 1-inch thick slices. Place in buttered muffin tins or close together in cake pan. Top with chopped nuts (optional) and bake 425° until golden brown. Glaze with mixture of a few drops of milk and powdered sugar.

Raised Corn Muffins

1 package dry yeast	½ cup shortening
¼ cup lukewarm water	2 eggs
2 cups scalded milk	4 to 4½ cups all-purpose flour, divided
1 cup yellow cornmeal	3 to 4 tablespoons butter, melted
1 tablespoon salt	
½ cup sugar	

Soften yeast in lukewarm water. Pour scalded milk over cornmeal, salt, sugar and shortening; stir well. Cool to lukewarm (85°). Beat in eggs and 2 cups flour. Add softened yeast, mixing well. Stir in enough flour to make a batter. Cover and let rise until doubled in size, about 1 hour. Stir down and spoon batter into greased muffin tins, filling half full. Cover and let rise again until doubled in size. Bake in 400° oven about 20 minutes. Remove and brush tops with melted butter.

Yield: 3 to 4 dozen muffins

Whole Wheat Bread
this is so easy!

2 packages dry yeast	2¼ cups milk
6 cups whole wheat flour	¼ cup oil
¼ cup sugar	1 egg, beaten
1 tablespoon salt	

Preheat oven to 350°. Grease 2 (5x9-inch) loaf pans. Combine yeast, flour, sugar, and salt in a mixing bowl. Heat milk and oil in saucepan until very warm (120 to 130°). Let cool until mixture reaches 98°. Stir milk, oil, and egg into the mixing bowl with flour to form a soft dough. Knead until smooth, about 5 minutes. Place in a large, greased bowl and turn to grease all sides. Cover and leave in warm place until light and doubled in size. Punch down dough and shape into 2 loaves; put into pans. Cover and let rise again until doubled in size. Bake 45 to 50 minutes or until done. Remove from pans to cool.

Yield: 2 (5x9-inch) loaves

Easy Yeast Rolls

1	cup buttermilk	1	cup whole wheat flour
¾	cup water	1	cup self-rising flour
¼	cup margarine	2	eggs, beaten
2	packages dry yeast	3¼	cups all-purpose flour,
1	teaspoon salt		divided
¼	cup sugar		

Combine buttermilk, water and margarine in saucepan. Warm over low heat to melt margarine. Combine yeast, salt, sugar, whole wheat flour and self-rising flour in mixing bowl. Add warm buttermilk mixture. Beat well. Add beaten eggs and ½ cup all-purpose flour. Mix well. Add remaining flour. Turn onto floured surface. Knead. (Oiling hands eliminates the need for a lot of extra flour in kneading which makes a lighter finished roll.) Put dough in a greased or oiled bowl, oil top of dough, cover and put in a warm place (75 to 80°) for 1 hour. Lightly grease cookie sheet. Punch dough down. Shape into desired rolls. Place on lightly greased pans. Cover and let rise in warm place about one hour. Bake in 350 to 375° oven 12 to 15 minutes.

Yield: 30 rolls

BEAR IN MIND:

(1) For sandwich rolls, roll out small sections of dough as thinly as possible. Rub with softened margarine on dough surface. Cut to desired shape and approximately half the desired size. Place one cut piece on top of another. Cover and let rise on lightly greased cookie sheet. Bake as directed above. Note: This is not delicate stuff— you can smush the layers together and they will still rise and separate easily.

(2) Eggs should be at room temperature before combining with other ingredients.

(3) If you put rolls close together, the finished product will be higher and lighter with soft sides; however, if you space apart on cookie sheet, they will be flatter and have crispier crusts and sides.

Irish Potato Rolls

1 **package dry yeast**	½ **cup sugar**
½ **cup lukewarm water**	2 **eggs, beaten**
1 **teaspoon sugar**	1 **cup mashed potatoes**
1 **cup milk, scalded,**	6½ **cups all-purpose flour**
then cooled to lukewarm	1 **egg yolk**
⅔ **cup shortening**	1½ **teaspoons milk**
1 **teaspoon salt**	

In saucepan dissolve yeast in water with 1 teaspoon sugar; add to luke-warm milk. In a separate bowl, add shortening, salt, sugar, and eggs to the mashed potatoes. Cream well. Add yeast and milk mixture to potato mixture. Mix well. Add flour to make a stiff dough. Knead on floured sur-face about 5 minutes. Place in buttered bowl. Turn dough over so all sides are coated with butter. Cover with dish towel. Let rise in warm place until doubled in size. Knead lightly on floured surface. Rub with butter, cover with plastic wrap, and chill. About 2 hours before dinner, pinch off about one fourth of dough; roll into "quarter"-size balls. Put into buttered muffin tins (2 per cup). Let rise about an hour. Lightly brush tops with beaten egg yolk and milk. Bake in 400° oven 20 to 25 minutes.

Yield: About 4 dozen rolls

BEAR IN MIND:
- *(1) These take a little time, but they are well worth the effort. Dough will keep in the refrigerator 7 to 10 days. Use as needed, just be sure it is kept covered.*
- *(2) Can be baked ahead and just reheated in foil in 325° oven 10 minutes.*

Sourdough Starter

1 **package dry yeast**	½ **cup sugar**
½ **cup warm water**	2 **teaspoons salt**
½ **cup instant potatoes**	1½ **cups warm water**

Once it's made, feed with:

½ **cup sugar**	1 **cup warm water**
3 **tablespoons instant potatoes**	

Dissolve yeast in ½ cup warm water. Add remaining ingredients. Stir well and let sit at room temperature (80 to 85°) 3 to 4 days until mixture is "bubbly". It is ready to use or refrigerate. Every 4 to 6 days feed with sugar, instant potatoes, and warm water. Use one cup to make sourdough rolls and put one cup back in refrigerator.

Yield: About 2 cups sourdough starter

BEAR IN MIND:

(1) Store in a covered quart glass jar in refrigerator.

(2) Starter can be frozen (with lid or seal off, when completely frozen, seal). Thaw at room temperature and feed as directed above.

(3) Starter can also be dehydrated using a dehydrator, then re-constituted with warm water.

Sourdough Parmesan/Chive Rolls

6	**cups bread flour, sifted**	**5**	**ounces Parmesan cheese, grated**
½	**cup sugar**		
1	**tablespoon salt**	**⅔**	**cup chopped fresh chives**
1½	**cups warm water**		**Dash freshly grated**
½	**cup corn oil**		**nutmeg**
1	**cup Sourdough Starter, room temperature**		

Put bread flour, sugar and salt in a large mixing bowl, stir to blend. Pour in warm water, oil, and Sourdough Starter and mix with wooden spoon until well blended. Dough will be sticky. Put dough in large greased mixing bowl. Cover with tin foil. Leave at room temperature 12 to 18 hours. It will increase in size, double or even triple on some days.

Turn dough out onto floured surface. With floured hands, knead dough until it's smooth and manageable. Divide in half. Let dough "rest" 10 to 15 minutes. Roll out each half in a circle about 15 inches in diameter. Sprinkle ¼ of the grated cheese and snipped chives onto the dough. Sprinkle with nutmeg. Fold in "quarters", pressing cheese and chives into the dough. Roll out again. Sprinkle another ¼ of the cheese and chives and more nutmeg. Fold dough over once again into "quarters". Pinch off 2½-inch circle of dough. Shape by hand. Put on lightly greased cookie sheet. Cover with lightweight cloth. Leave at room temperature while you go shopping, 4 to 9 hours. Bake in 400° oven 12 to 15 minutes.

Yield: 3 ½ dozen (3-inch) dinner rolls

BEAR IN MIND:

(1) Can pinch off ½ to 1-inch pieces of dough and make miniature rolls for tea sandwiches or snacks.

(2) Use sharp cheddar cheese and lots of freshly ground pepper to sprinkle into dough and fold in "quarters".

(3) Sprinkle with cinnamon/sugar/nuts or raisins and fold into dough. Can add dash of cardamom to sugar also.

Sourdough Bear Bread

3	cups whole wheat flour	1	cup Sourdough Starter,
3	cups bread flour, sifted		page 94
½	cup sugar		Handful of raisins
1	tablespoon salt	2	egg yolks
1½	cups warm water	1	tablespoon milk
½	cup corn oil		

Put flours, sugar and salt in large mixing bowl, stir with spoon to blend. Pour in warm water, oil and sourdough starter. Stir with spoon until well blended. Dough will be sticky. Put dough into well-greased large glass or plastic bowl. Cover bowl with tin foil. Leave at room temperature 10 to 12 hours.

Turn dough out onto floured surface. Knead dough until it is smooth and manageable, adding bread flour as needed to eliminate excess stickiness. Separate dough into 8 equal portions. Use 6 of these portions for the main body and head of 6 bears. Use the other 2 portions to shape the 24 paws (4 for each bear), 12 ears and 6 noses. Pinch the round shapes together to form bear shape on lightly greased cookie sheet. Press raisins into the dough for the eyes and navel of each bear. Cover with lightweight cloth and leave at room temperature 8 to 12 hours.

Beat egg yolks and milk in small cup with fork. Brush onto each bear. Bake in preheated 350° oven 15 to 20 minutes or until done. Cool on racks. Store in airtight containers.

Yield: 6 bear breads

BEAR IN MIND: *Freezes well.*

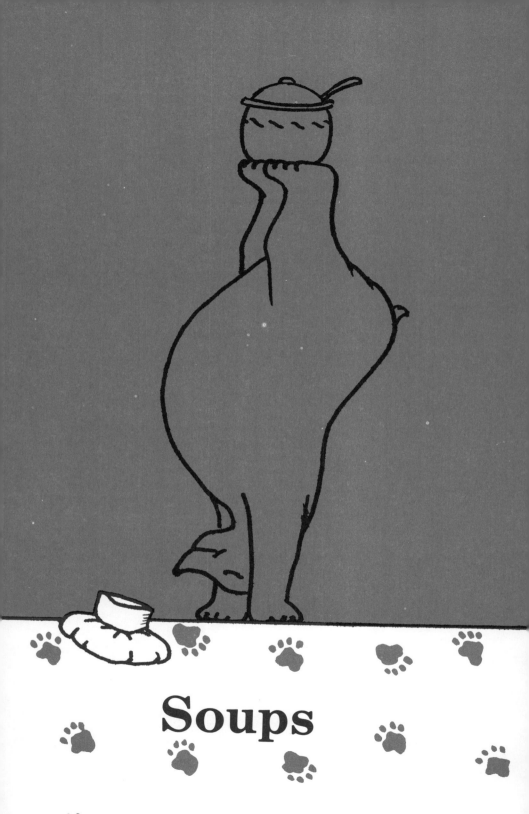

Soups

"BEARING GIFTS"

*CREAM OF ASPARAGUS SOUP, page 100 ... buy a white tureen, fill with soup. Makes a great housewarming gift.

*COUNTRY CHICKEN SOUP, page 100 ... pour into a wine carafe, snap on lid and tie a gingham cloth around the neck of carafe. A curing gift for victim of the common cold.

*GAZPACHO, page 103 ... pour into glass jar; add a dash or two of PESTO SAUCE, page 44, and stir.

*MULLIGATAWNEY SOUP, page 101 ... has a unique flavor — a good gift for new mothers. Freezes well too; give in freezer containers.

*VICHYSSOISE, page 104 ... for gift-giving put this delicious soup in clear plastic containers with colorful lids; add a box of imported fine biscuits or wafers.

*SHRIMP GUMBO, page 106 ... put into unmarked whipped margarine containers; attach a couple of fresh flowers on the top.

*SPIRITED FRENCH ONION SOUP, page 102 ... give the recipe with a set of ovenproof bowls.

*KENTUCKY BEARGOO, page 99 ... purchase a large stockpot; present with the recipe for a bridal shower gift.

*JAMBALAYA, page 105 ... give a large sea shell filled with this tasty dish!

*Make a soup mix using dried beans. Put in a plastic bag tied with a bow. If you grow your own herbs, dry some and add to the mix in a cheesecloth bouquet garni. Include a recipe card.

"BEAR ESSENTIALS FOR ENTERTAINING"

*On thick, cream-type soups, add a paprika monogram (using a paper stencil).

*Freeze any leftover chicken broth in freezer trays or mini muffin tins. Remove from trays or tins and store in labeled freezer bags. Add to fresh vegetables or canned vegetables when cooking or add to basic white sauce for added flavor.

*Simmer bones for soup (never boil!) to extract best flavor and gelatin from bone marrow. Adjust salt after cooking. If soup is too salty add a sliced raw potato to absorb extra salt; then remove potato.

*Have a soup party! In summer, use cold soups; in winter, hot soups. Prepare all soups in advance; have plenty of breads, butters, some cheeses. Serve buffet-style using over-sized ladles and old-fashioned enameled pots.

*Serve VICHYSSOISE, page 104, in beautiful bowls. Have bowls of hard-cooked eggs, fresh chives, fresh parsley, boiled potato cubes and chiffonade of Bibb lettuce. Guests add their own garnish!

Kentucky Beargoo

2½ pounds beef chuck, cubed
1 (3-pound) chicken, cut up
1½ teaspoons hot pepper sauce, divided
3 teaspoons salt, divided
3 quarts water
2 cups diced potatoes
2 cups chopped onions
1 garlic clove, minced
2 cups carrots, sliced
1 cup chopped fresh parsley
1 (1-pound 12-ounce) can tomatoes
1 (8-ounce) can tomato sauce
5 beef bouillon cubes
1 (10-ounce) package frozen cut green beans
2 (10-ounce) packages frozen corn
2 (10-ounce) packages frozen cut okra

In large soup pot, combine beef, chicken, 1 teaspoon hot pepper sauce, 1 teaspoon salt and water. Cover and simmer 1 hour. Remove chicken and set aside to cool. Add remaining ½ teaspoon hot pepper sauce, 2 teaspoons salt and remaining ingredients to beef. Cover and simmer 1 to 1½ hours. Skin cooled chicken and remove meat from bones. Cut into bite sized pieces. Add to beef mixture and heat.
Yield: 12 servings

Beer and Cheese Soup

1 cup chopped carrots
1 cup chopped celery
1 cup chopped yellow onions
2 teaspoons peanut oil
6 cups chicken stock
1 cup grated cheddar cheese
2 teaspoons all-purpose flour
  Salt and pepper to taste
½ teaspoon dry mustard
⅛ teaspoon hot pepper sauce
⅛ teaspoon Worcestershire sauce
1 (12-ounce) can of beer
  Polish sausage or knackwurst, optional
  Parsley for garnish

In skillet sauté carrots, celery and onions in oil until brown. In large saucepan boil soup stock, add vegetables and simmer 45 minutes. Dredge cheese in flour and mix into soup, stirring constantly until mixture thickens. Add salt, pepper, mustard, hot sauce and Worcestershire sauce. Add beer and keep stirring until soup is hot. Sausage may be sliced and added to soup just before serving. Sprinkle with parsley.
Yield: 6 to 8 servings

Cream of Asparagus Soup

1	small bunch green onions	1	tablespoon sugar	
2	medium onions, sliced	4	tablespoons all-purpose flour	
1	stick butter, unsalted			
1½	pounds fresh asparagus or 2 (10-ounce) packages frozen	2	cups chicken stock	
		3	cups milk	
		½	teaspoon white pepper	
1	cup water	2	teaspoons salt	
	Salt and pepper to taste		Sour cream to garnish	

Wash and slice green onions, including green tops. In 4½-quart saucepan, sauté green onions and other onions in butter. Simmer 30 minutes covered. Cut tips from asparagus 1 inch long. Cook tips in 1 cup water 5 minutes with salt, pepper and sugar; set aside for garnish. Add asparagus stalks to onions and cook a few minutes longer. Stir flour into vegetables until smooth. Add stock, milk, white pepper and salt. Simmer 2 to 3 hours, stirring occasionally. Cool. Put in blender and purée. When ready to serve add 1 dollop of sour cream to each bowl and garnish with drained asparagus tips.

Yield: 6 to 8 servings

BEAR IN MIND: *You may add some sherry to soup when cool.*

Country Chicken Soup

2	medium onions, chopped	¼	teaspoon thyme	
2	to 3 carrots, sliced	3	tablespoons parsley flakes	
2	celery stalks, sliced	1	(2½-pound) fryer, whole	
2	teaspoons salt	4	cups water	
¼	teaspoon pepper	1	cup uncooked noodles	
½	teaspoon basil			

Place all ingredients in crock pot, except noodles, in order listed. Cover and cook on LOW, 8 to 10 hours. One hour before serving, remove chicken and cool slightly. Remove meat from bones and return to crock pot. Add noodles and turn to HIGH, cover and cook 1 hour longer.

Yield: 6 servings

Broccoli Soup

2   pounds fresh broccoli
2   tablespoons butter
½   cup chopped yellow onions
¼   cup chopped bell pepper
2   tablespoons all-purpose
     flour
6   cups chicken stock
1   bay leaf

Parsley to taste
1   teaspoon ground thyme
6   black peppercorns
     Pinch of nutmeg
3   egg yolks, whipped
1   cup half and half or milk,
     blended with yolks

Chop broccoli, saving some of the small buds and flowerets for garnish.
In skillet, sauté broccoli in butter along with the onions and bell pepper.
Sprinkle with the flour and stir. Combine this mixture and the soup stock
in large saucepan. Add bay leaf, parsley, thyme and peppercorns. Cook
30 minutes and purée the mixture in a blender or sieve. Add the nutmeg,
then strain the soup. Return to pan. Add egg yolks and half and half to
hot soup. Garnish with broccoli buds.

Yield: 6 to 8 servings

BEAR IN MIND: *You may add ¼ to ½ teaspoon curry powder and/or 2
to 4 ounces grated Swiss cheese to the soup for a different taste.*

Mulligatawney Soup For Dieters

1½   cups chopped cooked
     chicken
3   cups chicken broth (skim
     fat off)
⅔   cup chopped carrots
½   medium bell pepper,
     chopped
2   apples, peeled, cored and
     chopped

1   tablespoon chopped onion
2   teaspoons chopped parsley
     flakes
½   teaspoon curry powder
⅛   teaspoon mace
2   to 4 whole cloves
     Salt and pepper to taste
10   ounces tomato juice

Place all ingredients except tomato juice in a 4 or 5-quart saucepot.
Bring to boil, reduce heat and cover. Simmer until carrots are tender. Add
tomato juice and heat, but do not boil. Remove cloves. Serve hot.

Yield: 6 servings

Egg Drop Soup

2½ cups chicken broth,
     homemade, divided
¼   teaspoon soy sauce
2   eggs, beaten
1   teaspoon cornstarch
½   teaspoon salt
¼   teaspoon freshly ground
     pepper

2   to 3 green onions, sliced
1   cup peeled and sliced fresh
     broccoli stems
½   cup sliced fresh mushrooms
     Fresh mushroom slices for
     garnish

Bring 2 cups broth to a boil in 2-quart saucepan; add soy sauce. Beat eggs in a cup and pour in a thin stream into broth, stirring constantly. Mix cornstarch, ½ cup broth, salt and pepper together in a covered jar until smooth. Stir into soup to thicken slightly. Add the onions, broccoli and mushrooms. Cook until broccoli is almost tender. Serve while hot. Float fresh mushroom slices on soup for garnish.

Yield: 4 servings

BEAR IN MIND:
   (1) If you use canned chicken broth, you might want to decrease salt.
   (2) For variation, add fresh spinach, tiny fresh shrimp and bamboo
        shoots.

Spirited French Onion Soup

4   cups thinly sliced onions
1   stick butter
¼   teaspoon sugar
1   teaspoon salt
½   teaspoon white pepper
1   tablespoon all-purpose
     flour
5   (14½-ounce) cans beef
     broth

¾   cup dry red wine
1   bay leaf
¼   teaspoon thyme
3   tablespoons cognac or
     brandy
4   to 6 large toasted rounds
     of bread
1   to 1½ cups grated Swiss
     cheese

Sauté onions in butter in large Dutch oven 10 to 15 minutes. Stir in sugar, salt and white pepper. Cook over medium heat, stirring frequently, 30 to 40 minutes or until onions are golden brown. Sprinkle flour over onions and stir constantly 3 minutes. Stir in broth, wine, bay leaf and thyme. Heat to boil, then simmer 30 to 40 minutes. Stir in cognac. Pour into oven-proof bowls. Make toast rounds to float in each bowl. Sprinkle with cheese and put under broiler until cheese is melted.

Yield: 4 to 6 servings

Gazpacho

1	(10¾-ounce) can tomato soup	½	cup chopped bell pepper
1	tablespoon Italian dressing	¼	teaspoon pepper
1½	cups tomato juice	½	cup chopped Spanish onion
1	tablespoon lemon or lime juice	2	tablespoons olive oil
1¼	cups water	¼	teaspoon hot pepper sauce
1	cup chopped cucumber	⅛	teaspoon garlic salt
1	garlic clove, pressed	2	tablespoons red wine vinegar
1	cup chopped fresh tomato	1	teaspoon Worcestershire sauce
¼	teaspoon salt		Cucumber slices to garnish

Combine all ingredients except cucumber slices in large bowl. Chill at least 6 hours. Garnish each serving with cucumber slices.

Yield: 6 servings

BEAR FLAIR: You may also garnish this refreshing soup with a dollop of sour cream sprinkled with fresh dill.

BEAR IN MIND: For gazpacho ice, freeze in ice cube trays or 2-inch deep baking pans until firm; process in food processor until smooth. Scoop into 6 round shapes. Freeze on plastic-lined metal tray until ready to serve. Serve on thinly sliced cucumbers in chilled bowl.

Hot Herb Tomato "Soup"

6	small green onions	½	teaspoon dried dill weed
1	tablespoon Worcestershire sauce	2	tablespoons freshly squeezed lemon juice
2	(18-ounce) cans tomato juice		

Slice bulb end from onions and chop. Reserve onion tops for garnish. Combine all ingredients, including the chopped onion, in large saucepan. Bring to a boil. Blend mixture in food processor until smooth. Serve hot in mugs. Garnish with onion curls if desired.

Yield: 6 to 8 servings

BEAR FLAIR: Make onion curls with green end of onion by making thin lengthwise cuts to, but not through, the ends. May also be garnished with thin lemon slice and/or dollop of sour cream.

Minestrone

¼	pound salt pork, minced	2	potatoes, peeled and diced
3	garlic cloves, minced	¼	head cabbage, chopped
2	tablespoons olive oil	2	bell peppers, chopped
1	large onion, chopped	2	zucchini, thinly sliced
2	carrots, thinly sliced	1	bunch fresh spinach, finely
3	cups thinly sliced celery		chopped
1	(6-ounce) can tomato paste	¾	cup cooked macaroni
4	quarts water	1	(12-ounce) can tomatoes,
3	beef bouillon cubes		drained and chopped
3	tablespoons salt	1	(12-ounce) can garbanzo
½	teaspoon white pepper		beans, drained
1	teaspoon oregano	1	(12-ounce) can kidney
1	teaspoon thyme		beans, drained

In stockpot, sauté pork and garlic in hot olive oil. Add onion, carrots and celery; cook 10 minutes over medium heat. Add tomato paste, cook 5 more minutes. Add water and bring to a boil. Let simmer 5 minutes. Add bouillon and seasonings. Also add potatoes, cabbage and bell pepper. Cook another 5 minutes. Turn to low and add zucchini and spinach. Cook until all vegetables are tender. Add cooked macaroni, tomatoes, garbanzo beans and kidney beans. Heat through to the simmering stage; serve.

Yield: 10 to 12 servings

BEAR IN MIND: *Don't let the number of ingredients put you off—it's really a matter of dumping things in the pot!*

 Vichyssoise

1	medium onion, chopped	8	cups chicken stock
2	leeks, sliced	½	pint whipping cream
2	tablespoons margarine		Chopped chives to taste
2	tablespoons all-purpose		Ground nutmeg to taste
	flour		
4	medium potatoes, peeled		
	and diced		

Brown onions and leeks in margarine. Blend in flour. Add potatoes and stock, cook 40 minutes or until potatoes are soft. Force through sieve. Stir in cream. Chill. Garnish with chives and nutmeg.

Yield: 4 servings

BEAR FLAIR: *Tie 4 (3 to 4-inch long) fresh chive blades with another (3 to 4-inch long) chive. Float in each bowl of soup.*

Cheesy-Cream of Potato Soup

1 medium onion, chopped	1 (10¾-ounce) can cream of
4 tablespoons butter	chicken soup
6 to 7 medium potatoes	12 ounces processed cheese
Garlic salt to taste	2 cups milk
Salt and pepper to taste	

In saucepan, sauté onion in butter. Peel potatoes and cut into small cubes. Add potatoes to onion and barely cover with hot water. Season with garlic salt, salt, and pepper. Cook until mushy. Stir in can of soup. Cut cheese into thin slices and stir into potato mixture. Stir until cheese has melted. Add milk. May be served hot or cold.

Yield: 6 servings

BEAR FLAIR: Garnish each bowl with fresh cut chives or grated sharp cheese.

Jambalaya

1 pound smoked sausage, sliced	2 tablespoons chopped fresh parsley
1 cup chopped bell pepper	2 cups uncooked regular rice
1 cup chopped onion	2 tablespoons Worcestershire sauce
1 garlic clove, pressed	2 teaspoons salt
1 tablespoon all-purpose flour	½ teaspoon thyme
1 (28-ounce) can tomatoes, with liquid	¼ teaspoon red pepper
2½ cups water	2 pounds fresh shrimp, peeled and deveined

Cook sausage until brown in large Dutch oven. Drain off all but 2 tablespoons of pan drippings. Add bell pepper, onion and garlic. Cook until tender. Add flour and stir until blended. Stir in tomatoes with liquid, water and parsley; bring to a boil. Add remaining ingredients except shrimp. Return to a boil. Reduce heat and simmer covered 20 minutes. Add shrimp and cook covered 10 more minutes.

Yield: 8 servings

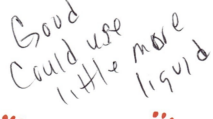

Good
Could use little more liquid

Shrimp Gumbo

1	pound fresh shrimp, peeled and deveined	1½	teaspoons salt
2	cups sliced fresh or 1 (11-ounce) package frozen okra	½	teaspoon pepper
		2	cups hot water
½	cup shortening, melted	1	cup canned tomatoes
⅓	cup chopped green onions with tops	2	bay leaves
		4	drops hot pepper sauce
3	garlic cloves, pressed	1½	cups cooked rice, seasoned to taste

Prepare shrimp. In large saucepan, sauté okra in shortening about 10 minutes or until it appears dry, stirring constantly. Add onions, garlic, salt, pepper and shrimp. Cook about 5 minutes more. Add water, tomatoes and bay leaves. Cover and simmer 20 to 25 minutes. Remove bay leaves. Add hot pepper sauce. Place ¼ cup rice in bottom of 6 soup bowls. Fill with gumbo.

Yield: 6 servings

Crab Bisque

2	cups crabmeat, cartilage removed	2	(10¾-ounce) cans tomato bisque soup
1	cup sherry, optional	½	teaspoon curry powder
2	(10¾-ounce) cans split pea soup	1	teaspoon paprika
			Sour cream for garnish
1	pint half and half		

Toss crabmeat with sherry. In large double boiler over low heat, mix all ingredients together until hot. Garnish with about 1 teaspoon sour cream per bowl.

Yield: 6 servings

BEAR FLAIR: *To enhance the natural delicate color of this bisque, garnish the sour cream with tiny cooked shrimp.*

Salads

"BEARING GIFTS"

*AVOCADO MOUSSE, page 114 ... mold in scooped-out cantaloupe halves or melon of your choice (be sure the melon is well-drained, patted dry before pouring in the mousse). No containers to return! For a striking garnish, arrange sliced radishes and a sprig of parsley.

*POOH-BEAR PEAR SALAD, page 109, or SUMMER STUFFED TOMATOES, page 121 ... put either of these salads on disposable "plastic" frozen dinner tray lined with ruby lettuce. Cover with clear wrap.

*SAUERKRAUT SALAD, page 119 ... easy do-ahead dish; scoop out a gorgeous head of red cabbage, leaving large outer leaves intact; fill with salad, a fantastic gift!

*STACKABLE SALAD, page 121, or SNOOKY'S POTATO SALAD, page 118 ... sensational gift when presented in a straight-sided glass bowl.

*NEIMAN MARCUS SEAFOOD SALAD, page 126 ... place each serving in a whole romaine lettuce leaf on a fish-shaped platter.

*JAN'S CRABMEAT AND BEANSPROUT SALAD, page 126 ... an unusual dish made dramatic when given in a large sea shell and garnished with a couple of crab claws.

*FRESH BROCCOLI SALAD, page 115 ... this is especially pretty in large fresh tomato "flowers", made by cutting vertically 3 times to, but not through, base of the tomato.

*ITALIAN SAUSAGE PASTA SALAD, page 125, or TORTELLINI SALAD, page 124 ... purchase a trifle dish, put in box of tortellini pasta, and copies of these recipes.

*CORA'S FROZEN FRUIT SALAD, page 110 ... freeze in paper-lined muffin tins. Remove from tins when frozen. Store in airtight bags. Instant gifts when needed.

*SPICED PEACH SALAD, page 110 ... purchase an unusual mold and give with the prepared dish and the recipe.

*SHRIMP AND PASTA SALAD, page 123 ... for an exotic gift, place salad on lotus leaves or in a coconut shell.

*HOT SHRIMP SALAD IN CHEDDAR CHEESE CRUST, page 128 ... a delicious, memorable gift; can be prepared the day before and baked at last minute.

*Any of the dressings on the last pages of this section make excellent gifts. You can use dressing bottles, other unusual shaped jars or antique Mason jars as containers for these gift treasures.

"BEAR ESSENTIALS FOR ENTERTAINING"

*For a unique salad presentation, reserve outer leaves of lettuce head. Shred and toss remaining lettuce with crumbled bacon and a cucumber dressing. Spoon onto each reserved leaf ¼ cup salad mixture and 2 partially-cooked broccoli spears, roll and secure with toothpick. Garnish with additional dressing and more crumbled bacon. Instant salad pickup.

*Use the flower/herb nasturtium for its colorful blossoms and peppery-flavored leaves to add zip to any salad.

*Use gladioluses to hold CHICKEN SALAD SENSATIONAL, page 129. Each blossom will hold up to ¼ cup finely chopped salad, so you'll need to use 2 or 3 flowers per serving. Nestle the blossoms in a small basket or bowl for serving. Use leaves to prop the flowers.

*Make carrot rose for your favorite carrot salad; make long thin slices, using a vegetable peeler. Arrange in rose shape, using more than one slice, if needed. Can also use raw kolhrabi, turnip or sweet potato.

Pooh-Bear Pear Salad

1   (8-ounce) package cream
    cheese
½   cup chopped pecans
1   tablespoon finely diced
    crystallized ginger
2   (29-ounce) cans pear
    halves, well-drained,

    and 1 tablespoon pear
    juice reserved
1   drop red food coloring
    Lettuce
    Mint sprigs

Cream the cream cheese, pecans and ginger with ½ tablespoon of pear juice and stuff the pear halves. Place two pear halves together making whole pear. Dilute red food coloring with ½ tablespoon pear juice and gently rub over hump of pear, giving a blush effect. Place on lettuce leaf and garnish top or stem end of pear with a sprig of mint.

Yield: 8 servings

Orange Grapefruit Salad

1   (6-ounce) package orange-
     flavored gelatin
1½   cups boiling water
1   (6-ounce) can frozen
     orange juice concentrate,
     thawed
1   cup cold water

1   (11-ounce) can mandarin
     oranges
1   (16-ounce) can grapefruit
     sections, drained and cut
     into pieces
     Mayonnaise to taste

Lightly oil a 6½-cup ring mold or 2-quart casserole. Dissolve gelatin in boiling water. Add orange juice concentrate and cold water. Drain mandarin oranges, reserving syrup. Add syrup to gelatin mixture. Chill until partially set. Fold in oranges and grapefruit. Pour into mold. Chill until set. Unmold and serve with mayonnaise.

Yield: 8 to 10 servings

BEAR FLAIR: *May chill and serve salad in fresh grapefruit halves that have been scooped out.*

Cora's Frozen Fruit Salad

½   **pint whipping cream**
1   **cup mayonnaise**
12 **pitted Bing cherries,**
    with juice
2   **tablespoons powdered**
    sugar

4   **bananas, diced**
2   **tablespoons French**
    dressing
2   **cups diced pineapple**
10 **large marshmallows,**
    diced

Whip cream, add mayonnaise. Add remaining ingredients. Put in 8-inch square pan. Freeze.

Yield: 12 to 14 servings

BEAR FLAIR: *Freeze in individual muffin tins or in quart-size paper milk container and slice for serving.*

Spiced Peach Salad
fabulous with pork or seafood

2   **envelopes unflavored**
    gelatin
¼   **cup cold water**
1¼ **cups juice from canned**
    spiced (pickled) peaches

6   **ice cubes (1x2-inch size)**
7   **sliced peaches, cut small**
½   **cup chopped nuts or celery**

Lightly coat 6 to 8 individual molds with vegetable cooking spray. Soften gelatin in cold water, dissolve in peach juice by heating in saucepan to boiling point. Then add ice cubes and chill. When mixture congeals slightly, add peaches and nuts. Pour into individual molds (or 1 large mold) and chill until set.

Yield: 6 to 8 servings

BEAR IN MIND:
(1) *You may add ¼ cup chopped maraschino cherries for additional color.*
(2) *When using individual molds use 1 (3-ounce) package cream cheese, softened, and 1 cup chopped pecans. Roll cream cheese into 1-inch balls, then roll in pecans. Place in center of each mold. Pour gelatin mixture into molds. Chill.*

Tangy Cranberry Mold

1	pound fresh cranberries	½	cup orange juice
1½	cups sugar	1	(8-ounce) can crushed
2	tablespoons unflavored		pineapple with juice
	gelatin	1	cup chopped pecans
2	teaspoons orange-flavored liqueur	2	teaspoons grated orange rind

Lightly coat 6-cup mold or 9x13-inch casserole with vegetable cooking spray. Wash cranberries and process in food processor (5 pulses) or until coarse. Mix with sugar and let stand 15 minutes. Soak gelatin in liqueur and orange juice 15 minutes. Heat over hot water in double boiler. Mix all ingredients and pour into casserole or mold. Chill 3 hours.

Yield: 10 servings

Pineapple Pimiento Salad

1	(20-ounce) can crushed pineapple, packed in heavy syrup	2	(3-ounce) packages cream cheese, softened
1	(3-ounce) package lemon-flavored gelatin	¾	cup chopped celery
		¾	cup chopped pecans
1	(4-ounce) jar pimiento, drained and chopped	⅛	teaspoon salt
		½	pint whipping cream, whipped

Coat 6-cup mold with cooking spray. Drain pineapple and heat juice. Pour over gelatin and stir. Chill. Mash pimiento and softened cream cheese with fork until blended. Add drained pineapple and blend. Then add celery, pecans and salt. Blend together. Pour into partially set gelatin. Fold in whipped cream. Chill.

Yield: 12 servings

BEAR FLAIR: *Put in individual molds or in pineapple mold; garnish with pimiento strips.*

Ribbon Salad

a colorful addition to Christmas dinner

1 (3-ounce) package cherry-flavored gelatin	1 (3-ounce) package cream cheese, softened
1½ cups hot water	1 cup chopped pecans
1 cup diced apple	1½ cups hot water
1 (16-ounce) can crushed pineapple, drained and reserve juice	1 (3-ounce) package lime-flavored gelatin
1 (3-ounce) package lemon-flavored gelatin	

To make bottom layer, combine cherry-flavored gelatin with 1½ cups hot water. Stir until gelatin is dissolved. Add apples to mixture and pour in large loaf pan. Chill until set. For second layer, add enough water to pineapple juice to make 1½ cups liquid. (Reserve pineapple for third layer.) Heat juice, add lemon-flavored gelatin and cream cheese. Mix well. Add pecans. Pour mixture over bottom layer in pan. Chill until set. For top layer, heat 1½ cups water and add lime-flavored gelatin. Stir until gelatin is dissolved. Add the pineapple. Mix well. Pour mixture over middle layer. Chill until set.

Yield: 25 servings

BEAR IN MIND: *Be sure each layer is set before adding next layer.*

 # Original 24-Hour Salad

2 cups halved, seeded white cherries	2 eggs
2 cups orange sections	2 tablespoons sugar
2 cups diced pineapple	1½ cups whipping cream, divided
2 cups quartered marshmallows	Juice of 1 lemon
¾ cup chopped, blanched almonds	Lettuce

Combine cherries, orange, pineapple, marshmallows and almonds. Set aside. In separate bowl, beat eggs until light. Gradually add sugar, ¼ cup cream and lemon juice. Mix thoroughly and cook in double boiler until smooth and thick, stirring constantly. Cool. Whip remaining cream and fold into cooled mixture. Pour dressing over fruit and mix lightly. Chill 24 hours. Serve on crisp lettuce.

Yield: 12 to 16 servings

Tangy Fruit Salad

1	(11-ounce) can mandarin oranges, drained (reserve juice)	1	pint fresh strawberries
2	(17-ounce) cans chunky mixed fruit, drained (reserve juice)	½	pound seedless grapes
		½	cup chopped nuts
		½	cup raisins
2	apples, cored and sliced	1	(3-ounce) package instant vanilla pudding mix
3	bananas, sliced	½	cup orange-flavored breakfast drink mix

In a large bowl, place prepared fruit. Combine drink mix and pudding mix in a medium bowl and add enough of the reserved fruit juices to make "dressing" consistency. Pour over fruits, stir gently. Chill several hours or overnight.

Yield: 10 to 12 generous servings

Asparagus Salad

1½	cups cold water, divided	1	(10½-ounce) can cut asparagus spears
½	cup sugar		
½	cup vinegar	1	small onion, grated
½	teaspoon salt	1	(2-ounce) jar pimiento
2	packages unflavored gelatin	1	cup chopped celery
		½	cup chopped pecans

Mix 1 cup cold water, sugar, vinegar and salt and boil five minutes. In separate bowl dissolve gelatin in remaining ½ cup cold water. Pour hot mixture into dissolved gelatin. Set aside to cool. When this begins to thicken, add asparagus, onion, pimiento, celery and pecans. Chill several hours.

Yield: 4 to 6 servings

BEAR IN MIND: *This is a colorful salad for a luncheon. May serve with cream cheese.*

 # Avocado Mousse

2	avocados, diced	2	tablespoons unflavored
	Juice of 2 limes		gelatin, dissolved in
1	small onion, grated		small amount of cold
1	garlic clove, pressed		water
½	teaspoon salt		Few drops green food
2	cups mayonnaise		coloring

Lightly oil 5-cup mold. Place avocado in bowl, sprinkle with lime juice, onion, garlic and salt. Fold in mayonnaise. Add gelatin to mixture. Place in mold. Chill until set.

Yield: 6 servings

BEAR IN MIND: *You may place this in a melon mold.*

Artichoke and Rice Salad

1	(8-ounce) package chicken	1	large onion, chopped
	flavored rice mix	1	teaspoon curry powder
1	(6½-ounce) jar	4	celery stalks, chopped
	marinated artichokes	2	tablespoons mayonnaise

Cook rice mix as directed on package. While hot, add remaining ingredients and stir well. May be served while hot or may be chilled and served cold. Will keep 4 to 5 days in refrigerator.

Yield: 6 to 8 half-cup servings

BEAR IN MIND: *Add cold, cooked chicken pieces and serve as cold main dish.*

Green Bean Salad

1	(16-ounce) can French-cut green beans, drained	2	medium onions, sliced
1	(16-ounce) can green peas, drained	½	cup vinegar
1	(4-ounce) jar pimiento, drained	¼	cup sugar
1	celery stalk, sliced	½	cup oil
		1	teaspoon salt
			Pepper to taste

Mix all ingredients 24 hours before using. Cover and chill until ready to serve.

Yield: 4 to 6 servings

BEAR IN MIND: *Can use 1 pound fresh green beans, cooked crisp-tender and omit the canned beans and peas. Just before serving, toss in shredded Gruyère or Swiss cheese and 1 cup sliced fresh mushrooms.*

Fresh Broccoli Salad

1	large bunch fresh broccoli	12	bacon slices, cooked and crumbled
1	small red onion, thinly sliced	½	cup vinegar
2	cups diced small fresh mushrooms	⅓	cup sugar
1	(8-ounce) can sliced water chestnuts, drained	⅔	cup mayonnaise
		½	teaspoon salt
		1	teaspoon celery seeds

Wash broccoli. Cut flowerets away from stems. (Save stems for broccoli soup.) Place flowerets in boiling water 1 to 2 minutes. Drain and rinse in cold water immediately. Place broccoli into large bowl, add onion, mushrooms, water chestnuts and bacon. Set aside. Combine vinegar, sugar, mayonnaise, salt and celery seeds. Pour over broccoli and toss gently. Cover and chill overnight.

Yield: 6 servings

BEAR IN MIND: *A nice variation is to substitute ½ cup raisins for mushrooms and water chestnuts.*

Cucumbers on Ice

2	quarts thinly sliced cucumbers	1½	cups sugar
1	medium onion, thinly sliced	½	cup apple cider vinegar
1	tablespoon plus 2 teaspoons uniodized salt, divided		

Place sliced cucumbers and onions in bowl. Sprinkle with 1 tablespoon salt. Let stand at room temperature 2 hours. Drain and return to bowl. Sprinkle with remaining salt, sugar and vinegar and stir well. Put in freezer containers and freeze. Serve anytime after freezing. After thawing, store in refrigerator.

Yield: 7 cups

Cucumber Salad

great for barbecues

3	tablespoons vinegar	¾	teaspoon salt
2	tablespoons water	3	large cucumbers, thinly sliced
1	tablespoon sugar		
½	small garlic clove, pressed	1	red bell pepper, thinly sliced
⅛	teaspoon ground red pepper	1	small red onion, thinly sliced

Combine vinegar, water, sugar, garlic, red pepper and salt. Stir well. Add cucumber, bell pepper and onion. Toss well. Cover and chill at least one hour before serving.

Yield: 10 to 12 servings

BEAR IN MIND: *Use thinly sliced radishes instead of red bell pepper, for variation.*

Skillet Salad

6	bacon slices	1	teaspoon salt
¼	cup vinegar	4	cups shredded cabbage
1	tablespoon brown sugar	½	cup chopped parsley
2	tablespoons chopped onion	1	cup shredded lettuce

Cook bacon until crisp. Drain bacon, crumble and set aside. Add vinegar, brown sugar, onion and salt to bacon grease in skillet and heat well. Add crumbled bacon to this mixture. Remove skillet from heat and toss cabbage, parsley and lettuce in the hot mixture. Serve immediately.

Yield: 4 servings

BEAR IN MIND: *You may substitute 1 cup shredded fresh spinach instead of lettuce, or you may use both.*

Mushroom Salad Bowl

1	pound fresh mushrooms	¼	cup vinegar
1	pound boiled ham, sliced	4	teaspoons crumbled dried basil leaves
3	cups sliced cooked potatoes	1	tablespoon salt
1	(17-ounce) can green peas	½	teaspoon pepper
½	cup sliced green onions including tops	¼	teaspoon ground cumin seed
¾	cup salad oil		

Rinse, pat dry and slice fresh mushrooms. Combine mushrooms, ham, potatoes, peas and onions. In separate bowl mix salad oil, vinegar, basil leaves, salt, pepper and cumin seed. Pour this mixture over the mushroom-ham mixture. Toss gently. Chill.

Yield: 6 servings

BEAR IN MIND: *Use 2 (8-ounce) cans sliced mushrooms instead of fresh mushrooms. Use ½ cup chopped onion instead of green onions.*

Palm Salad

1   **(14-ounce) can hearts**
    of palm, drained, sliced
    ½-inch thick
1   **(11-ounce) can mandarin**
    oranges, drained

⅓   **cup chopped dates**
    Lettuce leaves, left whole
    (ruby or red leaf lettuce
    is the prettiest)

Place lettuce on salad plates, followed by hearts of palm, oranges and dates. Drizzle on Easy Fruit Dressing, page 131.

Yield: 4 servings

BEAR IN MIND: *Use pineapple chunks instead of oranges. Sprinkle with toasted pine nuts and a vinaigrette dressing.*

Snooky's Potato Salad
a classic dish

8   **medium potatoes, boiled**
     in jacket
1½   **cups mayonnaise**
½   **pint sour cream**
1½   **teaspoons horseradish**

1   **teaspoon celery seed**
½   **teaspoon salt**
1   **cup chopped fresh parsley**
2   **medium onions,**
     finely minced

Peel potatoes and cut in ⅛-inch slices. Combine mayonnaise, sour cream, horseradish, celery seed and salt. Set aside. In another bowl mix parsley and onion. In a large serving bowl arrange layer of potatoes, salt lightly, cover with a layer of sour cream-mayonnaise mixture, then layer of onion mixture. Continue layering, ending with parsley and onion. DO NOT MIX. Cover and refrigerate 8 hours before serving.

Yield: 4 to 6 servings

Curried Rice Salad

5	cups cooked rice	1	to 1½ cups mayonnaise
¾	cup raisins, steeped in hot water to soften	2	to 3 teaspoons curry powder
3	celery stalks, chopped	½	teaspoon salt
1	carrot, grated	½	teaspoon freshly ground pepper
½	(6-ounce) can pitted olives, sliced		Juice of 1 lemon
¾	cup peanuts		

Place cooked rice in mixing bowl. Drain raisins and add to rice, then add celery, carrot, olives and peanuts. Mix with mayonnaise, curry powder, salt, pepper and lemon juice. Toss lightly, place in serving bowl and chill.

Yield: 6 to 8 servings

BEAR IN MIND: *If preparing a day ahead, add peanuts just before serving, so they will be crunchy.*

Sauerkraut Salad

1	large bell pepper, chopped	1	(2-ounce) jar pimiento
1	large onion, chopped	1	quart sauerkraut, drained
1	cup sliced celery		

Dressing:

2	cups sugar	¾	cup vinegar
¼	cup water	1	tablespoon celery seed
½	cup oil		

In bowl, combine bell pepper, onion, celery, pimiento, and sauerkraut. In medium saucepan, bring all ingredients in the dressing recipe to a boil. Add dressing to vegetable mixture. Put in covered container and refrigerate 24 hours or longer. Drain before serving.

Yield: 8 servings

BEAR IN MIND: *For a St. Patrick's Day salad you may add a few drops of green food coloring to the dressing ingredients.*

Spinach Chow-Mein Salad

6   cups spinach, torn in
     small pieces
1   small sweet onion,
     chopped
½   cup sliced celery
4   hard-cooked eggs, diced

Salt to taste
Lemon pepper seasoning,
to taste
1   (3-ounce) can rice chow
     mein noodles

Dressing:
½   pint sour cream
3   tablespoons lemon juice

1   (0.6-ounce) package
     Italian dry dressing mix

Combine and toss spinach, onion, celery, eggs, salt and lemon pepper.
Prepare dressing in separate bowl by combining sour cream, lemon
juice and Italian dressing. Pour dressing over spinach mixture. Top salad
with chow mein noodles.

Yield: 6 servings

Ring Around the Shrimp

2   envelopes unflavored
     gelatin
½   cup cold water
1   (10¾-ounce) can tomato
     soup
1   (8-ounce) package cream
     cheese
½   cup diced celery
¼   cup instant minced onion

Salt to taste
1   cup mayonnaise
1½   pounds fresh shrimp,
     peeled, deveined, cooked
     and chopped
1   pound fresh shrimp,
     peeled, deveined, cooked
     and left whole
     Red leaf lettuce

Lightly oil 5-cup ring mold. Sprinkle gelatin into cold water in small
bowl. Set aside. In saucepan, bring soup to a boil. Add cream cheese,
stirring until cheese melts. Remove from heat, add softened gelatin. Stir
well. Cool. Add celery, onion, salt, mayonnaise and chopped shrimp. Pour
into mold. Chill several hours or overnight. Unmold onto red leaf lettuce
and fill center of "ring" with whole cooked shrimp.

Yield: 6 to 8 servings

BEAR FLAIR: *Add a celery top or two to the cooked shrimp in ring.*

BEAR IN MIND: *Could marinate the whole cooked shrimp for center of
ring.*

Summer Stuffed Tomatoes

2 cups canned artichoke hearts, drained and chopped	½ teaspoon garlic salt
¾ cup chopped celery	6 medium to large firm ripe tomatoes
½ cup chopped green onions with tops	3 bacon slices, cooked
1 cup mayonnaise	½ cup grated Parmesan cheese
	Lettuce

Combine artichoke hearts with celery, green onions, mayonnaise and garlic salt. Scoop out tomatoes. Stuff with mixture. Place on lettuce leaf. Sprinkle with crumbled bacon and Parmesan cheese.

Yield: 6 servings

BEAR IN MIND: *A wonderful treatment for summer's "bright red beauties".*

Stackable Salad

3 cups chopped potatoes, cooked	5 to 6 bacon slices, cooked and crumbled
1½ cups frozen peas, thawed	½ teaspoon dill weed
1 teaspoon salt	2 cucumbers, chopped
2 tomatoes, chopped	1 cup grated cheddar cheese
½ teaspoon pepper	
1½ cups chopped cooked chicken	

Dill sauce:

1 cup mayonnaise	1¼ teaspoons dill weed
½ pint sour cream	½ teaspoon salt
1 tablespoon chopped chives	Dash curry
1½ tablespoons chopped parsley	Dash dry mustard

For the first layer, combine the potatoes and peas and sprinkle with salt. For the second layer, add tomatoes and sprinkle with pepper. The third layer is a combination of chicken, bacon and dill weed tossed together. The fourth layer is chopped cucumbers followed by grated cheese. Cover with dill sauce. Chill.

To prepare dill sauce combine all ingredients together.

Yield: 8 servings

BEAR FLAIR: *Pretty in a medium-size glass bowl.*

Marinated Tomatoes

4	large fresh tomatoes, sliced	1	teaspoon Italian seasoning
⅓	cup olive oil	1	teaspoon salt
¼	cup red wine vinegar	½	teaspoon sugar
2	teaspoons parsley flakes	¼	teaspoon garlic salt
1	teaspoon chopped onion	¼	teaspoon coarsely ground pepper

Arrange tomato slices in shallow container. Combine remaining ingredients and mix well. Pour mixture over tomatoes. Cover and marinate in refrigerator several hours or overnight.

Yield: 8 servings

BEAR FLAIR: Fresh chopped basil leaves in the summer months would give a super taste and a lovely garnish.

Vegetable Pasta Salad

easy, refreshing and pretty

1	(16-ounce) box spiral pasta, cooked and drained	1	(1⅝-ounce) package dry vegetable soup mix
1	(10-ounce) package frozen spinach	1½	cups sour cream
1	(10-ounce) package frozen green peas	1	cup mayonnaise
2	cups julienned carrots	1	(8-ounce) can water chestnuts, drained and chopped
		3	chopped green onions

Cook pasta according to package directions and drain. Thaw and squeeze spinach until dry. Cook peas and carrots until tender. Do not overcook. Combine soup mix with sour cream and mayonnaise. Next add water chestnuts and green onions to soup mixture. Add spinach, peas and carrots to mixture. Gently stir in pasta. Be sure everything is well-coated. Refrigerate at least 3 hours.

Yield: 6 to 8 servings

BEAR IN MIND: You may substitute low calorie mayonnaise for fewer calories. Use Knorr's vegetable soup mix if available.

Congealed Salmon Salad

1	(15½-ounce) can salmon	1	cup chopped celery
2	envelopes unflavored gelatin	¾	cup mayonnaise
		3	tablespoons lemon juice
1	teaspoon finely chopped onion	½	teaspoon salt
		2	hard-cooked eggs, sliced

Drain salmon, reserving liquid. Add enough hot water to salmon liquid to make 1 cup. Bring liquid to a boil, pour over gelatin, stirring well. Chill until slightly thickened. Flake salmon, add gelatin mixture, onion, celery, mayonnaise, lemon juice and salt. Stir until blended. Arrange egg slices at bottom of lightly oiled 4-cup mold. Spoon salmon over egg. Refrigerate.

Yield: 6 to 8 servings

Shrimp and Pasta Salad

great hot weather dish

3	cups water	½	cup sliced water chestnuts
1	pound fresh shrimp, peeled and deveined	¾	cup mayonnaise
⅓	(16-ounce) package spiral pasta	2	tablespoons sugar, optional
½	cup diced celery	1	tablespoon vinegar
½	cup sliced ripe olives	1	tablespoon lemon juice, or more to taste
½	cup sliced fresh mushrooms	½	teaspoon salt
		⅛	teaspoon pepper

Bring water to a boil; add shrimp and return to a boil. Reduce heat and simmer 3 to 5 minutes. Drain well; rinse with cold water. Chill. Cook pasta according to package directions and drain. Rinse with cold water. Combine pasta, shrimp, celery, olives, mushrooms and water chestnuts. Combine mayonnaise, sugar, vinegar, lemon juice, salt and pepper. Pour over pasta mixture and toss until coated. Cover and chill.

Yield: 4 to 6 servings

BEAR IN MIND: *For a more colorful dish you may use multi-colored spiral pasta.*

Summer Pasta Salad

1   (16-ounce) box linguine
1   (16-ounce) bottle zesty
    Italian salad dressing
1   (4-ounce) can mushrooms,
    drained
1   cucumber, chopped
3   tomatoes, chopped in
    large pieces
1   onion, chopped
½   (2.75-ounce) jar McCor-
    mick's Salad Supreme

Break linguine into fourths. Cook according to package directions and drain. Mix remaining ingredients with linguine and refrigerate.

Yield: 6 to 8 servings

BEAR IN MIND: *If dieting, use oil-free Italian dressing. You may add fresh broccoli and other fresh vegetables and herbs.*

Tortellini Salad

2   (7-ounce) packages
    tortellini pasta
½   cup virgin olive oil
¼   (8-ounce) bottle Italian
    dressing
½   teaspoon freshly ground
    pepper
1   teaspoon salt
1   small garlic clove, pressed
    Dash nutmeg
    Dash oregano
2   teaspoons dried tarragon
4   teaspoons dried basil or
    ¼ cup chopped fresh basil
½   cup chopped fresh parsley
2   to 3 tomatoes, sliced
½   cup sliced pitted ripe
    olives
4   ounces feta cheese, cubed

Cook tortellini according to package directions. In jar, combine oil, salad dressing, pepper, salt, garlic, nutmeg, oregano, tarragon, basil and parsley. Shake well. Place cooked pasta, tomatoes, olives and feta cheese in large bowl. Pour dressing over salad and toss gently. Chill until ready to serve.

Yield: 12 servings

BEAR FLAIR: *Fresh basil leaves look smashing perched on top of this salad.*

Italian Sausage Pasta Salad

6	Italian-style link sausages, sweet or hot	3	tablespoons chopped Italian parsley
½	pound elbow macaroni or twists	¼	cup olive oil
4	bell peppers, chopped	3	tablespoons wine vinegar
2	red onions, sliced	1	garlic clove, chopped
2	cups canned kidney beans, drained	½	teaspoon salt
3	hard-cooked eggs, quartered		Freshly ground black pepper to taste
			Pinch oregano

To cook the sausages, prick the skins with a fork, then place in skillet with water to cover. Bring to a boil, reduce the heat and poach 1 minute. Drain off the water. Slice sausages into ½-inch lengths and fry over medium heat in dry skillet until browned. Cook and drain macaroni according to directions on package. Combine the sausage, macaroni, peppers, onions, kidney beans, eggs and parsley in large salad bowl. In second bowl, combine olive oil, wine vinegar, garlic, salt, pepper and oregano. Beat vigorously with a fork. Pour mixture over salad, tossing gently. Chill a few hours. Serve chilled.

Yield: 6 to 8 servings

Egg Salad

1	dozen hard-cooked eggs	¼	cup chopped almonds
2	cups mayonnaise	¼	pound saltine crackers, crushed
½	cup chopped dill pickles		Salt and pepper to taste
½	cup chopped celery		Lemon juice to taste
½	cup chopped pimiento		
½	large onion, chopped		

Peel eggs and chop finely. Add remaining ingredients and mix well. Adjust seasonings to taste.

Yield: 6 to 8 regular sandwiches

BEAR IN MIND: *This is a new twist to traditional egg salad. The saltine crackers add a crunch!*

Neiman Marcus Seafood Salad

2 cups cooked rice, chilled	1 tablespoon chopped chives
½ cup crabmeat or chopped lobster	¼ cup chopped parsley
½ cup slivered ham	1 tablespoon olive oil
½ cup finely chopped celery	1 tablespoon red wine vinegar
2 hard-cooked eggs, finely chopped	½ cup mayonnaise
	Salt and pepper to taste

Combine and toss (lightly) rice, crabmeat, ham, celery, eggs, chives and parsley. Sprinkle with olive oil and red wine vinegar. Add mayonnaise, salt and pepper and mix all together. Chill several hours before serving.

Yield: 6 servings

Jan's Crabmeat and Beansprout Salad

1 cup mayonnaise	1 pound fresh crabmeat (canned may be substituted), cartilage removed
4 tablespoons soy sauce	
3 tablespoons lemon juice	
½ teaspoon paprika	3 tablespoons chopped green onions
2½ tablespoons curry powder	
1 (16-ounce) can beansprouts, drained	½ cup chopped almonds, toasted
1 cup diced celery	Salt and pepper to taste
	Lettuce

Mix mayonnaise, soy sauce, lemon juice, paprika and curry powder. Cover and refrigerate overnight. Mix beansprouts, celery, crabmeat, green onions and almonds. Pour dressing over and toss gently. Salt and pepper to taste. Arrange on lettuce leaves.

Yield: 8 servings

BEAR IN MIND: *An unusual curried crabmeat salad with some surprises.*

Basic Crab Salad

1	pound king crabmeat, fresh or frozen, cartilage removed	1½	teaspoons Worcestershire sauce
½	cup mayonnaise	½	teaspoon lemon juice
2	tablespoons chopped parsley	1	cup diced, pared cucumber Crisp lettuce
2	tablespoons snipped chives	4	hard-cooked eggs, quartered

Separate crabmeat to a fine texture. In separate medium-size bowl, combine mayonnaise, parsley, chives, Worcestershire sauce and lemon juice; mix well. Add crabmeat and cucumber. Toss. Cover and refrigerate until well-chilled (about 1½ hours). When serving, arrange lettuce on salad plate and top with salad. Garnish with egg.

Yield: 4 servings

BEAR IN MIND: *Substitute low-calorie mayonnaise for a delicious diet salad.*

Marinated Shrimp and Vegetable Salad

1	to 2 cups fresh cauliflower flowerets	1	cup lemon juice concentrate
1	to 2 cups cherry tomatoes, pierced with fork	1	cup vegetable oil
1	to 2 cups sliced zucchini	2	tablespoons chopped chives
1	cup small whole fresh mushrooms	1	tablespoon sugar
1	pound fresh shrimp, peeled, deveined and cooked	2	teaspoons salt
		2	teaspoons lemon pepper
		½	teaspoon dried dill weed
		6	drops hot pepper sauce

Combine vegetables and shrimp in shallow 1½-quart baking dish. In small bowl, combine lemon juice, oil, chives, sugar, salt, lemon pepper, dill weed and pepper sauce. Mix well. Pour this mixture over vegetables and shrimp. Cover. Chill several hours or overnight, stirring occasionally.

Yield: 8 servings

BEAR FLAIR: *Can be served in large bowl as either a salad or an appetizer, using toothpicks to spear shrimp and vegetables.*

Hot Shrimp Salad in Cheddar Cheese Crust

1	cup all-purpose flour
½	teaspoon salt
½	cup grated sharp cheddar cheese (grate while very cold)
⅓	cup plus 1 tablespoon shortening, refrigerated 1 hour ahead
1	to 2 tablespoons cold water
2	cups cooked and chopped shrimp, reserve 3 whole shrimp for garnish if desired
1	cup chopped celery
2	hard-cooked eggs, chopped
1	cup mayonnaise

1	teaspoon lemon juice
1	teaspoon sugar
1	teaspoon Worcestershire sauce
2	teaspoons chopped green onion
2	tablespoons chopped pimiento
1	tablespoon finely snipped fresh dill weed
½	teaspoon salt
¼	teaspoon freshly ground pepper
½	cup grated sharp cheddar cheese
½	cup crushed potato chips

Preheat oven to 475°. Put flour, salt, cold cheese and cold shortening in processor with steel blade. Pulse 3 to 4 times or until shortening is evenly distributed and resembles coarse meal. With processor on, slowly add cold water until dough forms a ball. Do this with a minimum amount of water, being careful not to over-process. Roll out between 2 sheets of waxed paper. Put in 9-inch pie pan. Bake 8 to 10 minutes.

While cooking, put shrimp, celery and eggs in medium-size bowl. Mix mayonnaise, lemon juice, sugar, Worcestershire sauce, onion, pimiento, dill weed, salt and pepper. Pour over the shrimp mixture and toss well. Reset oven to 450°. Pour shrimp salad over the baked crust and sprinkle with grated cheese and potato chips. Bake 15 minutes or until bubbly and golden brown.

Yield: 6 to 8 servings

BEAR FLAIR: Garnish with whole cooked shrimp and sprigs of fresh dill.

BEAR IN MIND:
(1) This can be prepared in mini muffin pans for appetizers or 3-inch pie pans for individual servings for ladies' luncheon.
(2) Also try chicken instead of shrimp. Just use marjoram or tarragon instead of dill weed.
(3) Substitute sour cream for mayonnaise and omit the eggs and you can make ahead and freeze.

Chicken Salad Sensational

2	(3-pound) fryers, whole
3	carrots, each cut into 3 sections
3	medium onions, quartered

4	celery stalks, with leaves, each cut into 3 sections
6	chicken breast halves
3	chicken bouillon cubes

Chicken Salad Dressing:

3	tablespoons sugar
1	teaspoon salt
1	teaspoon Dijon-style mustard
1½	tablespoons all-purpose flour
1	egg, beaten
¾	cup milk

4	tablespoons red wine vinegar
1	tablespoon butter
2	to 3 cups finely chopped celery
	Mayonnaise to taste
	Salt and pepper to taste

Stuff whole fryers with carrots, onion and celery. Place in very large saucepot and add chicken breasts. Cover with water and add bouillon cubes. Bring to a boil. Reduce heat and simmer until chicken is tender. Discard vegetables. Cool chicken in broth. Bone and chop chicken. Set aside.

To prepare Chicken Salad Dressing: In double boiler, combine sugar, salt, mustard, flour, egg, milk and vinegar. Cook over hot water until thickened, stirring constantly. Remove from heat, add butter. Blend well. Cool dressing before combining with chicken. Mix with chicken and chill several hours or overnight. Just before serving, add celery, mayonnaise, salt and pepper.

Yield: 3 to 4 quarts chicken salad

BEAR FLAIR: *Heavenly when served in cantaloupe halves or wedges!*

BEAR IN MIND: *This broth is priceless in flavor! Freeze every drop for use in cooking fresh vegetables and other special recipes.*

Honey Bear Dressing

½	cup mayonnaise
½	cup sour cream
2	tablespoons lemon juice

1	tablespoon honey
1	tablespoon milk
½	teaspoon sesame oil

Combine all ingredients, blending well. Chill until ready to serve.

Yield: 1 cup dressing

BEAR FLAIR: *Really "jazzes up" a fresh fruit salad. Also use as a dip for fruit.*

Cole Slaw Dressing

2	tablespoons sugar	¼	teaspoon dry mustard
2	tablespoons vinegar	¼	teaspoon savory
2	tablespoons sour cream	¼	teaspoon marjoram
2	tablespoons mayonnaise	¼	teaspoon dill seed
¼	teaspoon salt	¼	teaspoon onion salt

Blend all ingredients well. Toss with slaw mixture and chill overnight.

BEAR FLAIR: Enough dressing for 4 cups slaw mixture.

"Mock" Caesar Dressing

1	garlic clove, minced	2	tablespoons grated Parmesan cheese
½	teaspoon salt		
¼	teaspoon pepper	¼	cup salad oil
	Dash dry mustard	1	head romaine lettuce, washed, dried and torn
1	tablespoon lemon juice		

Blend well all ingredients except lettuce. Put in large serving bowl. Add torn lettuce and chill until ready to serve. Toss gently and serve. Can add a sprinkle of additional grated Parmesan cheese, if desired.

Yield: 6 servings

Bleu French
delicious and different

⅔	cup vinegar	1	cup corn oil
1	garlic clove	1	teaspoon sugar
1	(10¾-ounce) can tomato soup		Dash oregano
		3	ounces bleu cheese

In blender, pulverize vinegar and garlic. Add tomato soup, corn oil, sugar and oregano. Blend. Add bleu cheese and blend slightly. If you like it "more bleu", crumble additional bleu cheese after blending.

Yield: about 2 cups dressing

BEAR IN MIND: Stores several weeks in refrigerator.

Easy Fruit Dressing

½	cup powdered sugar	½	teaspoon paprika
3	tablespoons vinegar	1	teaspoon poppy seeds
½	teaspoon salt	¾	cup oil
1	teaspoon dry mustard		

Combine all ingredients, except oil, in bowl of food processor with steel blade. With processor on, slowly pour in oil and process about 30 seconds. Chill.

Yield: about 1 cup

 Green Goddess

1	can anchovy fillets	2	scant tablespoons wine
1	garlic clove		or tarragon vinegar
1	cup parsley, packed	1	cup Homemade
2	green onions or 1 small		Mayonnaise
	white onion		Anchovy paste to taste

Put anchovy fillets, garlic, parsley, onion and vinegar in blender. Blend until smooth. Add mayonnaise and anchovy paste. Blend well.

Yield: about 1 cup dressing (enough for 10 to 12 salads)

BEAR IN MIND: *This is fabulous served over a combination of leaf lettuce, escarole and endive.*

Homemade Mayonnaise

2	egg yolks	1	teaspoon dry mustard
1	whole egg		Dash salt
1½	tablespoons fresh		Dash white pepper
	lemon juice	2	cups salad oil

Process all ingredients except oil in food processor, using steel blade, 5 to 10 seconds or until combined and light in color. With machine running, slowly add oil. Process until thickened. May try different herbs or flavorings.

Yield: 2½ cups mayonnaise

BEAR IN MIND: *This really makes a chicken salad extra special.*

Summer Dressing

1	cup plain yogurt	½	teaspoon garlic powder
3	tablespoons chili sauce	½	teaspoon salt
1	teaspoon crumbled dry		Pepper to taste
	rosemary or dill weed	½	cup chopped green onions,
1	teaspoon horseradish,		with tops
	optional		

In medium bowl, blend all ingredients except onions until smooth. Stir in onions. Cover and chill several hours or overnight.

Yield: 1 cup dressing

BEAR IN MIND:
(1) Great over cold meat cuts, salads, baked fish and baked potatoes.
(2) Can substitute Dijon-style mustard for chili sauce.

Shrimp Vinaigrette Dressing

1	(8-ounce) package frozen tiny uncooked shrimp, thawed	3	tablespoons Dijon-style mustard
1	bay leaf	1	tablespoon chopped shallots
⅓	cup olive oil	1	tablespoon finely snipped fresh dill weed
2	teaspoons fresh lemon juice	½	teaspoon salt
4	tablespoons white wine vinegar	¼	teaspoon freshly ground pepper
1	garlic clove, minced	½	teaspoon sugar

Rinse and devein shrimp. Add bay leaf to 2 quarts water in 3-quart saucepan. Bring to a boil. Stir in shrimp. Cook and stir until shrimp are cooked (2 to 3 minutes). Drain shrimp in collander. Cool under running water to stop cooking. Mix the remaining ingredients and shake well in dressing bottle or covered jar. Pour over shrimp in a bowl. Cover and refrigerate at least several hours, preferably overnight.

Yield: about ¾ cup dressing

BEAR FLAIR: *You'll like this over fresh spinach and mushroom salad.*

Vegetables and Side Dishes

"BEARING GIFTS"

*THREE BEARS CASSEROLE, page 135 ... prepare this dish; scoop out a round, unsliced loaf of bread and butter the inside of loaf. Spoon in the vegetable mixture; bake as usual. Neat gift; no need to return a dish. Can also use the recipes **JALAPEÑO SPINACH,** page 152, or **ORIENTAL PEAS,** page 148.

*VIDALIA "CHRYSANTHEMUMS", page 145 ... this makes a gorgeous gift and is so quick and easy to prepare.

*VEGETABLE SAUTÉ, page 147 ... for a young bride, give a nonstick omelet skillet (with sloping sides) and a copy of this recipe. Or even better, give her a wok!

*GREEN PEA & TOMATO CASSEROLE, page 147 ... good to have ingredients in pantry for emergency gifts. Give with recipe and a 2-quart casserole to complete the gift.

*ROSEMARY RED POTATOES, page 149 ... if you grow your own fresh vegetables, you can delight anyone with fresh potatoes and fresh rosemary and a copy of this recipe.

*SOUR CREAM POTATOES, page 149 ... an excellent dish to carry for covered dish supper, as well as **SPINACH KUGEL,** page 152.

*APPLE SQUASH, page 153 ... don't overlook this unusual winter squash to surprise and delight hearts with a gift of food!

*SOUTH OF THE BORDER SQUASH, page 154 ... an easy dish to do in advance for delivering later.

*HOLLANDAISE SAUCE, page 163 ... transferred to a covered container is a precious gift when accompanied in early spring with fresh asparagus spears and in the fall with fresh broccoli.

"BEAR ESSENTIALS FOR ENTERTAINING"

*Vegetable exotics are becoming increasingly available. For instance, "Mache", also known as lamb's lettuce, has a sweet hazelnut flavor and can be cooked or used raw in salads. "Fiddlehead ferns", coiled tips of young ferns tasting a little like asparagus can be steamed, blanched or sautéed and served hot or cold. "Wing beans" can be steamed or stir-fried or served raw with dip. Entire pod is edible.

*For drama, stuff large mushrooms with tiny green peas or pearl onions.

*Half a tomato, scoop and fill with carrot purée; broil and add to tray for roast accompaniment.

*Try cutting cucumbers in thin, spaghetti-like strips; place on plate and top with zesty, red salsa, or **SPICY TOMATO SAUCE,** page 175.

*Serve sweet potato soufflé in scooped-out orange halves, especially for Thanksgiving and Christmas buffets.

*For pasta party centerpiece, bake French bread, scoop out the center of loaf, insert small plastic container and add oasis. Create a fresh flower arrangement, using uncooked pasta extended with wire (so pasta doesn't get damp) for "filler" in arrangement. If you're in a hurry, simply put uncooked pasta in an apothecary jar or make bundles of dried wheat for centerpiece.

*Mold hot rice in custard cups, unmold immediately onto platter; garnish with tiny fresh tomato rose and sprig of watercress. At the base of rice add 3 steamed snowpeas.

Three Bears Casserole

1 bunch fresh broccoli	1 pound processed cheese
1 head fresh cauliflower	1 stick margarine
5 small carrots	

Preheat oven to 350°. Cut vegetables into bite-sized pieces and steam 5 minutes. Place all vegetables into 2-quart casserole. Melt cheese and margarine together. Pour cheese mixture over vegetables and bake 30 minutes or until bubbly.

Yield: 6 to 8 servings

Hong Kong Asparagus

2 pounds fresh asparagus	2 tablespoons soy sauce
2 tablespoons vegetable oil	⅛ teaspoon black pepper
2 cloves garlic, minced	½ cup sliced almonds
¾ cup chicken broth	2 to 3 cups cooked rice or
1 tablespoon cornstarch	Chinese noodles
1 tablespoon cold water	

Break off and discard tough ends of asparagus, then wash. Using a diagonal cut, slice into ½-inch pieces. Put oil in large skillet or wok on medium heat. Sauté garlic and asparagus 2 minutes. Add chicken broth, bring to a boil. Whisk together cornstarch, cold water and soy sauce. Add to asparagus in skillet and bring to a slow boil. This will thicken. Add pepper and almonds. Add salt to taste, if needed. Serve over hot, fluffy rice or Chinese noodles.

Yield: 4 to 6 servings

BEAR IN MIND: *Store fresh asparagus in a quart jar with small amount of water (stems in water, tips coming out of jar).*

Asparagus Mousse

2	tablespoons butter		Salt and pepper to taste
2	tablespoons all-purpose flour		Juice of 1 lemon
1	(16-ounce) can asparagus, chopped and liquid reserved	1	tablespoon onion juice
		1	cup slivered almonds
4	egg yolks, beaten	1	pint whipping cream, whipped
2	tablespoons gelatin, dissolved in ¼ cup water		

Melt butter in double boiler, add flour and mix thoroughly. Add reserved asparagus juice. Stir until thick. Pouring slowly, whisk into egg yolks. Put back in double boiler and cook another 2 minutes. Add gelatin, salt, pepper, lemon and onion juice. Cool mixture and fold in asparagus, almonds and whipped cream. Pour into lightly oiled 5-cup mold; refrigerate until congealed. Serve with Homemade Mayonnaise, page 131.

Yield: 10 to 12 servings

BEAR FLAIR: *Unmold onto platter and circle with fresh asparagus tips and lemon bows (made from thin strips of lemon rind).*

Artichoke and Spinach Gourmet

1	cup sour cream	1	(6½-ounce) jar marinated artichoke hearts
1	(0.7-ounce) package cheesy Italian dry salad dressing mix	½	to 1 cup cherry tomatoes
2	(10-ounce) packages frozen chopped spinach		

Combine sour cream and salad dressing mix. Let stand while cooking spinach. Unwrap frozen blocks spinach and place in 1½-quart casserole. Cover. Place in microwave oven and cook 6 minutes on HIGH or until thawed. Fold undrained artichoke hearts into spinach along with sour cream mixture. Cover dish and return to microwave oven to cook 8 minutes on MEDIUM HIGH. Remove from oven and stir spinach. Top with cherry tomatoes, cover and continue cooking 1 to 2 more minutes.

Yield: 6 servings

BEAR IN MIND: *Round, shallow, straight-sided casseroles are the best shapes for cooking food in the microwave. Food cooks more evenly than in square, deep, sloping-sided dishes or casseroles.*

Beans with Basil 'n' Bacon

1	pound fresh pole beans	½	teaspoon salt
½	cup chicken broth	¼	teaspoon freshly ground
2	teaspoons chopped fresh		black pepper
	basil	4	bacon slices, cooked and
1	teaspoon chopped fresh		crumbled
	oregano		

Wash and string beans. Cut into 1-inch pieces, using diagonal slice. In saucepan, bring chicken broth to a boil, add beans along with basil, oregano, salt, pepper and bring back to a boil. Cover and simmer about 15 minutes, or until tender. Meanwhile cook bacon until crisp. Crumble bacon and save to sprinkle on top, once beans are cooked. When ready to serve, add a sprig of basil on top of beans with the bacon.

Yield: 4 servings

BEAR IN MIND: If using canned chicken broth, you may want to decrease amount of salt.

Green Bean Bundles

2	pounds fresh green beans	1½	teaspoons minced fresh
1	pound thick sliced bacon		basil
4	quarts chicken broth	½	teaspoon pepper
1	teaspoon salt		

Wash and trim whole beans. Bundle 12 to 15 beans together in hand and place on top of a ¼-inch wide (lengthwise) bacon slice. Tie the bacon around the bundle of beans in a knot or bow. Continue making bundles until all beans are used. Bring broth and seasonings to a boil in 5-quart Dutch oven. Using a slotted spoon, slip bean bundles into the broth, cover and simmer about 25 minutes or until beans are tender but not mushy. Amazingly, they stay in the bundles!

Yield: 6 servings

BEAR IN MIND:
(1) Chill bacon in freezer about 10 minutes for ease in tying knots or bow.
(2) These can be "bundled" the day before and stored in covered container in refrigerator until ready to cook.

Marinated Green Beans

3 **(16-ounce) cans whole green beans, drained**	1 **tablespoon lemon juice**
1 **(8-ounce) bottle Italian dressing**	1 **tablespoon horseradish**
	½ **cup mayonnaise**
Salt and pepper to taste	2 **teaspoons dry mustard**
1 **cup sour cream**	**Dill sprig, optional**

Place beans in 2-quart casserole and pour dressing over all. Season with salt and pepper. Cover tightly. Marinate 5 to 6 hours or overnight. Stir beans several times to insure even marinating. Prepare sauce consisting of sour cream, lemon juice, horseradish, mayonnaise and dry mustard. Mix well. Drain Italian dressing from beans and discard. Carefully fold sour cream sauce into beans.

Yield: 6 servings

BEAR FLAIR: *A dill sprig adds the final touch.*

Swiss Green Beans

2 **tablespoons butter**	2 **tablespoons chopped onion**
2 **tablespoons flour**	1 **(16-ounce) can green beans, drained**
¼ **teaspoon salt**	
⅛ **teaspoon pepper**	½ **cup shredded Swiss cheese**
¾ **cup milk**	**Toasted bread crumbs for topping**
½ **cup sour cream**	

Preheat oven to 325°. In saucepan, melt butter over low heat. Blend in flour, salt and pepper. Cook over low heat until smooth and bubbly. Remove from heat and stir in milk. Return to heat and stir until thick and smooth. Remove from heat and stir in sour cream and onion. Place beans into 1½-quart casserole. Add sauce and mix well. Top with cheese and then bread crumbs. Bake 20 to 25 minutes.

Yield: 4 to 6 servings

Beets 'n' Balm

6	average-size beet roots and leaves or tops		Dash lemon pepper
4	tablespoons margarine	1	to 2 large lettuce leaves
½	teaspoon salt	½	tart apple
	Dash nutmeg, freshly grated	½	teaspoon sugar
¼	teaspoon seasoned salt	4	to 5 sprigs fresh lemon balm, chopped

Wash and pare beets; save the tops for garnish. Cut into chunks to feed food processor. Shred beets, using food processor. Melt margarine in 2-quart saucepan. Add salt, nutmeg, seasoned salt, and lemon pepper. Stir in shredded beets. Wash lettuce leaves, do not dry. Place lettuce on top of beets. Slice apple and put around edges of saucepan on top of lettuce. Sprinkle sugar on top of all. Cover and simmer 15 minutes, stirring occasionally. When ready to serve, sprinkle lemon balm on top of beets.

Yield: 4 servings

BEAR FLAIR: *Use the tiniest fresh beet leaves for garnish.*

Tasty Broccoli and Carrots

1½	cups water	1	to 2 tablespoons butter
1½	teaspoons salt, divided	2	tablespoons lemon juice
2	(10-ounce) packages frozen broccoli, thawed	1	teaspoon oregano
		½	teaspoon lemon pepper
1	(8-ounce) package carrots, sliced	2	tablespoons finely chopped parsley

Bring water to a boil with 1 teaspoon salt. Drop in vegetables and cook until tender. When done, drain well. Melt butter in small saucepan. Add seasonings except parsley and pour over drained vegetables. Sprinkle with parsley.

Yield: 6 to 8 servings

BEAR IN MIND: *You may substitute fresh broccoli. Cut broccoli and carrots in same sized pieces and steam until tender.*

Broccoli and Corn Carry-in

1	(10-ounce) package frozen broccoli, cooked and drained
1	egg, beaten
½	stick butter, melted
1	cup cracker crumbs, divided
½	teaspoon onion flakes
1	(16-ounce) can creamed corn

Preheat oven to 350°. Grease 1-quart casserole. Place broccoli in casserole. Mix together egg, butter, ¾ cup cracker crumbs, onion flakes and creamed corn. Pour mixture over broccoli. Sprinkle with remaining cracker crumbs. Bake 30 minutes.

Yield: 4 to 6 servings

Broccoli Pea Casserole

1	(15-ounce) can green peas
2	(10-ounce) packages frozen chopped broccoli, divided
1	(10½-ounce) can cream of mushroom soup
1	cup mayonnaise
1	teaspoon salt
½	teaspoon pepper
1	cup grated sharp cheddar cheese
1	medium onion, chopped
2	eggs, beaten
	Cracker crumbs for topping

Preheat oven to 350°. Grease 2-quart dish. Drain peas. Cook broccoli according to package directions. Drain well. Arrange half of broccoli in casserole. Top with peas. Mix soup, mayonnaise, salt, pepper, cheese, onion and eggs. Pour half over peas. Add remaining broccoli and top with remaining sauce. Sprinkle with cracker crumbs. Bake 30 minutes.

Yield: 6 to 8 servings

Red Cabbage

1	large red cabbage
1	medium onion
4	tablespoons margarine
2	tablespoons white vinegar
2	beef bouillon cubes
1	bay leaf
1	apple, cored and sliced
	Salt and pepper to taste
2	tablespoons red wine
2	tablespoons sugar
½	cup water

Cut up cabbage. Sauté onion in margarine in Dutch oven over medium heat. Add cabbage and remaining ingredients. Simmer 2 hours. Add more water during cooking, if necessary.

Yield: 6 servings

Cabbage and Celery Casserole

1	cup White Sauce, page 164	½	teaspoon salt
½	cup chopped celery	¼	teaspoon pepper
5	tablespoons butter, divided	1	tablespoon pimiento
3½	cups chopped cabbage	¼	cup dry bread crumbs

Preheat oven to 350°. Prepare white sauce using packaged mix or homemade. In saucepan, cook celery in 3 tablespoons butter 10 minutes, stirring frequently. Add cabbage and cook 10 minutes longer. Add salt, pepper, pimiento and white sauce. Pour into 9x13-inch glass baking dish. Sprinkle with bread crumbs, dot with remaining butter. Bake 20 to 25 minutes.

Yield: 4 to 6 servings

Carrots au Gratin

3	cups sliced carrots	2	tablespoons all-purpose
1	large onion, sliced		flour
4	tablespoons butter	½	cup grated cheddar cheese
½	teaspoon salt	½	cup buttered bread crumbs

Preheat oven to 350°. Butter 1½-quart casserole. Cook carrots and onion in water 10 minutes. Drain, reserving 2 cups liquid. Melt butter, blend in salt and flour. Gradually add reserved liquid. Cook until thickened. Remove from heat; add cheese and stir until melted. Place vegetables in casserole. Pour sauce over the vegetables. Sprinkle with bread crumbs. Bake 1 hour.

Yield: 6 servings

Ginger Carrots and Celery

12	medium carrots, cut in 2-inch julienne strips	2	teaspoons sugar
		½	teaspoon salt
4	large celery stalks, cut in 2-inch julienne strips	¼	teaspoon ground ginger
		½	stick butter, melted

Preheat oven to 350°. Combine carrots and celery in 1½-quart baking dish. Season with sugar, salt, ginger and melted butter. Cover and bake 1 hour or until vegetables are tender.

Yield: 6 servings

Clara's Carrot-Squash Casserole

2	cups cooked and mashed yellow squash	2	sticks melted butter
1	medium onion, minced	1	cup grated sharp cheddar cheese
1	(10¾-ounce) can cream of mushroom soup, undiluted	2	eggs, beaten
¾	cup grated carrots	1	cup sour cream
1	cup scalded milk	1	(8-ounce) package herb stuffing, divided

Preheat oven to 350°. Grease 3-quart casserole. Combine all ingredients except ¼ cup stuffing mix. Spoon into casserole. Top with remaining stuffing mix. Bake 45 minutes.

Yield: 10 (1-cup) servings

Marjie's Special Carrots

2	pounds carrots, sliced	1	(10¾-ounce) can tomato soup
1	head cauliflower, separated into bite-size pieces	1¼	cups vinegar
1	large onion, thinly sliced	¾	cup vegetable oil
1	bell pepper, thinly sliced	1	teaspoon salt
1	cup sugar	1	teaspoon dry mustard

Cook carrots in small amount of water until crisp-tender. Drain well. Put carrots, cauliflower, onions and peppers in large bowl. Mix well remaining ingredients and pour over vegetables. Marinate in refrigerator at least 24 hours. Drain marinade and serve cold.

Yield: 8 to 10 servings

BEAR IN MIND: *This gets better the longer it marinates. A terrific do-ahead dish.*

Fried Cauliflower Parmesan

1 cup all-purpose flour	2 tablespoons vegetable oil
1 teaspoon salt	2 (10-ounce) packages
Pinch of baking powder	frozen cauliflower, thawed
1 teaspoon paprika	Oil for deep fat frying
1 cup warm beer	Grated Parmesan cheese
1 egg, beaten	

Combine flour, salt, baking powder and paprika. Add beer, egg and vegetable oil; stir until smooth. Heat oil to 375°. Dip cauliflower into batter and fry in hot oil until golden. Drain well. Sprinkle with Parmesan cheese.

Yield: 4 to 6 servings

Vegetables Oriental

¼ stick butter	½ cup chopped almonds
1 bunch celery hearts	2 teaspoons soy sauce
½ pound fresh mushrooms	½ cup slivered almonds

Melt butter in wok or large skillet. Slice celery and mushrooms diagonally and sauté 10 minutes. Add chopped almonds and soy sauce. Stir quickly and remove to serving bowl. Decorate with slivered almonds.

Yield: 4 servings

 # Baked Eggplant

1 large eggplant	1 (16-ounce) can tomatoes
1 small onion, minced	1 cup cracker crumbs
Salt, pepper and sugar	6 bacon slices, 3 cooked
to taste	and crumbled

Preheat oven to 350°. Grease 2-quart casserole. Peel eggplant, slice or dice. Cook in water with onion, salt and sugar until tender. Drain well. Mash eggplant and add tomatoes, cracker crumbs, pepper, crumbled bacon and drippings. Spoon into casserole. Top with remaining bacon slices. Bake 45 minutes or until brown.

Yield: 6 servings

Eggplant Cajun with Green Noodles

a pretty, colorful dish

½	teaspoon freshly ground pepper	1	medium-size eggplant, cubed (do not peel)
½	teaspoon salt	3	tablespoons butter
½	teaspoon red pepper	1	tablespoon vegetable oil
½	teaspoon Hungarian sweet paprika	¼	cup chopped celery
½	teaspoon white pepper	¼	cup chopped bell pepper
¼	teaspoon onion powder	1	tablespoon minced garlic
¼	teaspoon oregano	1	(16-ounce) can tomatoes, drained
⅛	teaspoon thyme	1	(8-ounce) package spinach noodles
⅛	teaspoon cumin		
¼	cup chopped onion		

Combine in bowl pepper, salt, red pepper, paprika, white pepper, onion powder, oregano, thyme and cumin. Mix well and set aside. In large skillet sauté onions and eggplant in butter and oil 5 minutes. Add celery, bell pepper and garlic. Continue to sauté, stirring constantly, until vegetables are transparent. Stir in seasonings. Reduce heat to low and stir occasionally. Purée tomatoes and pour over simmering vegetables. Prepare noodles al dente according to package directions. Drain. Pour vegetables over noodles and serve hot.

Yield: 4 to 6 servings

BEAR FLAIR: *Mold cooked spinach noodles in (4 to 6-cup) ring mold. Unmold and pour brilliant-colored vegetables in center of ring.*

 Onion Pie

6	bacon slices	2	cups milk
2	cups chopped onions		Parmesan cheese for topping
3	eggs		

Preheat oven to 350°. Cook bacon, reserve bacon drippings. Sauté onions until tender in bacon drippings. Mix eggs and milk. Add onions, bacon and drippings. Mix well. Pour into 2-quart casserole. Top with Parmesan cheese. Bake 45 minutes or until brown.

Yield: 8 servings

Vidalia Chrysanthemums

4	large onions	1	cup grated sharp cheddar cheese
1	stick margarine		
1	(10¾-ounce) can of cream of chicken soup	2	tablespoons chopped pimiento

Preheat oven to 350°. Grease 2-quart casserole. Cut onions into 6 wedges each without cutting all the way through. Place onions in casserole. Melt margarine and pour over onions. Spread onions with soup and sprinkle with cheese and pimiento. Bake 40 to 45 minutes or until bubbly.

Yield: 4 to 6 servings

BEAR IN MIND: *This is fabulous served over cooked rice.*

Baked Stuffed Onions

6	large onions, peeled	Beef broth or butter, melted, optional
½	pound bulk pork sausage	Buttered bread crumbs, for topping
¾	cup soft bread crumbs	

Preheat oven to 350°. Cook onions 10 minutes in enough boiling salted water to cover; drain well and cool. Remove center of onions, leaving about a ½-inch shell. Invert to drain; chop onion centers. Cook sausage in skillet over medium heat until done, about 10 minutes, stirring with a fork to crumble; drain well. Combine sausage, bread crumbs and chopped onions. If desired, stir in enough broth or butter to moisten. Stuff mixture into onion shells. Sprinkle with buttered bread crumbs. Place onions in shallow baking dish with ½ cup hot water in bottom of dish. Bake 25 to 30 minutes or until stuffing is hot and onions are tender.

Yield: 6 servings

Unusual Creamed Onions

1	(20-ounce) jar whole onions
2	teaspoons sherry
1	(10¾-ounce) can cheddar cheese soup
1	(4-ounce) can pitted ripe olives, divided
	Cracker crumbs for topping
	Paprika to garnish

Preheat oven to 350°. Drain onions and blend liquid and sherry into soup. Add onions and generous amount of ripe olive wedges. Pour into 2½-quart casserole and top with cracker crumbs, paprika and remaining whole ripe olives. Bake until heated through, 15 to 20 minutes.

Yield: 4 to 6 servings

BEAR IN MIND: *Good with turkey or ham.*

Mushrooms Au Gratin

3	tablespoons butter
1	pound fresh mushrooms, halved
½	cup chopped onions
	Salt and pepper to taste
1	cup sour cream
1	tablespoon all-purpose flour
¼	cup grated Parmesan cheese
¼	cup dry bread crumbs

Lightly grease 1½-quart baking dish. Melt butter in large skillet. Add mushrooms, onions, salt and pepper. Cover and simmer over medium-low heat 7 to 10 minutes or until tender; drain. Spoon mushrooms into baking dish. Combine sour cream and flour; mix well and spread over mushrooms. Sprinkle with cheese and bread crumbs. Broil 3 to 5 minutes or until lightly browned.

Yield: 4 servings

Vegetable Sauté

2   tablespoons olive oil
2   tablespoons butter
1   large bell pepper, sliced
1   large onion, sliced
1   small cauliflower, sliced
1   large tomato, chopped
    coarsely
½   teaspoon garlic salt

¼   teaspoon red pepper
1   teaspoon Worcestershire
    sauce
2   tablespoons white wine
    or 2 tablespoons red wine
    vinegar

Heat large skillet over medium-high heat. Add oil and butter, then sauté bell pepper, onion and cauliflower until almost tender. Add tomatoes, garlic salt, pepper, Worcestershire sauce and wine. Simmer 5 minutes. Serve hot.

Yield: 4 to 6 servings

Green Pea and Tomato Casserole

1   stick margarine
1   (16-ounce) can tomatoes
1   (8-ounce) can tomato
    sauce
2   bay leaves
1   small onion, chopped
4   to 5 celery stalks, sliced
1   tablespoon all-purpose
    flour

1   tablespoon Worcestershire
    sauce
1   tablespoon ketchup
2   (8-ounce) cans green
    peas, drained
1   (8-ounce) can water
    chestnuts, drained
1   tablespoon chili sauce
1½   cups grated cheese

Preheat oven to 350°. Cook all ingredients except cheese in large pan on low heat 10 minutes. Pour into 2-quart casserole and bake 25 minutes. Sprinkle cheese on top and bake 5 minutes more.

Yield: 8 servings

Oriental Peas

2	(10-ounce) packages frozen peas, cooked	1	(8-ounce) can water chestnuts, drained and sliced
2	(10¾-ounce) cans cream of mushroom soup	1	teaspoon salt
1	(8-ounce) can mushrooms, drained	½	teaspoon seasoned salt
1	(16-ounce) can bean sprouts, drained	¼	teaspoon lemon pepper
		1	(6-ounce) can Chinese noodles

Preheat oven to 325°. Lightly butter 2-quart casserole dish. Mix all ingredients except noodles. Put in 2-quart casserole. Bake 15 minutes. Top with Chinese noodles and finish baking 15 to 20 minutes more or until bubbly.

Yield: 10 to 12 servings

BEAR FLAIR: *Just before serving garnish with a sprig of fresh lovage or fennel.*

Potatoes Dauphinoise

1	garlic clove, cut in half	2	pounds potatoes, thinly sliced (about 8 cups)
2	tablespoons butter	½	cup whipping cream
1½	cups milk	4	ounces Gruyère cheese, grated
	Salt and pepper to taste		
	Nutmeg to taste		

Preheat oven to 375°. Rub 8x12-inch baking dish with cut side of garlic, then with butter. In 5-quart Dutch oven, bring milk to a boil with salt, pepper and nutmeg. Add potatoes to boiling milk, a few at a time, to maintain milk at a simmer. Bring to a boil again and cook 5 minutes, stirring frequently to prevent potatoes from sticking to bottom of pan. Add cream, stir and pour into baking dish. Sprinkle with cheese. Bake 25 to 30 minutes.

Yield: 10 to 12 servings

Rosemary Red Potatoes

2	pounds small fresh red potatoes	1	stick margarine, melted
			Rosemary to taste

Preheat oven to 325°. Clean potatoes. Leave some unpeeled. Peel some around the middle. Place in shallow glass baking dish. Pour melted margarine over potatoes. Sprinkle rosemary generously over potatoes. Bake until tender. For last 10 minutes, place under broiler for crunchy finish.

Yield: 6 servings

Sour Cream Potatoes

8	medium potatoes, peeled and sliced	¾	stick margarine
1	(8-ounce) package cream cheese		Garlic salt to taste
			Chives to taste
1	cup sour cream		Paprika to taste

Preheat oven to 350°. Grease 2-quart casserole dish. Boil potatoes until done. Drain and let cool slightly. Beat cream cheese and sour cream together. Beat potatoes into cream cheese mixture. Add margarine, garlic salt and chives. Beat until smooth. Pour into dish. Brush with melted butter and sprinkle with paprika. Bake 30 minutes.

Yield: 6 to 8 servings

BEAR IN MIND: *This can be prepared up to the baking point, then refrigerated. Take out of refrigerator 45 minutes before serving and bake as directed.*

Elegant Hash Browns

2 cups sour cream	1½ sticks butter, divided
10 ounces grated cheddar cheese	1 (2-pound) bag frozen hash brown potatoes, thawed
1 small onion, minced	Salt and pepper to taste
1 (10¾-ounce) can cream of chicken soup	2 cups crushed corn flakes

Preheat oven to 350°. Grease 9x13-inch baking dish. Mix sour cream, cheese, onion, soup and 1 stick butter. Mix with thawed potatoes, salt and pepper. Spread in baking dish. Top with corn flakes and ½ stick of melted butter. Bake 45 minutes to 1 hour.

Yield: 12 to 14 servings

Cheesy Potatoes

4 large potatoes	1 teaspoon salt
4 tablespoons butter, cut into small pieces	¼ teaspoon pepper
1 medium onion, minced	1 cup shredded sharp cheddar cheese

Scrub potatoes and slice, with skin on, into ¼-inch slices. In large skillet, melt butter; add potatoes, onion, salt and pepper. Cover and cook potato mixture until potatoes are tender and browned, about 15 minutes. Turn potatoes occasionally with pancake turner. Remove skillet from heat; sprinkle potatoes with cheese. Cover skillet until cheese melts.

Yield: 6 servings

Baked Sliced Potatoes

8	large baking potatoes, with skin on	4	garlic cloves, pressed
½	cup butter, melted	1	to 2 teaspoons salt
½	cup salad oil	1	teaspoon dried thyme

Preheat oven to 400°. Butter two 9x13-inch baking dishes. Slice unpared potatoes into ¼-inch thick slices and overlap in baking dishes. Lightly brush slices with mixture of butter and oil; then pour remaining butter and oil equally over each dish of potatoes. Sprinkle with garlic, salt and thyme. Bake 25 to 35 minutes or until potatoes are done and brown on the edges.

Yield: 8 to 10 servings

 # Sweet Potato Alouette

4	to 5 medium-size sweet potatoes	1	cup sherry
1	cup sugar	½	to 1 pint whipping cream, whipped stiff

Boil potatoes. Peel and mash with sugar. Beat with mixer until light and fluffy. Add sherry and fold in cream that has been whipped stiff. Pile into silver or cut glass bowl and refrigerate until very cold, at least 6 hours. Serve cold.

Yield: 8 to 10 servings

BEAR FLAIR: *Garnish with fresh mint leaves or lemon balm leaves or a fresh flower blossom.*

Spinach Kugel

2	(10-ounce) packages noodles	6	eggs, beaten
2	sticks margarine	1	(2.5 ounce) box onion soup mix
2	(10-ounce) packages frozen chopped spinach, thawed and drained	1	(16-ounce) jar non-dairy coffee creamer
			Sesame seeds for topping

Preheat oven to 350°. Cook noodles according to package directions, about 15 minutes. Drain well. Do not rinse. Melt margarine and combine with cooked noodles, spinach, beaten eggs, onion soup mix and coffee creamer. Put in 9x13-inch shallow casserole. Sprinkle with sesame seeds. Bake 45 minutes or until lightly browned.

Yield: 10 to 12 servings

Jalapeño Spinach

2	eggs, hard-cooked		Salt and pepper to taste
1	(10-ounce) package frozen chopped spinach	¼	cup milk
3	green onions with tops, chopped	2	ounces Monterey Jack cheese with jalapeño peppers, shredded
1	tablespoon butter	4	bacon slices, cooked and crumbled
1	tablespoon flour		

Peel eggs, chop up whites, reserve yolks and set aside. Cook spinach with 2 tablespoons water in microwave on HIGH 2½ minutes. Stir and turn dish. Cook another 2 minutes. Drain spinach, reserving ¼ cup liquid. Sauté green onions in butter about 45 seconds on HIGH. Stir in flour, salt and pepper. Stir in milk and reserved spinach liquid. Microwave on MEDIUM-HIGH about 2 minutes, stirring after 1 minute, until sauce thickens. Fold in shredded cheese and chopped egg whites. Put in 1½-quart casserole and top with crumbled bacon. Microwave on HIGH 2 minutes until heated thoroughly. Press egg yolks through a sieve and sprinkle around edges of casserole.

Yield: 4 servings

Creamed Spinach

1	(10-ounce) package frozen chopped spinach	¼	teaspoon salt
1	small garlic clove, minced		Dash cayenne pepper
¼	cup minced onion		Dash nutmeg
2	tablespoons butter	2	bacon slices, cooked and crumbled
1	tablespoon all-purpose flour	½	cup sour cream at room temperature

Cook spinach as directed. Drain well. In saucepan, sauté garlic and onion in butter. Stir in flour and cook about 1 minute. Add drained spinach, salt, cayenne pepper and nutmeg. Cook over low heat until very thick. Fold in crumbled bacon and sour cream. Heat gently to serving temperature and serve at once.

Yield: 4 to 6 servings

Apple Squash

2	medium acorn squash, halved and seeds removed	½	stick butter, melted
½	cup water	2	small apples, peeled and cubed
¼	cup brown sugar, firmly packed	¼	cup chopped pecans

Place squash in large, shallow microwave dish, cut side up. Pour water in bottom and cover. Microwave 6 minutes on HIGH. Combine brown sugar, butter and apples in medium size bowl and stir well. Divide equally into squash halves. Rotate dish and cover. Microwave on HIGH until tender, about 8 minutes. Let stand 5 minutes. Uncover and sprinkle with pecans.

Yield: 4 servings

BEAR FLAIR: *This is terrific served with grilled fish fillets and a green salad.*

Yellow Squash and Tomatoes

2	tablespoons butter or margarine	1	teaspoon salt
½	cup chopped yellow onion	½	teaspoon pepper
2	large tomatoes, peeled, chopped and drained	⅛	teaspoon hot pepper sauce
1	teaspoon sugar	½	cup grated Parmesan cheese
2	pounds yellow squash, sliced	4	slices uncooked bacon, cut into small pieces

Preheat broiler. In large skillet, melt butter; sauté onion until tender, about 5 minutes. Add tomatoes and sugar; cook 10 minutes. Reduce heat; add squash and salt. Cover and cook until tender. Season with pepper and hot pepper sauce. Pour into 1½-quart shallow baking dish. Top with cheese and bacon. Broil until bacon is cooked, about 10 minutes.

Yield: 6 to 8 servings

South of the Border Squash

1	cup chopped onion	1½	cups grated Monterey Jack cheese
1½	pounds squash, sliced		
2	tablespoons butter	1	egg
1	(4-ounce) can green chilies	1	cup cottage cheese
2	tablespoons all-purpose flour	2	tablespoons chopped parsley
1	teaspoon salt Pepper to taste	½	cup freshly grated Parmesan cheese

Preheat oven to 375°. Butter 9x13-inch pan or 2-quart casserole dish. In skillet, sauté onion and squash in butter until tender. Stir in chilies, flour, salt and pepper. Pour into casserole. Sprinkle Monterey Jack cheese on top. Stir together the egg, cottage cheese and parsley. Spread this mixture on top of the Monterey Jack cheese. Sprinkle with Parmesan cheese. Bake 25 to 30 minutes.

Yield: 6 servings

BEAR FLAIR: *Put a sprig of fresh parsley and a couple of whole, cooked, tiny squash in center of casserole just before serving.*

BEAR IN MIND: *Mix ahead the morning of your party, or even the day before, and refrigerate up to the time you are ready to bake.*

Squash Rockefeller

11	tablespoons butter, divided	2	teaspoons minced fresh parsley
⅛	teaspoon garlic powder	1	teaspoon Worcestershire sauce
6	to 8 medium squash, washed and sliced	3	dashes hot pepper sauce
1	(10-ounce) package frozen chopped spinach, thawed and drained		Salt to taste
		¾	cup bread crumbs
1	bunch green onions, chopped	2	to 3 tablespoons grated Parmesan cheese

Preheat oven to 450°. Melt 4 tablespoons butter in large skillet. Add garlic powder and squash. Cover and steam until tender, about 15 minutes. Place squash in 9-inch square glass baking dish. Sauté spinach, onions and parsley in 5 tablespoons butter about 5 minutes. Season with Worcestershire sauce, pepper sauce and salt. Pour spinach mixture over squash. Melt remaining butter and stir in bread crumbs. Sprinkle bread crumbs over spinach and then sprinkle with Parmesan cheese. Bake uncovered 15 minutes or until golden brown.

Yield: 8 to 10 servings

BEAR IN MIND: *Instead of preparing this dish casserole-style, cut squash in half, scoop out and cook. Mix remaining ingredients and stuff squash with spinach mixture.*

Italian Baked Zucchini

½	pound fresh mushrooms, sliced	4	medium zucchini
2	tablespoons butter	2	tablespoons bread crumbs
½	teaspoon salt	4	eggs
⅛	teaspoon pepper	4	tablespoons grated Parmesan cheese
¼	teaspoon oregano		

Preheat oven to 325°. Grease 1-quart casserole dish. In skillet, sauté mushrooms about 5 minutes in butter. Stir in salt, pepper and oregano. Shred zucchini coarsely. Combine with bread crumbs and mushrooms. Spoon into casserole. Beat eggs and pour over zucchini and mushroom mixture. Top with grated Parmesan cheese. Bake 30 to 40 minutes.

Yield: 6 servings

Zucchini Supreme Pie

4	cups thinly sliced zucchini	¼	teaspoon chopped fresh oregano
1	cup chopped onion		
1	stick margarine	2	eggs, well-beaten
½	cup chopped fresh parsley	1	(8-ounce) package Mozza-rella cheese, shredded
½	teaspoon salt		
½	teaspoon black pepper	1	(8-ounce) can refrigerated cresent dinner rolls
¼	teaspoon garlic powder		
¼	teaspoon chopped fresh basil	2	teaspoons Dijon-style mustard

Preheat oven to 375°. In saucepan, sauté zucchini and onion in marga-rine until tender, about 10 minutes. Add parsley, salt, pepper, garlic powder, basil and oregano. In large bowl mix eggs and cheese. Stir in zuc-chini mixture. Set aside. Separate dough into 8 triangles and press into bottom of ungreased 11-inch quiche or pie pan. Press seams together and spread mustard over crust. Pour zucchini mixture into crust. Bake 20 minutes or until knife inserted in center comes out clean. Let stand 10 minutes before serving.

Yield: 6 servings

BEAR FLAIR: *Arrange zucchini slices in overlapping design on perime-ter of pie. Place parsley sprig in center.*

BEAR IN MIND: *Overlap tomato slices instead of zucchini for topping and nestle fresh basil leaves in center.*

Zucchini-Tomato Parmesan

6	to 8 zucchini, sliced	3	tablespoons olive oil
2	to 3 onions, sliced	½	cup grated Parmesan cheese
6	to 8 tomatoes, cut in wedges		

In large skillet, sauté zucchini, onions and tomatoes in olive oil 2 to 3 minutes. Cover and simmer 1 hour. Add parmesan cheese before serving.

Yield: 6 to 8 servings

Baked Stuffed Tomatoes

8	firm medium-size tomatoes		Salt and red pepper
¾	cup diced celery		to taste
½	cup diced bell pepper		Worcestershire sauce
2	tablespoons minced onion		to taste
1	cup cracker crumbs, divided	2	eggs, beaten
8	bacon slices, cooked crisp, reserve drippings	4	tablespoons butter, divided

Preheat oven to 350°. Leave peeling on tomatoes. Cut small slice from stem end and cut out hard center. With small spoon, scoop out pulp and reserve, leaving ½-inch outer layer. Rub inside with salt and turn upside down to drain. Chop tomato pulp fine, mix with celery, bell pepper, onion, ½ cup cracker crumbs, crumbled bacon and drippings. Season with salt, red pepper, Worcestershire sauce to taste. Add beaten eggs. Fill each tomato with mixture. Top each with remaining cracker crumbs and ½ tablespoon butter. Bake in shallow dish, with water to cover bottom of dish, 20 minutes or until topping is golden.

Yield: 8 servings

Curry Baked Tomato Slices

4	medium-size tomatoes, medium-ripe	1½	teaspoons curry powder
½	cup all-purpose flour	2	large eggs
2	cups soft bread crumbs	5½	tablespoons butter, melted
1	teaspoon salt		

Preheat oven to 375°. Line bottom of 15x10-inch jelly roll pan with foil; butter foil well. Cut stem ends from tomatoes. Cut each one into slices ½-inch thick. Mound the flour on sheet of waxed paper. In shallow dish or pie plate, stir together bread crumbs, salt and curry powder. In small bowl, beat eggs. Dip tomato slices, one at a time, in the flour; then in egg and then in crumb mixture, making sure the crumb mixture adheres well. As each slice is coated, place in single layer on the prepared pan. Drizzle with melted butter. Bake 10 to 15 minutes or until coating is crisp and lightly browned.

Yield: 4 servings

Herb Baked Tomatoes

3	large tomatoes
6	teaspoons margarine, divided
½	teaspoon salt
⅛	teaspoon pepper
¼	teaspoon basil

¼	teaspoon thyme
¼	teaspoon oregano
¼	teaspoon sugar
¼	cup crumbled potato chips

Preheat oven to 325°. Cut core from tomatoes and slice in half. Place in shallow baking dish, cut side up. Put 1 teaspoon of margarine on each piece. Combine remaining ingredients and sprinkle over tomatoes. Bake 30 minutes.

Yield: 6 servings

BEAR IN MIND: *If you object to tomato peels, peel tomatoes and place in muffin tins to keep shape.*

Baked Tomatoes Stuffed with Artichokes

3	(7-ounce) cans artichoke hearts, quartered
2	cups freshly grated Parmesan cheese, divided
½	cup bread crumbs
2	tablespoons dried minced onions
1	teaspoon minced garlic

1	teaspoon lemon pepper
¼	teaspoon salt
2	cups Homemade Mayonnaise, page 131
10	tomatoes
	Bread crumbs for topping
10	teaspoons butter

Preheat oven to 375°. Butter 8x12-inch baking dish. Drain artichoke hearts well and chop. Put in mixing bowl and add 1½ cups Parmesan cheese. Add ½ cup bread crumbs, onions, garlic, lemon pepper, salt and mayonnaise. Mix well. Set aside. Cut stem end off tomatoes and scoop out pulp with grapefruit knife. Reserve pulp. Fill tomatoes with artichoke mixture. Chop pulp and add to leftover artichoke mixture. Spread remaining filling on bottom of buttered dish. Set tomatoes on top, side by side. Sprinkle whole dish with remaining cheese. Sprinkle bread crumbs over top and put butter pat on each tomato. Bake 25 to 30 minutes.

Yield: 10 servings

BEAR IN MIND:
    (1) You may use artichoke mixture to fill crepes.
    (2) Place a layer of cooked rice and shrimp on bottom of baking dish
       to provide a complete meal.

Cheesy Rice Bake

1	(10½-ounce) can beef bouillon	4	ounces sharp cheddar cheese, shredded
1	cup uncooked regular rice	1	(4-ounce) can green chilies, drained and chopped
4	ounces Monterey Jack cheese, shredded	1	cup sour cream

Preheat oven to 350°. Grease 2-quart casserole. Add enough water to bouillon to make 2½ cups. Cook rice in bouillon and water. Let cool. Then add cheeses, chilies and sour cream. Bake 30 to 35 minutes.

Yield: 4 to 6 servings

Spaghetti Primavera

1	garlic clove, crushed	1	small bunch asparagus
¼	cup chopped fresh parsley	8	ounces fresh mushrooms, sliced
1	tablespoon olive oil	1	(1-pound) box spaghetti
1	(16-ounce) can tomatoes	½	cup grated Parmesan cheese
	Salt and pepper to taste		
2	cups sliced zucchini	½	pint warm whipping cream
1	stick plus 2 tablespoons butter, divided	⅓	cup chopped basil leaves
2	cups fresh broccoli flowerets		
1	(10-ounce) package frozen green peas, thawed and drained		

In skillet, sauté garlic and parsley in olive oil. Add tomatoes, salt and pepper. Simmer 15 minutes. Set aside. In another skillet, sauté sliced zucchini in ½ stick butter until almost tender. Set aside.

Bring large saucepot of water to a boil. Add broccoli, green peas and asparagus. Boil 5 to 7 minutes. Drain vegetables. Sauté sliced mushrooms in 2 tablespoons butter. Add blanched vegetables to mushroom pan, cooking just long enough to heat.

Cook spaghetti according to package directions. Drain and mix with Parmesan cheese, remaining butter, cream, basil and salt to taste. Arrange spaghetti on large platter. Top with vegetables. Add the tomato mixture last.

Yield: 6 to 8 servings

Spaghetti Carboñara

6	bacon slices	1	ounce Parmesan cheese, grated
8	ounces thin spaghetti	1	ounce Romano cheese, grated
2	green onions, thinly sliced		
1	(4-ounce) can sliced mushrooms, drained	3	eggs, well beaten
1	garlic clove, minced	¼	cup finely chopped parsley or chervil
2	tablespoons margarine		

Cook bacon until crisp, reserving drippings. While bacon is cooking, cook the spaghetti according to package directions. Sauté the green onions, mushrooms and garlic about 1 minute in 1 to 2 tablespoons of reserved bacon drippings. Heat a large bowl in microwave or oven (200°). Drain spaghetti. Put in heated bowl with margarine and stir. Add cheeses, onion, mushrooms and garlic to eggs and pour over spaghetti, stirring and tossing. (Heat will cook eggs to a smooth, creamy consistency.) Sprinkle with cooked, crumbled bacon and parsley. Serve at once.

Yield: 4 servings

Rice Barbados

4	tablespoons butter	1	cup cold water
2	medium onions, chopped	½	cup white wine
1	cup uncooked regular rice	2	tablespoons vinegar
1	teaspoon salt	1	(10-ounce) package frozen chopped okra, thawed
1	teaspoon marjoram		
1	teaspoon sage	4	pimientos, finely chopped
½	to 1 teaspoon minced garlic	2	to 3 tablespoons minced parsley
1	teaspoon lemon pepper		

Melt butter in saucepan. Add onions, rice, salt, marjoram, sage, garlic and lemon pepper. Mix. Add water, wine and vinegar and bring to a boil. Add okra on top, do not stir. Return to boil, lower heat and simmer covered 30 to 35 minutes. Stir only when put in serving bowl. Garnish with pimiento and parsley.

Yield: 6 servings

BEAR FLAIR: *Lightly oil a 4-cup ring mold. Press in cooked rice. Unmold and fill center of ring with chopped tomatoes or halved salad tomatoes.*

BEAR IN MIND: *Add 1 pint oysters, drained and finely chopped, after rice has been cooked. Cover and heat 10 to 15 minutes. Stir and garnish with pimiento and parsley.*

Wild Rice Casserole

¾ cup uncooked wild rice
2½ cups chicken broth
1 pound ground sausage
2 onions, finely chopped
1 pound mushrooms, sliced
2 tablespoons margarine
1 (10¾-ounce) can cream of mushroom soup

Pinch oregano
Pinch thyme
1 teaspoon salt
⅛ teaspoon pepper
½ cup sliced almonds, toasted

Preheat oven to 350°. Grease 3-quart casserole. Wash rice and combine with chicken broth in saucepan. Bring to a boil and reduce heat to cook slowly about 45 minutes until most of the liquid has been absorbed. Fry sausage and drain. Remove sausage and sauté onion in same pan until transparent. Cook mushrooms in margarine until they lose their juices (about 5 to 7 minutes). Add soup, oregano, thyme, salt, pepper along with the sausage, mushrooms and onions to the cooked rice. Blend well and put in casserole and bake 25 to 30 minutes. Top with toasted almonds a few minutes before removing from oven.

Yield: 10 servings

Savory Kugel

a nice change from potatoes or rice

8 ounces noodles, cooked
½ pint sour cream
8 ounces cottage cheese
1 onion, chopped and sautéed in 3 tablespoons margarine
1 teaspoon salt
¼ teaspoon freshly ground pepper

¼ teaspoon Worcestershire sauce mixed with 1 tablespoon Dijon-style mustard
4 tablespoons grated Parmesan cheese
2 tablespoons chopped fresh parsley

Preheat oven to 350°. Butter a 1½-quart casserole. Mix the cooked noodles, sour cream, cottage cheese, sautéed onion, salt, pepper, Worcestershire sauce and mustard together and put into casserole. Sprinkle with grated Parmesan cheese and parsley. Bake 30 to 35 minutes.

Yield: 6 to 8 servings

BEAR IN MIND: *Lightly oil 1 (4 to 6-cup) ring mold. Press noodle mixture into mold and bake. Unmold and fill with braised tiny finger carrots. Add a parsley sprig or fresh carrot top.*

Caponata

very versatile taste treat

3	celery stalks, chopped	1	(2½-ounce) package sliced almonds
1	bell pepper, chopped		
1	medium onion, chopped	3	tablespoons vinegar
3	tablespoons olive oil	½	teaspoon salt
1	small eggplant, peeled and cubed	1	tablespoon sugar
		½	teaspoon basil
1	(16-ounce) can tomatoes, undrained		Pepper to taste
		1	(6-ounce) can tomato paste
8	to 10 pitted ripe olives, sliced		

In large skillet simmer celery, bell pepper and onion in oil until tender. Add eggplant, tomatoes, olives, almonds, vinegar, salt, sugar, basil and pepper. Simmer 30 minutes. Stir in tomato paste.

Yield: 3 cups

BEAR FLAIR:
  (1) Serve hot or cold with French bread and green salad.
  (2) Layer with Parmesan and Mozzarella cheese and bake as a casserole.
  (3) Heat and fold into an omelet.
  (4) Add hot pepper sauce to taste and serve with crackers.

BEAR IN MIND: *Mixture can be kept refrigerated 2 to 3 weeks. The flavor is enhanced as it keeps.*

Squash Dressing

½	cup chopped onion	1	(10¾-ounce) can cream of chicken soup, undiluted
½	cup chopped green pepper		
½	cup chopped celery	3	cups chopped, cooked and drained yellow squash
1	stick margarine, melted		
5	cups crumbled cornbread	1	teaspoon salt
2½	cups milk	¼	teaspoon pepper

Preheat oven to 400°. Grease 9x13-inch baking dish. Sauté onion, pepper and celery in margarine until tender. Add to cornbread in large mixing bowl. Stir in milk, soup, drained squash, salt and pepper; stir well. Pour into baking dish. Bake 45 to 50 minutes or until lightly browned.

Yield: 10 to 12 servings

BEAR IN MIND: *A lovely change from the basic cornbread dressing, and a terrific way to utilize summer squash.*

Hollandaise Sauce

1	stick unsalted butter, cut in pieces	½	teaspoon salt
			Dash cayenne pepper
3	egg yolks	1	teaspoon hot water
	Juice of 1 lemon		

Process butter, yolks, lemon juice, salt and cayenne in food processor, using steel blade, about 20 seconds or until well-combined. Add hot water while machine is running. If it is quite stiff add a little more hot water. Heat and thicken over medium heat, stirring constantly. This keeps 2 weeks in refrigerator.

Yield: About ¾ cup sauce

BEAR IN MIND: *If salted butter is used, use only a dash of salt.*

Easy Lemon Sauce for Veggies

½	cup sour cream	1	teaspoon prepared mustard
½	cup mayonnaise	2	teaspoons lemon juice

Mix all ingredients and heat over very low heat.

Yield: About 1 cup sauce

BEAR IN MIND: *Great for asparagus and broccoli!*

Sour Cream Sauce

4	teaspoons light brown sugar	⅓	cup sour cream
			Worcestershire sauce to taste
¼	teaspoon dry mustard		
2½	teaspoons apple cider vinegar		Salt and pepper to taste

Combine sugar, mustard and vinegar. Stir until sugar is dissolved. Gently fold in sour cream. Add Worcestershire sauce, salt and pepper.

Yield: ½ cup sauce

BEAR FLAIR: *Serve over hot, cooked, drained vegetables of your choice.*

Thin White Sauce

1 tablespoon butter	¼ teaspoon salt
½ to 1 tablespoon all-purpose flour	⅛ teaspoon pepper
	1 cup milk

In saucepan over low heat melt butter. Stir in flour, salt and pepper. Cook and stir until mixture is smooth and bubbly. Remove from heat; stir in milk. Bring to a boil, stirring constantly; boil 1 minute.

Yield: 1 cup

BEAR IN MIND:

(1) *For medium white sauce, use 2 tablespoons butter, 2 tablespoons flour and 1 cup milk.*

(2) *For thick white sauce, use ½ stick butter, ¼ cup flour and 1 cup milk.*

Nothing Northern

HOW TO COOK VEGETABLES SOUTHERN-STYLE

Fresh vegetables have always played an important part in the Southern diet. Vegetables are prepared simply, but highly seasoned, predominately with cured pork. This method of seasoning came from the days before refrigeration. During the summer months, cured pork was the main meat available. Often vegetables were cooked with a large quantity of meat because that was the entire meal. A big ham hock in the beans went a long way toward helping a man plow a mule the rest of the day. Keep in mind that all these recipes originated before cholesterol-conscious diets.

Black-eyed peas: Shell and wash peas. Put in saucepan and cover with water. Season with 2-inch square piece of side meat that has been slashed several times, salt and 1 to 2 bouillon cubes. Boil slowly 1½ to 2 hours.

Purple hull peas: Cook same as black-eyed peas.

White Acre peas: Cook same as black-eyed peas. Add a few okra pods to peas during the last 30 minutes cooking time.

Butterbeans: Shell and wash butterbeans. Put in saucepan, cover with water, season with several tablespoons of butter and salt. Boil slowly 1½ to 2 hours.

Snap beans: Snap, string and wash beans thoroughly. Season with a ham hock or ham bone, salt, and cover with water. Boil slowly for 2 to 3 hours. For variety, add scraped new potatoes to pot and cook together.

Collards: Wash leaves and remove big central veins. Twist leaves in your hand and shred into small pieces with a sharp knife. Season with a ham hock and salt. Add some water and boil slowly 2 to 3 hours.

Corn: Tender young corn can be boiled on the cob after shucking and silking. Older corn should be cooked cream-style. Remove corn from cob with a corn cutter or knife. Put in a frying pan and cook slowly, stirring often, until corn tastes done and thickens. Season with bacon drippings and salt.

Eggplant: Trim ends and peel eggplant. Cut into bite-sized pieces. Beat 1 egg and ½ cup milk in a small bowl. Dip eggplant into egg mixture, then dredge with flour. Fry in one inch of moderately hot grease. Cook until golden brown, then drain on paper towels. Salt and serve hot.

Okra: Trim ends and cut in bite-size rounds. Fry in same manner as eggplant.

Okra variation: Leave 2 to 3-inch pods whole and boil until tender. Drain and dot with butter.

Okra and tomatoes: Trim and cut okra and peel and cut tomatoes. Put in saucepan and cook until okra is tender.

Summer squash: Wash squash and trim ends. Cut in ½-inch thick slices and put in heavy saucepan (or deep cast iron fryer). Add 1 or 2 chopped onions. Add enough water to almost cover. Boil rapidly until most of water is gone and squash is tender. Reduce heat, season with bacon drippings, salt and pepper, and continue cooking slowly until bits of squash brown slightly.

Sweet potatoes: To bake, preheat oven to 375⁰. Wash and grease potatoes lightly. Place on baking pan and cook 1 to 1½ hours or until potatoes are tender.

Candied sweet potatoes: Peel potatoes and slice in ¼-inch thick slices. Place in heavy saucepan and add ½ to 1 cup of sugar, 1 stick of margarine and 1 to 2 cups of white Karo syrup. Cook slowly uncovered until potatoes are tender and syrup has thickened.

Turnips: Wash leaves through 4 or 5 waters or until no grit remains in sink after draining. Put in a large pot and add a small amount of water. Season with fresh pork, preferably fresh neck bones, salt and 1 teaspoon sugar. Boil slowly for 2 to 3 hours.

Ard's Aardvark

2   teaspoons frozen orange
    juice concentrate, thawed
2   teaspoons frozen lemonade
    concentrate, thawed

1½ ounces bourbon
    Ice cubes and gingerale
    to mix

Place orange juice, lemonade and bourbon in 12-ounce glass. Stir well. Fill with ice cubes and gingerale. Serve immediately.

Yield: 1 (12-ounce) glass

BEAR IN MIND: *A dear friend's answer to making it through summer in the deep South!*

Southern Egg Nog

16 eggs, separated
16 tablespoons sugar
16 tablespoons whiskey

1   pint whipping cream
    Nutmeg to garnish

6 to 8 hours before serving, beat the egg yolks until thick. Add sugar gradually. Add whiskey, by the tablespoonful, beating until well blended and thickened. Chill until time to serve. Then beat egg whites until stiff. Set aside. Whip cream until stiff and fold into egg whites. Carefully fold egg yolk mixture into egg white mixture. Serve immediately.

Yield: 8 to 10 servings

BEAR FLAIR: *Freshly grated nutmeg for each serving adds the final touch!*

BEAR IN MIND: *A Sumter County favorite, over 100 years old. A must during the holidays.*

Frozen Watermelon Daiquiris

3   cups cubed and seeded
    watermelon
⅓   cup sugar

⅓   cup fresh lime juice
¼   cup light rum
    Mint leaves

Put watermelon, sugar, lime juice and rum into blender and process until slushy. Freeze mixture in a large metal bowl, about 2 hours or until thick. Spoon into glasses and garnish with mint leaves.

Yield: 4 servings

Real Lemonade

12	lemons	Ice
½	cup sugar	

Juice lemons, reserving rind. Place juice and sugar in 2½-quart pitcher; stir until sugar dissolves. Cut rinds into strips and add to sugar mixture. Fill the pitcher with ice and let melt for 30 minutes. Serve.

Yield: 10 servings

Mint Julep Syrup

4	to 6 cups loosely packed fresh mint leaves	3	cups water
3	cups sugar	6	lemons

Wash mint, pat dry. Mix sugar and water in large saucepan and bring to a boil. Add mint and crush against the sides of saucepan to release juices. Remove from heat. Squeeze lemons, reserving juice, and add rinds to hot mixture. Allow to cool 45 minutes, then add lemon juice. Remove rinds and strain to remove mint leaves. May refrigerate 2 to 3 weeks; freeze for 6 months.

Yield: 4 cups

BEAR IN MIND:
(1) Freeze the syrup in ice trays so you may remove 1 cube when needed. Thaw and add to 8-ounce glass of iced tea, club soda or lemonade.
(2) For mint juleps, fill 1 (8-ounce) cup with crushed ice, add 1½ ounces bourbon and fill with mint syrup.

Spiced Pecans

2	cups pecans	⅛	teaspoon salt
1	cup sugar	¼	cup water
¼	teaspoon cinnamon		

Grease cookie sheet. Mix all ingredients in large skillet. Stir over medium heat until all moisture is absorbed. Pour onto cookie sheet and separate. Allow to cool thoroughly.

Yield: 2 cups pecans

Tomato Aspic

3	envelopes unflavored gelatin	¼	cup lemon juice
½	cup cold water	1	tablespoon grated onion
3	cups tomato juice	1	tablespoon horseradish
½	cup ketchup	½	teaspoon salt

Lightly oil 4-cup mold. Sprinkle gelatin in cold water. Set aside. Bring tomato juice to a boil in medium saucepan. Add softened gelatin, ketchup, lemon juice, onion, horseradish and salt. Stir well. Pour into mold and chill several hours or overnight.

Yield: 8 (½-cup) servings

BEAR IN MIND: *May add artichoke hearts, celery, olives, chopped meats or seafood.*

Collard Greens Soup

3	to 4 pounds center-cut ham with bone, cut in chunks	½	teaspoon red pepper
		1	teaspoon oregano
1	beef soup bone	4	tablespoons Worcestershire sauce
4	medium onions, diced	1	gallon water
6	celery stalks, diced	2½	cups finely chopped collard greens
8	chorizo (Spanish) sausages, sliced	2	pounds dried lima beans, soaked 8 hours
1	bay leaf	3	potatoes, grated
½	teaspoon hot pepper sauce		Salt and pepper to taste
½	teaspoon thyme		

In stock pot, cook ham, ham bone, soup bone, onions, celery, sausage and seasonings in water. Simmer 2 hours. Add collard greens and soaked beans. Simmer 2 more hours. Add potatoes last 30 minutes to thicken. Salt and pepper to taste.

Yield: 8 to 10 servings

BEAR IN MIND: *You may add diced green pepper. Substitute canned garbanzo beans for dried. Substitute pepperoni or Polish sausage for Spanish sausage.*

A Good Biscuit Recipe

The finest Southern biscuits

2½	cups all-purpose flour	½	cup shortening
3	teaspoons baking powder	¾	cup milk
1	teaspoon salt		

Preheat oven to 450°. Mix flour, baking powder and salt. Cut in shortening with pastry blender or two knives. Stir in milk, then round up on lightly floured board. Knead very lightly. Roll or pat out ½-inch thick. Cut with floured biscuit cutter. Place on ungreased pan and bake 10 to 12 minutes.

Yield: 20 biscuits

BEAR IN MIND: *If you substitute buttermilk, use only 2 teaspoons baking powder, ½ teaspoon soda, 2 more tablespoons shortening, roll thinner and bake only 7 to 10 minutes.*

Flaky Pecan Biscuits

2	cups all-purpose flour	1	stick margarine
3	teaspoons baking powder	½	cup finely chopped pecans
3	tablespoons sugar	½	cup milk
½	teaspoon salt	1	egg, slightly beaten

Preheat oven to 425°. Sift dry ingredients together. Cut margarine into flour mixture with pastry blender until mixture looks like cornmeal. Add nuts. Combine milk and egg. Add to the flour mixture all at once, while stirring with fork. Turn dough out onto lightly floured board and knead gently a few times. Roll dough ½-inch thick; cut into one inch rounds with floured cutter. Bake on cookie sheet 12 to 15 minutes. Serve hot.

Yield: About 24 biscuits

Cracklin' Bread

1 cup cracklins, soaked in ½ cup warm water	1 teaspoon salt
3 cups cornmeal	Water, as needed, to make dough

Preheat oven to 450°. Pour cracklin mixture into cornmeal in large bowl. Add salt and more warm water, if necessary, to make dough. Let stand 5 to 10 minutes. Add a little more water if mixture is too stiff. Shape into small loaves or pones. Place on hot, shallow baking pan. Bake until brown on top. Reduce heat to 350° and bake 30 to 45 minutes longer, depending on the size of the pones.

Yield: 6 to 8 servings

Corn Muffins

1 cup cornmeal	1 tablespoon baking powder
2 tablespoons all-purpose flour	Pinch salt
2 tablespoons sugar	½ to 1 cup buttermilk
	1 egg

Preheat oven to 400°. Grease muffin tins or use paper muffin liners. Mix cornmeal, flour, sugar, baking powder and salt. Add buttermilk and egg. Mix until smooth and easy to pour. Spoon into muffin tins and bake 10 minutes or until brown.

Yield: 6 muffins

BEAR IN MIND: *Bake in 3 miniature muffin tins for special occasions.*

Pone Corn Bread

2 cups yellow cornmeal	2 teaspoons salt
1½ cups buttermilk	Bacon drippings
¼ teaspoon baking soda	

Preheat oven to 425°. Use iron skillet that is greased and hot. Mix cornmeal, buttermilk, soda and salt and form 5 to 7 pones (balls of batter) with hands. Pat in pan until about ½ to ¾-inch thick. Rub with bacon drippings. Bake until brown.

Yield: 5 to 7 pones

BEAR IN MIND: *Great with fresh vegetables, but a must with turnip greens or peas.*

Hush Puppies

2	cups yellow cornmeal	2	tablespoons oil
⅔	cup all-purpose flour	2	eggs
1	teaspoon salt	1½	cups milk
1½	tablespoons baking powder	1	medium onion, chopped

Sift together cornmeal, flour, salt and baking powder into medium-size mixing bowl. Add oil, eggs, milk and onion and stir until smooth. Hush puppies should be cooked after fish are fried, using the same grease. Set a glass of water by the frying pan (a Dutch oven or deep fat fryer is better). For small hush puppies use a teaspoon and for larger ones use a tablespoon. Dip spoon in water, then scoop up a spoonful of batter and drop into hot grease. Dip spoon in water each time to make batter drop off spoon easier. Turn hush puppies several times and cook until golden brown. Drain on rack or paper towels.

Yield: 8 to 10 servings

BEAR IN MIND: For an easy way to coat a large amount of fish, double a grocery bag and put 2 or 3 cups of cornmeal in it. Salt fish and drop in bag. Close bag and shake.

Okra-Tomato Gumbo

3	bacon slices, cut in small pieces	1	teaspoon sugar
6	to 8 medium tomatoes, peeled and chopped	1	teaspoon salt
			Pepper to taste
1	medium onion, chopped	2	cups sliced okra

Brown bacon in Dutch oven. Add tomatoes, onion, sugar, salt and pepper. Simmer uncovered until tomatoes are tender, about 30 minutes. Add okra and continue simmering about 20 minutes longer. Stir occasionally.

Yield: 6 servings

BEAR IN MIND:
(1) Can be frozen up to 6 months.
(2) ½ cup chopped bell pepper or ½ cup chopped celery may be added.

Nina's Parmesan Baked Vidalias

5	jumbo Vidalia onions	1	stick butter, divided
	Salt and pepper to taste	1	cup grated Parmesan
14	butter-flavored crackers,		cheese, divided
	crushed and divided	1	tablespoon milk

Preheat oven to 350°. Butter 8-inch square casserole. Peel and slice onions into ½-inch strips. In saucepan, cover onions with salted water and boil until onions are transparent. Do not overcook. Drain in colander. Place a third of the onions in casserole. Sprinkle with salt, pepper, a third of the crushed crackers, a third of the butter and a third of the Parmesan cheese. Repeat layers using one third each time. Sprinkle with milk. Bake 20 to 25 minutes or until onions are completely cooked.

Yield: 4 servings

BEAR IN MIND: *Recipe may be increased, but always use one onion more than the number of servings. For example, use nine onions for eight servings.*

Squash Soufflé

7	tablespoons margarine	2	eggs, beaten
7	tablespoons all-purpose		Salt and pepper to taste
	flour	½	cup grated sharp
2	cups cooked, mashed and		cheddar cheese
	drained yellow squash	¾	cup butter-flavored
2	cups milk		cracker crumbs

Preheat oven to 350°. Grease 2-quart casserole. Melt margarine in skillet. Add flour and blend. Add squash, milk and eggs. Salt and pepper to taste. Cook until mixture begins to thicken. Stir in cheese. Pour into casserole and top with cracker crumbs. Bake about 30 minutes or until golden brown.

Yield: 6 to 8 servings

Turnip Greens Casserole

1	(15-ounce) package frozen chopped turnip greens	½	cup mayonnaise
1	teaspoon sugar	2	tablespoons wine vinegar
	Salt and pepper to taste	2	eggs, slightly beaten
1	(10¾-ounce) can cream of mushroom soup		Bread crumbs for topping
		½	cup grated cheddar cheese

Preheat oven to 350°. Blend all ingredients except bread crumbs and cheese. Pour in 2-quart casserole. Bake 25 minutes. Remove from oven and add bread crumbs and cheese. Bake another 30 to 35 minutes.

Yield: 8 servings

 # Yam Turnout

2¼	pounds yams, cooked and peeled	6	tablespoons margarine, melted
⅓	cup granulated sugar	1	egg, beaten
⅓	cup brown sugar, firmly packed	1½	teaspoons grated orange rind
1½	teaspoons nutmeg	⅓	cup chopped pecans
¾	teaspoon salt		Flour to dredge

Dixie sauce:

1	cup maple syrup	1	teaspoon grated lemon rind
2	tablespoons lemon juice		

Preheat oven to 375°. Whip together yams, sugars, nutmeg, salt, margarine, egg and orange rind until smooth. Add chopped nuts. Coat an 8-inch ring mold with melted margarine. Place mold in refrigerator a few minutes to harden coating. Dredge mold with flour. Press yam mixture into mold. Bake 30 minutes. Turn out when cool. Mix sauce ingredients, heat and pour over yam mold.

Yield: 6 to 8 servings

Spicy Tomato Sauce

1 (16-ounce) can tomatoes	½ medium onion, chopped
½ cup sugar	½ stick butter
3 tablespoons vinegar	Salt and pepper to taste

Combine all ingredients in medium saucepan and bring to a boil. Cook over medium heat, stirring often until sauce thickens to desired consistency.

Yield: About 1½ cups sauce

BEAR FLAIR: *This is great on butter beans, black-eyed peas and other garden peas.*

New Era Chicken Pie

1 (4 to 5-pound) hen, cooked tender, reserving stock	Pepper to taste
Rich, flaky-type pastry for crust	1 stick butter
	Celery seed to taste
3 hard-cooked eggs, thinly sliced	2 tablespoons all-purpose flour
	2 tablespoons milk

Preheat oven to 350°. Remove chicken from bones. Discard skin and bones. Cut meat into bite-size pieces. Line sides and bottom of 3 to 4-inch deep casserole with thinly rolled pastry. Add layer of chicken. Top this with sliced egg. Sprinkle with pepper, dot with butter and sprinkle with celery seed. Dot with 1-inch squares of pastry. Add another layer each of chicken, egg, pepper and celery seed. Heat 1 pint of chicken stock. When it begins to boil, add paste made from flour and milk and let boil 1 to 2 minutes. Add another pint of stock and pour over chicken until it is covered. Top crust may be solid or made of two-way 1-inch strips of pastry. Seal to edges of pan carefully so stock won't boil out. Bake 1 hour or until light brown.

Yield: 8 to 10 servings

Cheese Grits

3	cups water	2	eggs, beaten
¾	cup grits	1	(4-ounce) can green
1	teaspoon salt		chilies, drained and
1	stick butter		chopped
8	ounces medium-sharp cheddar cheese, grated		

Preheat oven to 350°. Grease 7x11-inch baking dish. In saucepan bring to a boil the water, grits and salt. Add butter and cheese. Stir until melted. Add beaten eggs and chilies. Pour into dish and bake 1 hour.

Yield: 4 to 6 servings

Baked Country Cured Ham

1	whole country cured ham	2	cups brown sugar, firmly packed
4	teaspoons prepared mustard	24	to 48 whole cloves
¼	cup vinegar		

Using a brush, scrub ham thoroughly in a large pan of water, changing water often. Cover in cold water and soak overnight. Next day, put ham in large pot with enough cold water to more than cover it. Slowly bring to boiling point, then simmer gently 5 to 6 hours, depending on size of ham (about 28 minutes to the pound). Turn off heat and allow to cool in the cooking water, then remove from water and take off rind; it will peel off easily. Preheat oven to 375°. Put ham in an open roaster. Combine mustard, vinegar and brown sugar and blend well. Spread brown sugar mixture over ham and stud or insert whole cloves into ham. Bake 45 minutes. When cold, slice thin.

Yield: 15 to 20 servings

BEAR FLAIR: *For special serving at holidays, overlap ham slices in a semicircle on platter, leaving room for an ovenware container heaped with Baked Cranberries, page 206. Decorate platter with fresh sage leaves.*

BEAR IN MIND: *For a great finger food, cut slices into small pieces and serve with small buttered biscuits.*

Brunswick Stew

2	large fryers	1	to 2 cups vinegar
8	to 10-pound pork roast	6	lemons
3	pounds onions		Hot pepper sauce to taste
6	(28-ounce) cans tomatoes		Worcestershire sauce to
2	(12-ounce) cans tomato		taste
	paste		Salt and pepper to taste
2	(15-ounce) cans tomato		Red pepper to taste
	sauce	4	to 6 (15½-ounce) cans
2	(32-ounce) bottles		cream-style corn
	ketchup		Instant mashed potato
½	cup prepared mustard		flakes

Boil fryers and pork in large pot—cast iron is best. Cool meat and reserve broth. For easier handling, cook meat the day before and refrigerate overnight. Trim all fat from meat and grind. If you don't have a meat grinder, you can process a small amount at a time with the steel blade of your food processor. Refrigerate ground meat.

If you don't have one giant size pot, divide broth into two large pots (must be heavy gauge cookware). Grind onions and tomatoes and divide between the two pots. Add a can of tomato paste, tomato sauce and a bottle of ketchup to each pot. Divide mustard and vinegar between two pots (rinse ketchup bottles out with vinegar). Slice lemons, squeeze and drop halves in pots. Add a generous amount of hot pepper sauce, Worcestershire sauce, salt, pepper and red pepper. Boil slowly until onions taste done, about 2 hours, stirring occasionally.

Precise amounts for seasonings are not given because you must taste and add what is needed. Stew should be a little too spicy at this point because meat will cut it when it is added.

When onions are done, add cream corn and meat to both parts. Stew will stick easily after meat is added, so you must stir often. If the color is pale, add more tomato paste or ketchup. If flavor is weak, add more seasoning. Add instant potato flakes a cup at a time until stew is the correct thickness.

Yield: 50 servings

BEAR IN MIND:
(1) This recipe may seem a little haphazard, but it has always been the custom when cooking stew that everyone must taste it as you go and add seasoning until everyone thinks it is right.
(2) Brunswick Stew is standard fare for a Southern Bar-B-Que. There are as many recipes as there are people who make it. In years past, it would be cooked in a big pot over a fire in the yard. Today we cook it inside but try to retain the old-fashioned flavor.

Steak 'n' Potatoes

1½ pounds round steak	6 small potatoes, sliced
3 tablespoons butter	1 cup beef broth
2 medium-sized onions, sliced	⅛ teaspoon pepper
	Dash garlic salt

Preheat oven to 350°. Cut steak in slices ½-inch thick. In skillet, brown steaks quickly on both sides in butter. Remove from pan and cook onion slices until lightly browned. Put a layer of steak slices in shallow baking dish, add a layer of potatoes. Repeat layers if necessary. Combine broth, pepper and garlic salt. Pour over steaks. Cover with foil. Bake 1½ hours. Remove foil and bake another 30 minutes.

Yield: 4 servings

Barbecued Spareribs

Sauce:

¼ cup minced onion	½ teaspoon salt
2 tablespoons cooking oil	1 cup ketchup
2 tablespoons vinegar	3 tablespoons Worcestershire sauce
¼ cup lemon juice	
2 tablespoons brown sugar	1 cup water
1 teaspoon dry mustard	Dash hot pepper sauce

Spareribs:

3 pounds spareribs or pork chops	Salt and pepper to taste
	2 tablespoons cooking oil

Prepare sauce: In saucepan, sauté onion in 2 tablespoons cooking oil until yellow and transparent. Add remaining sauce ingredients to onions and simmer 5 to 10 minutes until blended. Season spareribs or pork chops with salt and pepper. Brown in skillet, turning once. Add browned ribs or pork chops to prepared sauce. Simmer 1½ hours or until tender.

Yield: 6 servings

BEAR IN MIND: *If you prefer lots of sauce, double the amounts of ingredients.*

Bearly Bourbon Pecan Pie

½	cup butter, melted	½	cup chocolate chips
1	cup sugar	1	cup chopped pecans
1	cup light corn syrup	2	(8-inch) pastry shells,
4	eggs, beaten		unbaked
1	to 2 tablespoons bourbon		Whipped cream for topping

Preheat oven to 350°. Combine butter, sugar, corn syrup, eggs, bourbon, chocolate chips and pecans. Mix well. Pour into pastry shells. Bake 40 to 45 minutes or until firm. Serve warm with whipped cream.

Yield: 12 to 16 servings

Buttermilk Pie

a rich Southern favorite

1	stick butter	½	cup buttermilk
1½	cups sugar	1	teaspoon vanilla extract
2	tablespoons all-purpose flour	1	egg white, lightly beaten
3	eggs	1	(9-inch) pastry shell, baked

Position rack in lower third of oven and preheat to 350°. Melt butter in small saucepan over low heat. Blend sugar and flour in large bowl. Add melted butter to sugar mixture and mix well. Add eggs one at a time, beating well after each. Stir in buttermilk and vanilla. Brush baked pastry shell with egg white to waterproof. Let dry 2 minutes. Pour in filling. Bake until filling is set, about 45 minutes. Cool.

Yield: 8 to 10 servings

BEAR FLAIR: *Serve warm or chilled.*

Classic Fresh Fruit Cobbler

4	cups sliced or chopped fresh fruit, sweetened with sugar to taste	2	teaspoons baking powder
1	stick margarine	¼	teaspoon salt
¾	cup milk	¾	cup all-purpose flour
		1	cup sugar

Preheat oven to 350°. Prepare fruit and set aside. Melt margarine in 1½-quart casserole. Blend remaining ingredients and pour over melted margarine. Do not stir. Pour fruit over mixture. Bake 1 hour.

Yield: 6 servings

 # Original Lane Cake

Cake:

3¼	cups cake flour	1	cup milk
2	teaspoons baking powder	8	egg whites, beaten stiff (but not dry)
2	sticks butter		
2	cups sugar	1	tablespoon vanilla extract

Filling:

8	egg yolks	1	cup finely chopped raisins
1	cup sugar	½	cup brandy
1	stick butter	1	teaspoon vanilla extract

For cake: Preheat oven to 375°. Line 4 (9-inch) cake pans with ungreased brown paper. Sift flour and baking powder together three times. Set aside. Cream butter and sugar until light. Add flour alternately with milk, beginning and ending with flour. Fold in beaten egg whites and vanilla. Pour batter into pans. Bake 15 to 20 minutes. Cool in pans 5 minutes. Remove and spread with filling.

For filling: In top of double boiler combine yolks, sugar and butter. Cook over simmering heat, stirring constantly until thick. Add raisins, brandy and vanilla. Use to spread between layers and as the frosting.

Yield: 1 (9-inch) 4-layer cake.

BEAR IN MIND:
   (1) This cake is much better if made a day or two in advance.
   (2) Use miniature muffin tins instead of 9-inch pans. These are gorgeous and easy to eat.

 # Peach Ice Cream

1	quart mashed peaches	1	(14-ounce) can sweetened
1½	cups sugar		condensed milk
	Juice of ½ lemon	2	cups milk
1	quart half and half	½	pint whipping cream

Add sugar and lemon juice to mashed peaches. Mix half and half, condensed milk, milk and whipping cream until well-blended. Stir in peach mixture. Pour into ice cream churn. Freeze until firm.

Yield: 3 quarts

Old-Fashioned Syrup Bread With Lemon Sauce

Syrup bread:

2½	cups all-purpose flour	2	cups pure sugar
1	teaspoon baking powder		cane syrup
1	teaspoon baking soda	½	stick butter, softened
1	teaspoon salt	2	eggs

Lemon sauce:

½	cup sugar	2	tablespoons butter
1	tablespoon cornstarch	2	tablespoons lemon juice
1	cup boiling water		
1	tablespoon grated lemon rind		

For syrup bread: Preheat oven to 350°. Grease 9x13-inch pan. Sift flour. Add baking powder, baking soda, salt and sift again. In separate bowl, pour cane syrup. Add eggs and butter, mixing well. Add dry ingredients to creamed mixture slowly, a small amount at a time, mixing well. Pour into pan and bake 30 to 40 minutes. Remove from pan and cut into 2-inch squares.

For lemon sauce: Combine sugar and cornstarch. Stir in water and lemon rind and cook over moderate heat until thick and clear. Remove from heat and add butter and lemon juice. Stir until smooth. Serve slightly warm over syrup bread.

Yield: 24 servings

BEAR IN MIND: A favorite from the plantation kitchens of Sumter County for generations, this recipe predates the War Between the States.

Pecan Pralines

3 cups sugar, divided	2 tablespoons butter
¾ cup milk	2½ cups pecan halves
¾ teaspoon vanilla extract	

In large saucepan, combine 2 cups sugar and milk. Cook on low heat. Meanwhile place remaining sugar in another saucepan on low heat. Stir until sugar melts. Pour and stir melted sugar slowly into milk and sugar mixture that should be almost to boiling point. Cook slowly to firm ball stage (when small amount of mixture dropped into cold water forms a firm ball, or candy thermometer reaches 242° to 248°) and remove from heat. Add vanilla and butter. Beat until mixture starts to thicken. Stir in pecans. Drop small spoonfuls onto waxed paper. Pralines "set" immediately.

Yield: 2½ dozen

Sweet Potato Pie

2 cups mashed, cooked sweet potatoes	2 teaspoons vanilla extract
½ stick butter	1 (9-inch) pastry shell, unbaked
½ cup sugar	½ cup chopped pecans
⅛ teaspoon salt	½ cup brown sugar, firmly packed
1 teaspoon lemon juice	2 tablespoons margarine, softened
3 eggs, slightly beaten	
2 cups milk	

Combine sweet potatoes and butter in saucepan over medium heat until butter is melted. Remove from heat. Add sugar, salt and lemon juice. Stir well. Add eggs, milk and vanilla. Pour into pastry shell and bake 45 minutes or until knife inserted in center comes out clean. Cool.

Combine pecans, brown sugar and margarine. Spread over cooled pie. Place under broiler 3 minutes. Cool.

Yield: 8 servings

Poultry

"BEARING GIFTS"

*CHICKEN AND CHERRY TOMATOES EN PAPILLOTE, page 185 ... give a copy of the recipe and a roll of parchment paper.

*CHICKEN BAKED WITH 40 CLOVES OF GARLIC, page 186 ... attach the recipe to a garlic braid.

*COLD NEW ORLEANS CHICKEN SPAGHETTI, page 205 ... prepare the dish and present on a white ceramic platter or give the recipe with a bottle of champagne vinegar.

*CHICKEN LASAGNE, page 206 ... would be a most enjoyed gift, especially in a baking dish with its own basket.

*GRILLED LEMONADE CHICKEN, page 202 ... jot the recipe on a card and give with long-handled thongs and a bottle of soy sauce.

*BAKED CRANBERRIES, page 206 ... add a ribbon to a cross-stitched mason jar top and fill with these wonderful cranberries. Smashing gift for Christmas.

*POPPY SEED CHICKEN, page 187, or **LEMON CHICKEN,** page 189 ... prepare dish and put into 2 (8-inch) square pans instead of the 8x12-inch pan. Freeze one and take to a new mother to have for a hectic day. Take along a gift for baby. She'll love you twice!

*CURRANT CORNISH HEN, page 186 ... place the recipe and a jar of currant jelly in an au gratin dish for a gift to be cherished a long time.

*CHICKEN OROBIANCO WITH FRUITED RICE, page 187 ... tie the recipe card and a package of dried fruit bits to a bottle of Orobiánco.

*BREAST OF CHICKEN WITH CAPERS, page 188 ... attach the recipe to a jar of capers and add a whisk with ribbon.

*BARE ELEGANCE, page 195 ... give shallots in an earthen garlic jar, as well as potted containers of tarragon and parsley with the recipe attached.

*CHICKEN RICE BAKE, page 200 ... an easy, economical gift to prepare in advance.

"BEAR ESSENTIALS FOR ENTERTAINING"

*Soaking chicken in buttermilk an hour or more before frying gives a great flavor and tenderizes as well.

*Casseroles wrapped completely in tin foil, then again in several layers of newspaper and placed in an insulated ice chest will stay hot for several hours.

*For leftover chicken, make and fill crepes; won't even seem like leftovers!

*Make bread cases by cutting 3-inch cubes from whole unsliced loaf of bread and then hollow out the cube, leaving ½-inch "walls". Brush melted butter on all surfaces of the cases. Bake in 325⁰ oven until bread cases are golden brown. Fill with **CHICKEN À LA KING,** page 194.

*Marinating chicken decreases its cooking time.

*To escape from boring chicken, pound skinned, boned chicken breasts to ⅛-inch thickness. Place julienned carrots, leeks and celery at one end of breast and roll up tightly. Place the chicken in a red cabbage leaf that has been simmered just long enough to make it pliable. Wrap tightly, folding edges in to create a snug package. Simmer these bundles in chicken broth for 20 to 30 minutes. A surprise awaits the diner!

Chicken and Cherry Tomatoes en Papillote

2	to 3 tablespoons vegetable oil	2	teaspoons finely chopped fresh basil
6	chicken breast halves, skinned and boned	½	pound fresh snow peas, trimmed
3	tablespoons lemon juice	1	cup cherry tomatoes, cut in halves
3	tablespoons teriyaki sauce		Salt and pepper to taste
1	tablespoon sesame oil		
⅓	cup chopped green onions		

Cut 6 (12x15-inch) pieces of parchment or aluminum foil. Fold in half lengthwise, creasing firmly. Trim each piece into a large heart shape. Place "hearts" on baking sheets, brush inside of each heart with vegetable oil, leaving 1½-inch of the edges unoiled. Pound chicken breasts to ¼-inch thickness. Combine lemon juice, teriyaki sauce, sesame oil, green onions and basil in a shallow dish. Add chicken and marinate in refrigerator at least 30 minutes. Arrange snow peas in fan design on half of each parchment heart, near the crease. Drain chicken breasts, reserving marinade. Arrange chicken on snow peas. Mix tomato halves with reserved marinade, and spoon evenly over each chicken breast. Sprinkle with salt and pepper. Fold over remaining halves of parchment hearts. Starting with rounded edge of each heart, pleat and crimp edges together to make a seal. Twist pointed end tightly. Bake at 350° for 20 to 30 minutes or until "hearts" are puffed and lightly browned and chicken is done. Serve the "hearts" on individual dinner plates, each person cutting open his own and eating "au natural".

Yield: 6 servings

BEAR FLAIR: *After baking, brush each parchment package with butter and add a fresh basil leaf.*

BEAR IN MIND:
(1) Can substitute julienned carrots and zucchini for snow peas and cherry tomatoes.
(2) May be prepared in advance, refrigerated and baked just before guests arrive or bake while enjoying hors d'oeuvres with your guests.
(3) Parchment paper may be purchased at specialty food shops or at art supply stores.

Chicken Baked with 40 Cloves of Garlic

3 chickens, cut up	40 garlic cloves, peeled
Olive oil to coat chicken	1 cup dry vermouth or
Salt and pepper to taste	white wine
2 carrots, sliced	1 ounce cognac
2 large onions, halved and sliced	Parsley for garnish

Preheat oven to 375°. Rub chicken pieces with olive oil. Sprinkle with salt and pepper. Place chicken pieces, vegetables and garlic in a 9x13-inch glass baking dish. Pour wine and cognac over chicken and vegetables. Cover tightly with a double layer of foil. Bake 1½ hours. (Do not remove foil while baking.)

Yield: 6 to 8 servings

BEAR FLAIR: *The garlic cloves that have been cooked with the chicken will spread like butter on French bread to serve with this tasty dish.*

Currant Cornish Hen

4 Cornish hens, halved	2 tablespoons butter, melted
Salt and pepper to taste	2 teaspoons lemon juice
¼ cup sherry	

Sauce:

1 tablespoon margarine	½ cup sherry
½ cup currant jelly	1 tablespoon cornstarch
1 tablespoon lemon juice	¼ cup cold water
½ cup water	

Preheat oven to 450°. Season hens with salt and pepper. Set aside. Mix together sherry, melted butter and lemon juice. Brush mixture on hens. Roast in oven uncovered 15 minutes. Reduce heat to 350° and continue roasting another hour uncovered, basting several times with the sherry mixture. For sauce, combine the margarine, jelly, lemon juice and water in saucepan and simmer 5 minutes. Add sherry and pan juices from the hen. Thicken with the cornstarch mixed with the cold water. Stir until thickened. Serve over hen.

Yield: 8 servings

BEAR FLAIR: *Surround hens with lemon twists for garnish.*

Chicken Orobianco with Fruited Rice

¼	cup olive oil	½	pound fresh mushrooms,
2	garlic cloves, quartered		sliced
8	chicken breast halves,	1	teaspoon salt
	skinned and boned	¼	cup water
2	pounds hot Italian sausage	2	tablespoons cornstarch
	links	1	cup uncooked regular rice
2	cups Orobianco or medium-	½	cup dried fruit bits
	dry white wine	½	cup boiling water

In large skillet over medium heat, add olive oil and cook garlic until golden. Remove garlic and discard. Cook chicken and sausage, a few pieces at a time, on medium-high heat in pan drippings until browned on all sides. Spoon off all but 2 tablespoons of the drippings. Return chicken and sausage to skillet. Stir in wine, mushrooms and salt; heat to boiling. Reduce heat to low, cover and simmer 30 minutes or until chicken is tender, basting occasionally with liquid in skillet. Arrange chicken and sausage on a warm platter. In small bowl, blend water and cornstarch until smooth. Gradually stir cornstarch mixture into hot liquid left in skillet. Cook over medium heat stirring constantly with a fork until mixture thickens; keep warm. Cook rice as directed on package. Put fruit bits into small bowl and cover with boiling water. Fruit will absorb water. Drain. Keep fruit bits warm. When rice is cooked, add fruit and toss to mix. Spoon some of the sauce over chicken and sausage. Put remaining sauce in gravy boat. Serve chicken and sausage over rice with sauce.

Yield: 8 servings

Poppy Seed Chicken

12	chicken breast halves,	1½	sticks butter, melted
	skinned, boned, cooked	2	(10¾-ounce) cans cream of
	and cut up		chicken soup
4½	dozen butter-flavored	1	pint sour cream
	crackers, crushed	2	teaspoons poppy seeds

Preheat oven to 350°. Mix melted butter with cracker crumbs. Set aside. Mix soup, sour cream and poppy seeds together. Layer the cooked chicken, soup mixture and cracker crumbs in an 8x12-inch glass baking dish. Repeat until all ingredients are used, ending with the cracker crumbs. Bake until hot and bubbly, about 40 minutes.

Yield: 10 to 12 servings

Breast of Chicken with Capers

4	chicken breast halves, skinned and boned
	Salt and freshly ground pepper to taste
1	teaspoon paprika
2	tablespoons butter
¼	cup finely chopped onions
¼	cup dry white wine
⅔	cup whipping cream
2	tablespoons capers, drained

Sprinkle chicken with salt, pepper and paprika. Heat butter in heavy skillet and sauté chicken over medium heat about 5 to 6 minutes on one side and turn over and brown on other. Sprinkle onions around chicken. Cover and cook on low heat about 8 minutes. Transfer to warm platter. Add wine to skillet and stir. Cook until most of wine evaporates. Add cream, capers, salt and pepper. Bring to boil over high heat and add any juices that have accumulated around the chicken. Stir and cook until reduced to about ¾ cup. Spoon over chicken and serve.

Yield: 4 servings

Chicken Niçoise

4	chicken breast halves, skinned and boned
½	teaspoon thyme
	Salt and pepper to taste
¼	cup finely chopped salt pork or bacon
1	tablespoon olive oil
½	cup chopped onion
1	(16-ounce) can tomatoes
1	garlic clove, pressed
¼	cup dry red wine
1	bay leaf
¼	cup halved ripe olives
2	tablespoons chopped fresh parsley

Sprinkle chicken with thyme, salt and pepper. Cook pork over low heat in large skillet until pieces are crispy. Remove meat and drain on paper towel. Set aside for garnish. Increase heat to medium-high and add chicken. Sauté about 5 minutes or until lightly brown. Remove chicken and set aside. Add olive oil and onion to skillet and cook until tender. Drain tomatoes and reserve juice. Chop tomatoes and add to skillet with juice, garlic, wine and bay leaf. Bring to a boil. Reduce heat to simmer and cook 10 minutes. Return chicken to sauce. Simmer 20 minutes longer. Remove bay leaf. Garnish with olives, pork pieces and parsley.

Yield: 4 servings

BEAR IN MIND: *Only 280 calories per serving!*

Chicken with Artichoke Hearts

Grated rind of 2 small lemons
2 cups bread crumbs
Salt and pepper to taste
6 chicken breast halves, skinned and boned
1 egg, beaten
1 stick unsalted butter, divided
2 tablespoons oil
6 shallots or green onions, sliced
6 tablespoons all-purpose flour
½ cup sauterne wine
½ cup chicken stock
1 pint whipping cream
Salt and pepper to taste
½ teaspoon fresh tarragon, chopped
3 (4-ounce) cans artichoke hearts, drained and quartered

Preheat oven to 350°. Butter 9x13-inch glass baking dish. Mix lemon rind and bread crumbs in small bowl. Salt and pepper chicken, then dip in beaten egg and in bread crumbs. Sauté chicken in 2 tablespoons butter and oil, on all sides until lightly browned. Set aside. In large saucepan, melt remaining butter and sauté shallots briefly. Add flour, stirring until smooth. Gradually add wine and chicken stock, stirring constantly. Whisking continuously, add whipping cream. Cook and stir until mixture almost reaches a boil. Add salt, pepper and tarragon. Add quartered artichoke hearts. Pour into baking dish and arrange chicken on top. May dot with more butter if desired. Bake 20 to 25 minutes.

Yield: 6 servings

BEAR FLAIR: *A fresh tarragon sprig for each serving is an easy garnish.*

Lemon Chicken

8 chicken breast halves
Salt and pepper to taste
Juice of 2 lemons
2 cups diced celery
1 (10¾-ounce) can cream of chicken soup
¾ cup mayonnaise
1 (8-ounce) can water chestnuts, sliced and drained
4 cups cooked rice
½ cup slivered almonds, toasted for topping

Boil chicken breasts in water until done. While warm, bone and skin. Chop into bite-size pieces. Add salt and pepper and cover with lemon juice. Refrigerate overnight. Preheat oven to 350°. Grease 9x12-inch baking dish. Combine all ingredients except almonds and place in baking dish. Sprinkle with almonds and bake 30 to 45 minutes or until bubbly.

Yield: 4 to 6 servings

Parsley, Sage, Rosemary and Thyme

10	large chicken breast halves, boned and skinned	¾	cup bread crumbs
1	stick butter, divided	1	tablespoon parsley
	Salt and pepper to taste	¼	teaspoon sage
10	slices Mozzarella cheese, room temperature	¼	teaspoon rosemary
		¼	teaspoon thyme
½	cup all-purpose flour	½	cup white wine
2	eggs, beaten	5	cups cooked wild rice

Preheat oven to 350°. Flatten each chicken breast half by pounding between two pieces of wax paper. Spread breast halves with ½ stick butter. Sprinkle with salt and pepper. Lay 1 piece of cheese on top of each breast half. Roll up and fasten with toothpicks. Take each rolled breast half and coat with flour, then with beaten eggs, then with bread crumbs. (May be frozen at this time.) Put chicken rolls into 9x13-inch glass baking dish. Melt remaining ½ stick butter. Add parsley, sage, rosemary and thyme. Pour over chicken breasts. Bake 30 minutes. Pour ½ cup wine over chicken breasts and bake 30 minutes longer. Serve over wild rice.

Yield: 10 servings

BEAR FLAIR:
(1) If fresh rosemary is available, garnish each serving with a sprig.
(2) For table centerpiece, why not arrange the fresh herbs, parsley, sage, rosemary and thyme, in a small wine carafe.

Buttermilk Pecan Chicken

¾	cup butter	1	tablespoon paprika
1	cup buttermilk	1	teaspoon salt
1	egg, beaten	¼	teaspoon pepper
1	cup all-purpose flour	8	chicken breast halves,
1	cup ground pecans		boned
¼	cup sesame seeds	½	cup pecan halves

Preheat oven to 350°. Place butter in 9x13-inch baking dish and melt in oven. Set aside. In small bowl mix buttermilk and egg, beat well. In another small bowl mix flour, ground pecans, sesame seeds and seasonings. Dip chicken into egg mixture and then coat in flour mixture. Place chicken in melted butter and turn over once, ending with skin side up. Scatter pecan halves over top, bake 1½ hours.

Yield: 8 servings

BEAR IN MIND: *Use two 3-pound fryers for family-style dinners.*

Chicken and Squash with Spinach Dumplings

4	large chicken breast halves	1	large carrot, quartered
12	small yellow squash	1	medium onion
3	quarts water	2	cups biscuit mix
2	chicken bouillon cubes	⅔	cup milk
2	celery stalks, cut in half crosswise	½	cup fresh spinach, chopped

Wash chicken and squash. Put chicken, water, bouillon cubes, celery, carrot and whole onion in 5-quart Dutch oven. Bring to a boil and simmer, covered, about 10 minutes. Take out celery, carrot and onion, then add whole squash. Cook another 10 minutes or until squash are tender. Mix biscuit mix with milk. Stir in spinach and drop by spoonfuls onto simmering chicken. Cook uncovered 10 minutes. Cover and cook another 10 minutes.

Yield: 4 servings

BEAR IN MIND: *If gravy is desired, take out chicken, squash and dumplings. To thicken broth, mix 2 to 3 tablespoons flour in ¼ cup water until smooth, salt and pepper to taste, then stir into broth. Cook 2 minutes.*

Chicken Chop Suey

2	tablespoons soy sauce	2	cups sliced fresh mushrooms
2	tablespoons cornstarch		
1¾	cups chicken broth	2	cups cooked chicken, cut in strips
3	tablespoons salad oil		
2	cups shredded cabbage	2	cups fresh bean sprouts
1	large onion, sliced	½	cup sliced water chestnuts
2	celery stalks, sliced diagonally	3	to 4 cups cooked rice or noodles

In small bowl, blend soy sauce and cornstarch. Stir in chicken broth. Set aside. In large skillet or wok, over high heat, add oil, then stir-fry cabbage, onions, celery and mushrooms. Using slotted spoon, remove vegetables and set aside. Add chicken to hot oil and stir about 3 minutes until lightly browned. Add vegetables and cook 1 minute more. Gradually add soy sauce mixture. Stir until thickened. Serve over hot fluffy rice or noodles.

Yield: 6 to 8 servings

BEAR IN MIND: *Having ingredients sliced, chopped or shredded in advance really makes this recipe quick and easy.*

Chicken Almondine

¼ cup margarine, melted
1 tablespoon paprika
1 tablespoon lemon juice
8 chicken breast halves, boned
  Garlic salt to taste
1 to 2 (4-ounce) cans mushroom stems and pieces, drained

1 teaspoon Worcestershire sauce
¼ cup slivered almonds
¼ cup water
2 tablespoons all-purpose flour
½ cup sour cream

Preheat oven to 350°. Blend margarine, paprika and lemon juice in a small bowl. Sprinkle chicken breasts with garlic salt and dip them into margarine mixture. Arrange chicken skin side up in 9x13-inch glass baking dish. Bake 30 minutes. Blend mushrooms, Worcestershire sauce, almonds and water. Pour over chicken. Bake an additional 30 minutes. Remove chicken from oven. Blend flour and sour cream until smooth. Remove chicken from baking dish and stir sour cream mixture into pan juices. Return chicken to baking dish and bake 5 more minutes.

Yield: 8 servings

Chicken in Rosé Sauce

4 tablespoons margarine, divided
8 chicken breast halves, skinned and boned
2 tablespoons all-purpose flour
¾ cup chicken broth
½ cup rosé wine

½ cup sliced fresh mushrooms
¼ cup thinly sliced green onions
1 (10-ounce) package frozen artichoke hearts, cooked or 1 (14-ounce) can artichoke hearts, drained

Preheat oven to 350°. Melt 2 tablespoons margarine in 9x13-inch glass baking dish. Add chicken breasts; bake 30 minutes. Melt remaining margarine in medium saucepan. Add flour and cook briefly, stirring constantly. While still stirring add chicken broth and wine. Stir until sauce is thick and smooth. Remove breast from oven. Turn and cover each with mushrooms, green onions and artichoke hearts. Pour sauce over and bake about 30 minutes, until tender.

Yield: 8 servings

BEAR IN MIND: *Good for low cholesterol and low salt diets.*

Poulet à la Crème

1	(3-pound) chicken	½	cup dry white wine
	Water to cover	¼	cup all-purpose flour
	Salt to taste	1	cup whipping cream
2	to 3 celery tops	⅛	teaspoon freshly ground
4	tablespoons butter, divided		nutmeg
¼	cup chopped onion		Pinch cayenne pepper
½	pound fresh mushrooms,	1	egg yolk
	sliced	3	tablespoons grated Gruyère
	Salt and pepper to taste		or Swiss cheese

In large Dutch oven, cook chicken in salted water, with celery tops, until done. Remove chicken and reduce stock by half. Bone and cut chicken into bite-size pieces. Heat 1 tablespoon of butter in large skillet. Add onions and cook until tender. Add mushrooms, salt and pepper. Cook 2 minutes and add wine. Cook over high heat until reduced by half. Add chicken and cook 4 minutes. Set aside. In 1-quart saucepan, melt remaining butter. Add flour and blend. Add ½ cup reduced chicken stock, stirring rapidly. Add cream, nutmeg and cayenne. Add two-thirds of this sauce to chicken mixture and simmer 5 minutes. Set aside. To remaining third of sauce add egg yolk and bring to a boil, stirring rapidly. Put chicken mixture in glass baking dish and pour remaining sauce over chicken. Sprinkle with cheese and bake at 425° about 10 minutes.

Yield: 6 servings

BEAR FLAIR: *For garnish, sprinkle finely chopped parsley and celery tops in diagonal rows. Place a slice of mushroom in center.*

Chicken à la Vallée d'Auge

10	chicken breast halves, boned and skinned		Dash pepper
¼	cup butter	1	tablespoon chopped parsley
2	small onions or 6 shallots, minced	¼	teaspoon thyme
		¼	teaspoon rosemary
1	teaspoon salt	¾	cup cider
		½	cup whipping cream

Brown chicken in butter until golden. Add onions and stir until lightly browned. Add remaining ingredients, except cream. Simmer about 20 minutes, stirring often. Remove chicken to platter. Add cream to skillet and heat but do not boil. Pour sauce over chicken and serve.

Yield: 10 servings

Chicken New Orleans

8	chicken breast halves	1	cup sliced fresh mushrooms
1	stick butter	1	tablespoon all-purpose
1	cup chopped celery		flour
1	cup sliced ripe olives	1	cup sherry
½	cup chopped pimientos	4	cups cooked wild rice
1	garlic clove, minced		

In large skillet, brown chicken in butter. Remove chicken. Sauté celery, olives, pimientos, garlic and mushrooms in skillet. Add flour, stirring well. When mixture has thickened a little, return chicken to skillet. Add sherry, cover and let simmer until chicken is tender, about 30 minutes. Serve over wild rice.

Yield: 8 servings

Chicken à la King

2	tablespoons chopped bell pepper	½	teaspoon paprika
½	cup sliced fresh mushrooms	2	cups milk
		2	egg yolks, beaten
1½	teaspoons salt, divided	2	cups cooked chicken, cut in cubes
4	tablespoons chopped pimiento	½	cup chopped celery
5	tablespoons butter	8	puff pastry cups or toast points
6	tablespoons all-purpose flour		Slivered almonds for garnish
	White pepper to taste		

In small amount of water, boil bell pepper, mushrooms and ½ teaspoon salt 5 minutes. Add pimiento and drain well. Set aside. Melt butter. Add flour, white pepper, paprika, remaining salt and milk, stirring constantly. Cook 3 minutes or until thick. Remove from heat and add beaten egg yolks. Add chicken, celery and mushroom mixture. Heat in double boiler and serve in puff pastry cups or on toast points. Sprinkle with slivered almonds and paprika.

Yield: 8 servings

Bare Elegance

8 large chicken breast halves, boned and skinned	1 teaspoon salt
2 tablespoons salad oil	1/8 teaspoon pepper
4 tablespoons butter, divided	1 cup half and half
6 shallots, chopped	1 egg yolk
2 carrots, pared and sliced into 1/4-inch rounds	1 tablespoon all-purpose flour
1/4 cup cognac or brandy	1/2 pound fresh mushrooms, thinly sliced
1 cup dry white wine	Sprigs of fresh tarragon or parsley to garnish
1/4 cup chopped fresh tarragon or 2 teaspoons dried tarragon	
1 1/2 tablespoons chopped fresh chervil or 1/2 teaspoon dried chervil	

In a 6-quart Dutch oven heat oil and add 2 tablespoons butter. Add chicken breasts; sauté on all sides until brown. Remove to platter. Add shallots and carrots to pan drippings and sauté 5 minutes or until golden brown. Return chicken to Dutch oven and heat. Slightly heat cognac in ladle and ignite. Add cognac, wine, tarragon, chervil, salt and pepper to Dutch oven. Bring this to a boil. Simmer gently, covered, 30 minutes. Remove chicken to heated platter. Strain drippings and return them to Dutch oven. In small bowl combine half and half, egg yolk and flour. Mix well with wire whisk. Add this mixture to drippings in Dutch oven. Bring just to a boil, stirring often. Add extra wine if sauce is too thick. In separate skillet, sauté mushrooms in remaining 2 tablespoons of butter. Spoon sauce over chicken and garnish with mushrooms and tarragon or parsley sprigs.

Yield: 8 servings

Chicken and Asparagus Olé

12	chicken breast halves, cooked in seasoned water	8	ounces sharp cheddar cheese, grated
1	medium onion, chopped	¼	teaspoon hot pepper sauce
1	stick butter	2	teaspoons soy sauce
1	(8-ounce) can sliced mushrooms	1	teaspoon salt
1	(10¾-ounce) can cream of mushroom soup	½	teaspoon pepper
		2	tablespoons chopped pimiento
1	(10¾-ounce) can cream of chicken soup	2	(10½-ounce) cans green asparagus, drained
1	(5-ounce) can evaporated milk	½	cup slivered almonds

Preheat oven to 350°. Butter 3-quart casserole. Remove chicken from bones and cut into small pieces. Set aside. In large skillet, sauté onion in butter. Add remaining ingredients except asparagus and almonds. Simmer until cheese melts. To assemble, place layer of chicken in casserole, then layer of asparagus and then layer of sauce. Repeat layers, ending with sauce. Sprinkle with almonds. Bake 45 minutes, or until hot and bubbly. Do not add liquid, even if it looks dry.

Yield: 10 to 12 servings

Turkey Cheese Puff

1	(10-ounce) package frozen broccoli	2	eggs, separated
2	cups sliced cooked turkey	¼	teaspoon salt
1	(10¾-ounce) can chicken gravy	¼	cup grated Parmesan cheese
		¼	cup slivered almonds, toasted

Preheat oven to 375°. Cook broccoli according to package directions. Drain well. Place in bottom of 8-inch square glass baking dish. Put turkey slices on top of broccoli. Then top turkey with gravy. Bake 10 minutes. Beat egg whites with salt until peaks form. Set aside. Beat egg yolks until thick. Fold in whites and then the Parmesan cheese. Pour egg mixture over turkey mixture. Top with almonds. Bake 15 to 20 minutes.

Yield: 6 servings

Dot's Chicken of the Vine

8	chicken breast halves, skinned and boned	4	tablespoons dry white wine
2	sticks butter	4	tablespoons cornstarch
1	medium onion, minced	1	teaspoon salt
1	garlic clove, minced	½	teaspoon pepper
3	cups whipping cream	2	cups green seedless grapes
4	tablespoons brandy	4	cups cooked egg noodles

In skillet, sauté chicken in butter 20 minutes, turning often. Remove chicken and set aside. Sauté onion and garlic in same pan 5 minutes. Add cream slowly. Blend brandy, wine and cornstarch until smooth and add to cream. Cook until thickened, stirring constantly. Add salt, pepper, grapes and chicken. Heat. Serve over egg noodles.

Yield: 8 servings

BEAR FLAIR: *Serve over green noodles. White asparagus spears would be a lovely vegetable to complement this dish.*

Chicken in Sour Cream

12	chicken breast halves, skinned and boned	1	teaspoon garlic salt
1	pint sour cream	½	teaspoon paprika
¼	cup fresh lemon juice	½	teaspoon pepper
2	teaspoons salt	2	to 3 cups bread crumbs
4	teaspoons Worcestershire sauce	1	stick butter
		1	stick margarine

Wash chicken breasts and pat dry. In medium bowl, combine sour cream, lemon juice and seasonings. Roll chicken breasts in sour cream mixture. Place chicken in large bowl. Top with any remaining sour cream. Cover and refrigerate overnight. Preheat oven to 350°. Remove chicken breasts, taking up as much of the sour cream mixture as possible. Roll chicken in bread crumbs and coat well. Place in 9x13-inch glass baking dish. Melt butter and margarine together. Pour half of the mixture over chicken and bake 45 minutes. Pour remaining butter over chicken and bake 15 minutes longer.

Yield: 12 servings

BEAR IN MIND: *Chicken may be frozen after it is breaded. Wrap individually for convenience.*

Chicken Veronique

4	chicken breast halves, boned and skinned
	Salt to taste
2	tablespoons butter
½	cup dry white wine
1½	tablespoons orange marmalade
½	teaspoon dry tarragon, crushed
½	cup whipping cream
2	teaspoons cornstarch dissolved in small amount of water
1½	cups seedless green grapes
4	cups cooked rice

Lightly salt chicken breasts. Melt butter in large skillet over medium heat. Add chicken and brown lightly on each side. Add the wine; blend in the marmalade and tarragon. Cover the pan and simmer very gently about 20 minutes, or until thickest part of the breasts are white in the center. Remove chicken to separate dish. To pan juices add whipping cream and bring to a rolling boil. Stir cornstarch/water mixture into sauce. Return to a boil stirring constantly. Add grapes and chicken breasts. Heat through and serve over rice.

Yield: 4 servings

BEAR FLAIR: *Garnish with a fresh sprig of tarragon.*

Saucy Chicken and Scampi

6	chicken breast halves, skinned and boned
½	tablespoon salt
½	teaspoon pepper
½	stick butter
1	garlic clove, minced
3	small onions, sliced
3	tablespoons chopped parsley
½	cup port wine
1	(8-ounce) can tomato sauce
1	teaspoon chopped fresh basil or ⅓ teaspoon dried basil
1	pound fresh shrimp, peeled and deveined
3	cups cooked pasta

Rub chicken with salt and pepper. In large skillet, heat butter and sauté chicken until golden on all sides. Add garlic, onions, parsley, port wine, tomato sauce and basil. Simmer covered about 30 minutes or until tender. Remove chicken and set aside. Turn up heat so tomato mixture boils. Add shrimp and cook uncovered 3 to 4 minutes or until shrimp are just pink and tender. Return chicken to skillet and stir. Serve over cooked pasta.

Yield: 6 servings

BEAR IN MIND: *Shallots may be substituted for garlic and onions. Their delicate and distinctive flavor is found in the red, greenish-white and the purple varieties of shallots.*

Chicken and Shrimp Supreme

12	chicken breast halves		Pinch of sugar
1	small onion	8	ounces cheddar cheese, grated
1	celery stalk		
	Salt and pepper to taste	½	cup sherry
1	cup sliced mushrooms	2	pounds shrimp, peeled and deveined (frozen shrimp which has been defrosted and drained can be used)
9	tablespoons butter, divided		
1	cup flour		
1	quart milk		
3	egg yolks, beaten	1	dozen small pastry shells or rosette shells
	Salt and white pepper to taste		

Steam chicken in small amount of water with onion, celery, salt and pepper about 45 minutes. Bone and leave in large pieces. Sauté mushrooms in 1 tablespoon butter. Set aside. Make sauce of remaining butter, flour and milk. Add beaten egg yolks and cook until thick, stirring constantly. Salt and white pepper to taste. Add pinch of sugar. Add cheese, sherry and mushrooms. Heat until cheese melts. Pour sauce over chicken. Cover and refrigerate overnight. About 30 minutes before serving add shrimp. Heat to bubbling, but do not overcook. Serve in small pastry shells or rosette shells.

Yield: 12 servings

Maggie's Casserole

1	large chicken, seasoned with lemon pepper and salt	1	(10¾-ounce) can mushroom soup
1	onion, quartered	1	cup chicken broth
1	celery stalk, cut in half	½	cup milk
1	(16-ounce) package vermicelli	12	ounces processed cheese
	Salt and pepper to taste	1	pound fresh shrimp, peeled, deveined and cooked
1	(10-ounce) package frozen broccoli	1	(6-ounce) can crabmeat, cartilage removed

Boil chicken in water to cover. Put onion and celery in water to season chicken as it boils. Reserve broth. Bone chicken. Boil vermicelli in chicken broth. Add salt and pepper to taste. Cook broccoli as directed on package. Drain. Preheat oven to 350°. In saucepan over low heat melt soup, broth, milk and cheese. Add chicken, shrimp, crabmeat and broccoli. Mix with well-drained vermicelli. Put in a greased 9x13-inch casserole. Bake 30 minutes.

Yield: 10 to 12 servings

Chicken Rice Bake

½	cup chopped celery	1	(2-ounce) jar pimiento, drained
1	(4-ounce) can sliced mushrooms, drained	1½	cups cubed cooked chicken
½	cup slivered almonds	1½	cups chicken broth
½	stick butter		Salt and pepper to taste
3	cups cooked rice	1½	tablespoons flour

Preheat oven to 350°. Grease 2-quart casserole. In skillet, sauté celery, mushrooms and almonds in butter. Combine rice and pimiento. Place one third of rice in casserole. Alternate with chicken, celery, mushroom mixture. Repeat until all are used. Pour chicken broth, seasoned with salt and pepper and blended with flour, over chicken rice mixture. Bake 1 hour.

Yield: 6 to 8 servings

Chicken Lobster Bake

D2

8 boneless chicken breast halves
1½ teaspoons salt
¼ teaspoon pepper
1 stick butter
½ pound mushrooms, sliced
2 tablespoons flour
3 cups chicken broth

1 tablespoon tomato paste
1 bay leaf, crushed
2 tablespoons chopped chives
2 tablespoons white wine
2 (10-ounce) packages frozen lobster tails, cooked
3 fresh tomatoes, quartered
4 to 5 cups cooked rice

Preheat oven to 300°. Season chicken with salt and pepper and brown in butter. Place in shallow baking pan, cover and bake 40 minutes. Sauté mushrooms in same pan used for browning chicken. Remove mushrooms. Blend in flour. Add broth and cook until thick and smooth. Add tomato paste, bay leaves, chives, and wine. Simmer 10 minutes. Remove cooked lobster from shells and cut each piece in half lengthwise. Add lobster, mushrooms and tomatoes to sauce in skillet. Simmer 5 minutes. Spoon over chicken and serve with rice.

Yield: 8 to 10 servings

BEAR IN MIND: *1 pound shrimp can be substituted for lobster.*

Grilled Sesame Chicken Breasts

½ cup white grape juice
¼ cup reduced-sodium soy sauce
¼ cup dry white wine
1 tablespoon sesame seeds

2 tablespoons vegetable oil
¼ teaspoon garlic powder
¼ teaspoon ginger
4 chicken breast halves, skinned and boned

Combine all ingredients, except chicken, in shallow dish and mix well. Add chicken, turning to coat. Cover and marinate in the refrigerator at least 2 to 3 hours. Remove chicken from marinade, reserving marinade. Grill 4 to 5 inches from medium hot coals 15 to 20 minutes, turning and basting frequently with reserved marinade.

Yield: 4 servings

BEAR IN MIND: *There are 254 calories per serving.*

Granddaddy's Grilled Chicken

Surprisingly different and tasty

3	chickens, halved	3	tablespoons mustard
2	tablespoons Worcestershire sauce	3	tablespoons butter
		4	teaspoons salt
3	tablespoons mayonnaise	½	cup vinegar
3	tablespoons peanut butter	2	teaspoons black pepper

In saucepan mix well all ingredients except chicken and bring to boil. Coat both sides of chicken halves with sauce. Cook over hot coals, basting frequently, until done (45 to 60 minutes).

Yield: 6 servings

Grilled Lemonade Chicken

1	(6-ounce) can frozen lemonade concentrate, thawed	1	teaspoon lemon pepper
		⅛	teaspoon garlic powder
⅓	cup soy sauce	1	chicken, cut up
1	teaspoon seasoned salt		

Blend all ingredients together and marinate chicken in mixture 1 hour. Cook chicken on grill over hot coals. Baste with marinade several times during last 10 minutes of cooking.

Yield: 4 servings

Low-Cal Oven-Fried Chicken

½	cup fine, dry bread crumbs	¼	teaspoon pepper
⅓	cup grated Parmesan cheese	6	chicken breast halves
2	tablespoons chopped fresh parsley	¼	cup Italian reduced-calorie salad dressing
¼	teaspoon garlic salt		Vegetable cooking spray

Preheat oven to 350°. Prepare 9x13-inch pan with cooking spray. Combine bread crumbs, cheese, parsley, garlic salt and pepper; set aside. Dip chicken in salad dressing; dredge in bread crumb mixture. Place chicken in pan. Bake uncovered 45 minutes or until tender.

Yield: 6 servings

BEAR IN MIND: *This is delicious and has only 230 calories per serving!*

Suprèmes de Volaille Florentine

4	chicken breast halves, boned and skinned	3	tablespoons finely chopped shallots
	Salt and pepper to taste	⅛	teaspoon grated fresh nutmeg
1	(10-ounce) package of frozen leaf spinach, thawed	4	to 8 tablespoons grated Parmesan cheese
½	stick butter, divided		
½	pound fresh mushrooms		

Sauce Suprème:

2	tablespoons butter		Juice of ½ lemon
2	tablespoons all-purpose flour		Salt and pepper to taste
1¼	cups chicken broth	1	garlic clove, crushed
½	cup whipping cream	½	teaspoon minced fresh tarragon

Preheat oven to 375°. Sprinkle chicken with salt and pepper and set aside. Rinse spinach in cold water and drain well; set aside. Heat 2 tablespoons butter in heavy skillet, add the chicken breasts. Cook about 2 minutes on each side or until brown. Set aside. Add the remaining butter to the skillet; stir in the mushrooms and shallots. Cook, stirring often, until the mushrooms give up their liquid. Cook until the liquid is almost evaporated. Add spinach and cook until wilted. Add nutmeg and stir. In an 8-inch square baking dish make 4 mounds of spinach of equal size. Sprinkle each mound with Parmesan cheese. Place 1 chicken breast half on top of each mound. Cover baking dish with foil and seal tightly. Bake 40 to 50 minutes or until tender. Top with sauce suprème and serve.

To make sauce: Melt butter in a saucepan. Add flour, stirring with a wire whisk. Add broth, stirring rapidly, until mixture is smooth and thickened. Let it simmer about 5 minutes longer. Add the cream, lemon juice, salt, pepper, garlic and tarragon. Pour over chicken and spinach mounds.

Yield: 4 servings

BEAR FLAIR: *Fresh spinach leaves make a quick and easy garnish, or use them to frame the serving plate.*

Tangerine Peel Chicken

24 chicken thighs, skinned, boned, and cut in bite-size pieces
1½ tablespoons soy sauce
1½ tablespoons sherry
1 tablespoon water
¼ to ½ teaspoon ginger powder or 1½ teaspoons grated fresh ginger-root
1 teaspoon sesame or peanut oil
2 teaspoons cornstarch
Dash orange-flavored liqueur

4 tablespoons peanut oil, divided, for stir frying
Grated rind of 3 oranges or tangerines
1 tablespoon dried red (hot) pepper
½ cup chicken broth
1 teaspoon sugar
Salt to taste
½ teaspoon pepper
1 (8-ounce) package egg noodles or Chinese cello-phane noodles, cooked

Combine chicken with soy sauce, sherry, water, ginger, sesame oil, corn-starch and liqueur. Chill and marinate several hours or overnight. At dinnertime, heat wok or skillet to medium-high heat. Add 2 tablespoons cold peanut oil. Then add drained chicken, reserving marinade. Stir-fry chicken 2 to 4 minutes. Transfer to a dish. Wipe wok and add remaining oil. Toss in orange rind and red pepper. Stir-fry 1 minute. Return chicken to wok. Add marinade, chicken broth, sugar, salt and pepper to wok and stir until sauce thickens, 1 to 2 minutes. Serve over cooked noodles.

Yield: 8 servings

Cold New Orleans Chicken Spaghetti

Great to make ahead for parties

1	(7-ounce) package spaghetti	3	celery stalks, chopped
	Dash seasoned salt	1	tablespoon peppercorns
	Dash hot pepper sauce		Dash salt
½	cup champagne vinegar	3	celery stalks, chopped
⅔	cup olive oil	½	cup mayonnaise
1	teaspoon salt		Juice of 1 lemon
1	teaspoon sugar		Toasted chopped walnuts,
1	teaspoon paprika		avocado slices, marinated
	Dash hot pepper sauce		artichoke hearts, tomatoes,
¼	teaspoon garlic powder		mushrooms and spinach
1	(4-pound) hen		leaves for garnish
1	onion, chopped		

Cook spaghetti according to package directions and season with salt and hot pepper sauce; set aside. Put vinegar and oil in pint jar; shake. Add salt, sugar, paprika, hot pepper sauce and garlic powder; shake well. Pour enough of this over cooked spaghetti to coat, tossing well. Chill overnight. Cook hen in large saucepot with onion, celery, peppercorns and salt. When cool, remove from bone and cube chicken. Add celery, mayonnaise and lemon juice and mix gently. Adjust seasonings to taste. Mix with spaghetti. Chill overnight. Just before serving, top with walnuts.

Yield: 6 to 8 servings

BEAR FLAIR: *This dish is gorgeous when served on a bed of fresh spinach leaves, lightly coated with the French dressing. Arrange fresh mushrooms, avocado, fresh tomato wedges and marinated artichoke hearts around New Orleans Spaghetti.*

BEAR IN MIND: *The marinating really makes this dish. The leftover French dressing is great on tossed salad or mixed with hot pasta and steamed vegetables.*

Chicken Lasagne

1	(10-ounce) package frozen spinach
6	lasagne noodles
12	mushrooms, sliced
2	tablespoons butter
¼	cup cornstarch
2	cups milk
½	cup chicken broth
½	teaspoon salt
½	teaspoon white pepper (to taste)
	Dash nutmeg
6	tablespoons butter
4	tablespoons grated Parmesan cheese
1	egg, beaten
2	cups cubed cooked chicken
½	cup grated Parmesan cheese

Preheat oven to 350°. Cook spinach, strain and squeeze out all water. Set aside. Prepare noodles according to package directions. Set aside. In large skillet sauté mushrooms in butter. Remove mushrooms and set aside. Dissolve cornstarch in milk and add chicken broth, salt, white pepper, nutmeg, butter and cheese. Bring mixture to a boil stirring constantly, then simmer 2 minutes to thicken. Remove one cup mixture and add beaten egg to it. Set aside. Add chicken, spinach and mushrooms to remaining mixture in pan. In a 9x13-inch pan, layer noodles, sauce mixture, noodles again and then reserved sauce with egg. Sprinkle liberally with Parmesan cheese and bake 35 to 40 minutes.

Yield: 6 to 8 servings

Baked Cranberries

2	cups fresh cranberries
1	cup water
1	cup plus 2 tablespoons sugar
½	teaspoon cinnamon
½	cup chopped walnuts

Sort and wash cranberries. Combine cranberries, water and sugar in 1-quart casserole. Cover and bake in 400° oven 45 minutes. Remove from oven and sprinkle with cinnamon (do not stir). Return to oven and bake 15 minutes more. Sprinkle with walnuts. May be served hot or cold.

Yield: 4 servings

BEAR IN MIND: *This is especially delicious with poultry. It is also great as a dessert topped with whipped cream.*

Seafood

"BEARING GIFTS"

*   ***MAGGIE'S CASSEROLE,** page 200 ... a handy dish to prepare for covered dish meals.
*   ***SHRIMP, MUSHROOM AND ARTICHOKE CASSEROLE,** page 212 ... attach the recipe to a 1½-quart casserole dish.
*   ***OYSTERS AND WILD RICE CASSEROLE,** page 221 ... have these ingredients on hand so you'll have a thankfully simple dish to give when needed in a hurry.
*   ***CRAB 'N' CAPERS,** page 222 ... give a set of scallop or crab shells with this recipe.
*   ***DEVILED CRAB À LA HELEN,** page 223, or **AUNTIE'S DEVILED CRAB,** page 222 ... give a set of au gratin dishes.
*   ***OYSTERS PIERRE,** page 220 ... next time you go to the beach get large oyster shells, clean them well; give with the recipe for this dish.
*   ***SHRIMP LE MAISTRE,** page 213 ... give the recipe, attached to one of those handy shrimp peelers.
*   ***SHRIMP NEW ORLEANS,** page 214 ... prepare and freeze as directed in Bear in Mind, under the recipe. Your gift will be ready at any time.
*   ***BLANCHE GRANDY'S SHRIMP CREOLE,** page 215 ... prepare the sauce for this dish and freeze in gift containers. When ready to present, give with a couple pounds of fresh shrimp and the recipe.
*   ***PROCESSOR BÉARNAISE SAUCE,** page 231 ... give in scooped-out lemon, garnished with fresh parsley or dill sprigs.
*   ***PINK HOMEMADE MAYONNAISE,** page 232 ... put in mason jar, add a snappy bow.

"BEAR ESSENTIALS FOR ENTERTAINING"

*   *Remember that fish should be as fresh as possible when purchased, kept ice cold during storage and cooked only briefly. Fish is done when it flakes easily with a fork. Serve immediately.
*   *Try making your own "pastry scallop shells" to use for serving seafood dishes; using lightly oiled 4 or 5-inch scallop shells, line with your favorite homemade pastry (or use the prerolled pastry from refrigerator case). Use pie weights and bake at 375⁰ for 10 minutes. Two crusts will make 6 pastry shells. Fill as desired.
*   *Soak canned seafood in diluted lemon juice at least 30 minutes before incorporating into recipe. This will improve the flavor.
*   *To poach any whole fish, tie fish in cheesecloth, lower into boiling water to which a bouquet garni of leek or onion, celery rib, parsley sprigs, bay leaf, sprig of thyme, 2 whole cloves and 2 black peppercorns, has been added. Simmer 6 to 10 minutes per pound, depending on thickness of fish. Serve with **PINK HOMEMADE MAYONNAISE,** page 232, or use in salads or add with crabmeat and a white sauce and finish En Papillote (place in piece of heart-shaped parchment paper and bake in 425⁰ oven for 15 minutes).
*   *For a simple cocktail sauce, combine ½ cup chili sauce, ½ cup ketchup, 4 tablespoons horseradish, ¼ teaspoon salt, dash pepper, 1½ teaspoons Worcestershire sauce and a few drops hot pepper sauce.

Bacon Wrapped Scallops

10	bacon slices	¾	cup whipping cream
6	green onions, cut into 1½-inch lengths	1	tablespoon Dijon-style mustard
1	pound fresh scallops, halved or quartered if large		

Broil bacon until partially cooked. Cut bacon slices in half. "Thread" pieces of green onion and scallops with bacon intertwining onto short skewers. Arrange in single layer on broiler pan rack. Combine cream and mustard in saucepan. Heat gently until it thickens slightly. Brush on skewered scallops. Broil until scallops are firm, turning once and brushing with cream sauce.

Yield: 20 skewers

Seaside Scallops

40	large scallops	4	tablespoons chopped shallots
12	tablespoons olive oil	1	tablespoon finely chopped garlic
8	tablespoons Italian tomato sauce		
12	tablespoons unsalted butter		

In large skillet, sauté scallops in hot olive oil. Sear 3 to 5 minutes. Remove from oil and drain. In saucepan, heat tomato sauce and place 2 tablespoons on each plate as a bed for scallops. In another skillet, lightly sauté shallots and garlic in butter. Top scallops with shallots and garlic.

Yield: 4 servings

BEAR IN MIND: *This recipe comes from Bud and Alley's Restaurant in Seaside, Florida.*

Shish-Kabob Scallops

1	pound fresh scallops	10	cherry tomatoes
3	tablespoons soy sauce	1	large bell pepper, cut into
1½	tablespoons fresh lemon		1-inch squares
	juice	10	large fresh mushrooms,
¾	teaspoon ground ginger		cleaned and stemmed
½	teaspoon dry mustard		

Place scallops in shallow glass pan. Combine soy sauce, lemon juice, ginger and mustard. Pour over scallops. Cover and chill for 1 hour. Drain and reserve marinade. On 6 skewers, alternate scallops, tomatoes, bell pepper and mushrooms. Place on broiler pan rack. Broil about 5 inches from heating element 7 to 8 minutes per side. Baste often with reserved marinade while broiling.

Yield: 6 servings

BEAR IN MIND:
   (1) Easy to do on grill as well.
   (2) Fresh scallops are highly perishable. Keep on ice until ready to cook, within 24 hours of purchasing.

Coquille

1½	pounds bay scallops	1	cup half and half
1	tablespoon chopped	1	tablespoon all-purpose
	shallots		flour
¼	teaspoon salt	4	tablespoons butter, room
	Dash white pepper		temperature
½	cup dry vermouth	¼	cup chopped parsley

Preheat oven to 425°. Wash scallops. Cut large ones in quarters. Place scallops in saucepan with shallots, salt, pepper and vermouth. Bring to a boil. Cover and simmer 2 to 5 minutes. Remove scallops with slotted spoon and divide them evenly among 4 ramekins or scallop baking shells. Cook remaining liquid in saucepan over high heat until reduced by half. Add half and half and continue boiling until consistency of syrup. Combine flour and butter. Reduce heat on cream sauce and add flour mixture gradually, stirring with whisk to avoid lumps. Pour sauce over scallops. Sprinkle parsley on top. Bake 5 minutes.

Yield: 4 servings

BEAR IN MIND: *This can be prepared in advance. Refrigerate a few hours until ready to bake. Bake 15 minutes, since they will be chilled.*

Shrimp and Scallops Gruyère

2½ sticks butter, divided	½ teaspoon salt
1 cup flour	3 tablespoons fresh lemon
4 cups milk	juice
16 ounces Gruyere cheese, shredded	½ cup sherry, optional
¼ teaspoon garlic powder	¾ pound fresh mushrooms, sliced
¼ teaspoon white pepper	1½ pounds fresh shrimp, peeled, deveined and cooked
¼ teaspoon dry mustard	
1½ pounds fresh scallops	5 cups cooked wild rice

In large saucepan melt 2 sticks butter. Add flour, stirring constantly then add milk. Cook and stir until thickened. Add cheese and continue stirring until cheese has melted. Add garlic powder, pepper and mustard. Poach scallops 10 minutes in water with salt and lemon juice. Add 1 cup of poaching liquid to cream sauce, discarding the rest, or add ½ cup poaching liquid and ½ cup sherry. Sauté mushrooms in remaining butter and add to sauce along with well-drained scallops and shrimp. Heat 10 to 15 minutes and serve over wild rice.

Yield: 10 servings

BEAR FLAIR: *Using a lemon zester, cut around lemon or lime, creating one continuous thin strip at least 8 inches long. Tie a bow or use as swirl to garnish dish.*

🐾 Shrimp Remoulade

2 pounds fresh shrimp, peeled, deveined and cooked	4 garlic cloves, minced
	1 tablespoon prepared mustard
6 tablespoons olive oil	
6 tablespoons lemon juice	1 tablespoon horseradish
1 (3½-ounce) jar capers and juice	½ teaspoon salt
	Pepper to taste
3 onions, sliced	

Mix all ingredients except shrimp. Pour over cooked shrimp when ready to serve.

Yield: 6 to 8 servings

BEAR IN MIND: *The flavor of the sauce improves if allowed to stand several hours before using.*

Shrimp, Mushroom and Artichoke Casserole

Company caliber and delicious

6½	tablespoons butter	2	tablespoons butter
4½	tablespoons flour	¼	pound fresh mushrooms, sliced
	Salt and white pepper to taste	¼	cup dry sherry
¾	cup whipping cream	2	tablespoons Worcestershire sauce
1	(13¾-ounce) can artichoke hearts, drained	¼	cup grated Parmesan cheese
1	pound fresh shrimp, peeled, deveined and cooked		Paprika to garnish

Preheat oven to 350°. Butter 1½-quart casserole. In saucepan melt butter, then stir in flour and cook stirring constantly until smooth and bubbly. Add salt and white pepper. Slowly stir in cream and cook until thickened. Keep sauce warm. Cut artichokes into quarters and arrange in bottom of buttered casserole. Scatter shrimp over artichokes. Sauté sliced mushrooms in 2 tablespoons butter. Spoon over shrimp. Add sherry and Worcerstershire sauce to sauce. Pour sauce over contents of casserole. Sprinkle with Parmesan cheese and paprika. Bake 20 to 30 minutes or until bubbly.

Yield: 4 servings

BEAR IN MIND: *If you are desperate, you may substitute tuna for shrimp.*

Peel Your Own Shrimp Bake

2	(0.7-ounce) packages dry Italian dressing mix	¼	to ¾ teaspoon pepper
1	stick butter, melted	5	pounds fresh, unpeeled shrimp, washed
	Juice of 2 lemons		

Preheat oven to 350°. Mix dressing according to package directions. Combine butter, lemon juice, pepper and dressing. Mix well. Put shrimp in large oven-proof dish. Pour sauce over shrimp. Cover and bake 1 hour.

Yield: 8 servings

BEAR FLAIR: *Place the sauce (in which shrimp was cooked) into 8 bowls. This sauce is wonderful for dipping. A salad and French bread are all you need.*

Shrimp Pilaf

6	bacon slices	1	tablespoon all-purpose
2	cups water		flour
1	teaspoon salt	¾	cup chopped celery
1	cup uncooked regular rice	¼	cup chopped bell pepper
3	cups shrimp, peeled and	3	tablespoons butter
	deveined	1	teaspoon salt
2	teaspoons Worcestershire	½	teaspoon pepper
	sauce		

Fry bacon in large skillet until crisp. Drain bacon, reserving 3 tablespoons drippings. Crumble bacon and set aside. Combine water, salt and drippings in large saucepan. Bring to a boil, stir in rice, and reduce heat. Cover saucepan and cook 20 minutes. Sprinkle shrimp with Worcestershire sauce and dredge in flour. Sauté shrimp, celery and bell pepper in butter 3 minutes. Remove from heat and stir into rice. Add salt, pepper and crumbled bacon; stir well. Serve hot.

Yield: 6 to 8 servings

Shrimp le Maistre

1½	pounds medium-size	1	garlic clove, minced, or 1
	shrimp, peeled, deveined		teaspoon garlic powder
	and cooked		Salt and pepper to taste
1	(16-ounce) box wild rice		Dash cooking sherry
	mix	2	teaspoons chopped
2	(10¾-ounce) cans cream		pimiento
	of mushroom soup	1	(6-ounce) can sliced
1	cup mayonnaise		mushrooms, drained
1	(8-ounce) can sliced water	1½	cups grated mild cheddar
	chestnuts		cheese
2	teaspoons Worcestershire		
	sauce		

Prepare shrimp, set aside. Preheat oven to 350°. Cook rice according to package directions, until rice is almost done (about 20 minutes). Remove from heat and add soup, mayonnaise, water chestnuts, Worcestershire sauce, garlic, salt, pepper, sherry, pimiento and mushrooms. Mix well. Add shrimp and stir. Pour into 9x13-inch baking dish. Top with grated cheese. Bake 30 minutes or until hot and bubbly.

Yield: 6 to 8 servings

Shrimp New Orleans

3	cups fresh shrimp, peeled, deveined and cooked	¾	cup half and half
2	cups cooked rice	½	cup cooking sherry
½	cup chopped bell pepper	1	tablespoon lemon juice
½	cup chopped onion	¼	teaspoon salt
2	tablespoons butter	¼	teaspoon nutmeg
1	(10½-ounce) can condensed tomato soup	¼	cup slivered almonds, toasted

Prepare shrimp and rice, set aside. Preheat oven to 350°. Cook bell pepper and onion in butter until tender. Add soup. Gradually add half and half and sherry (may adjust amount of sherry to taste). Blend until smooth. Add lemon juice, salt and nutmeg. Toss sauce mixture with shrimp and rice. Pour into baking dish and top with slivered almonds. Bake until hot and bubbly.

Yield: 6 to 8 servings

BEAR IN MIND: *To freeze, line baking dish with heavy foil, leaving long ends. Fill with cooled shrimp mixture. Fold ends over mixture, seal and freeze. When frozen, remove foil package from dish. To serve, remove foil, place back in dish, cover with foil, bake at 350°, 1 hour and 45 minutes. Top with almonds last 5 minutes.*

 # Creamed Shrimp and Avocado

Lovely for luncheon

3	medium avocados	½	teaspoon Worcestershire sauce
2	tablespoons butter		
3	tablespoons all-purpose flour	1	tablespoon lemon juice
½	teaspoon salt	½	cup grated cheddar cheese
⅔	cup half and half		Dash cayenne pepper
⅓	cup dry white wine	2	cups fresh shrimp, peeled, deveined and cooked

Preheat oven to 300°. Cut avocados in half and place in shallow pan. Add an inch of warm water and bake 10 minutes. In saucepan, melt butter and blend in flour and salt. Stir in half and half and cook until thickened. Slowly stir in wine, Worcestershire sauce, lemon juice, cheese and cayenne pepper. Stir over low heat until cheese melts. Add shrimp. Keep warm. Spoon hot shrimp mixture into avocado halves and serve immediately.

Yield: 6 servings

 # Curried Shrimp

1	pound fresh shrimp, peeled, deveined and cooked	1	tablespoon curry powder
2	tablespoons butter	¾	cup tomato juice
1	small onion, finely chopped	¾	cup chicken stock
3	tablespoons all-purpose flour	1	tablespoon whipping cream
		2	cups cooked rice

Side dishes:

1	(9-ounce) jar chutney	1	raw onion, chopped
10	bacon slices, cooked and crumbled	3	hard-cooked eggs, chopped

Prepare shrimp, set aside. Melt butter in saucepan, add onion and sauté 3 to 4 minutes until tender. Add flour and curry powder; blend thoroughly. Slowly add tomato juice and chicken stock, stirring constantly until thickened. Add cream and cook 2 minutes longer. Add shrimp and cook until heated through. Serve over rice with side dishes.

Yield: 4 servings

BEAR IN MIND: *When boiling shrimp, add 1 tablespoon caraway seeds to eliminate odor.*

Blanche Grandy's Shrimp Creole

2	pounds fresh shrimp, peeled, deveined and cooked	1	(15-ounce) can tomato sauce
8	bacon slices, cooked, reserve drippings	1	cup chili sauce
1	cup chopped bell pepper	2	teaspoons Worcestershire sauce
1	cup chopped onion	½	teaspoon black pepper
1	cup chopped celery	2	teaspoons salt
2	(16-ounce) cans tomatoes	8	drops hot pepper sauce
		4	cups cooked rice

Prepare shrimp, set aside. Use drippings from bacon to sauté bell pepper, onion and celery. Add tomatoes, tomato sauce, chili sauce, Worcestershire sauce, pepper, salt and hot pepper sauce. Cook until thickened then add shrimp. Serve with rice.

Yield: 8 servings

BEAR IN MIND: *To freeze this dish, prepare sauce, omitting shrimp. Add cooked shrimp when ready to serve.*

Shrimp Mull
A Cajun treat

½	cup uncooked diced bacon	16	drops hot pepper sauce
1½	cups diced onion	1	(14-ounce) bottle ketchup
1	cup chopped celery	3	tablespoons Worcestershire
1	quart water		sauce
2	(16-ounce) cans peeled	¼	teaspoon allspice
	tomatoes	¼	teaspoon curry powder
1	(10½-ounce) can tomato	1½	sticks butter, divided
	soup	5	pounds fresh shrimp,
2	garlic cloves, minced		peeled and deveined
	Juice of 1 lemon	1	cup sherry
1	teaspoon celery seed	2	cups uncooked regular rice

In frying pan sauté bacon, onion and celery until limp. Transfer to
5-quart Dutch oven and add water, tomatoes, soup, garlic, lemon juice,
celery seed, hot pepper sauce, ketchup, Worcestershire sauce, allspice,
curry and 1 stick butter. Boil gently 2 hours. Then add shrimp and sherry.
Simmer 10 minutes. Cook rice according to package directions, with
remaining butter. Serve shrimp sauce over rice.

Yield: 10 servings

Shrimp and Mushrooms in Garlic Sauce

4	teaspoons minced shallots	16	fresh shrimp, peeled and
4	teaspoons minced garlic		deveined
1	cup sliced fresh mushrooms	1	cup dry white wine
4	teaspoons chopped fresh	½	stick cold unsalted butter
	parsley		Salt and pepper to taste
4	teaspoons butter		

Sauté shallots, garlic, mushrooms and parsley in 4 teaspoons melted
butter. Add shrimp and sear. Add white wine and reduce heat. Whisk in
cold butter over low heat. Add salt and pepper. Serve as soon as butter
melts.

Yield: 4 servings

BEAR IN MIND: *This recipe comes from Bud and Alley's Restaurant in Seaside, Florida.*

Seaside Shrimp

4	teaspoons rosemary	48	to 50 medium-size fresh
	Dash basil		shrimp, peeled and deveined
	Dash oregano	1	cup white wine
	Dash thyme	8	teaspoons lemon juice
4	teaspoons chopped garlic	1	cup finely diced tomato
4	teaspoons chopped shallots	2	cups cooked rice
8	teaspoons olive oil		

In large skillet sauté rosemary, basil, oregano, thyme, garlic and shallots in olive oil. Bring oil to high heat and sear shrimp until pink. Remove shrimp. Add white wine, lemon juice and tomato. Simmer sauce 5 to 10 minutes. Serve over rice.

Yield: 4 servings

BEAR IN MIND: *This recipe comes from Bud and Alley's Restaurant in Seaside, Florida.*

Crevettes en Salsa Verde

1	pound fresh shrimp	¾	cup fish broth or clam juice
	Salt and freshly ground	½	cup dry white wine
	pepper to taste	¼	teaspoon dried hot red
2	tablespoons plus 4 tea-		pepper flakes
	spoons all-purpose flour,	½	cup finely chopped parsley
	divided	½	cup fresh green peas, cooked
⅓	cup olive oil		briefly in salted water and
¼	cup chopped green onions		drained
1	tablespoon finely chopped	2	to 3 cups cooked rice
	garlic		

Peel and devein shrimp but leave last segment and tail. Sprinkle shrimp with salt and pepper and coat on all sides with 2 tablespoons of flour. Shake off excess flour. In skillet large enough to hold shrimp in one layer, heat oil and add shrimp. Cook about 1 minute on each side. Quickly transfer shrimp to second skillet. Leave oil in original skillet, add remaining 4 teaspoons flour, stirring with whisk. Add onion, garlic, fish broth and wine. Stir. Cook over medium-high heat, stirring often, about 1 minute. Add pepper flakes and parsley. Stir to blend. Spoon sauce over shrimp in second skillet and add peas. Bring to a boil, then simmer about 2 minutes. Serve with piping hot rice.

Yield: 4 servings

Shrimp with Feta Cheese and Pasta

4	tablespoons butter
2	pounds fresh shrimp, peeled and deveined
1	(28-ounce) can Italian plum tomatoes
¼	cup olive oil
1	teaspoon crushed garlic
¼	cup bottled clam juice or dry Vermouth
1	teaspoon crushed dried oregano leaves
1	teaspoon dried red pepper flakes
2	tablespoons drained capers
	Salt and freshly ground pepper to taste
1	pound linguine, cooked according to package directions
¼	to ½ pound feta cheese
1	to 2 tablespoons Greek ouzo or pernod

Preheat oven to 350°. Melt butter in skillet. Add shrimp and cook 2 minutes, just until they turn pink. Remove from skillet and keep warm. Put tomatoes in saucepan and cook until liquid is reduced about a third. Stir often to prevent burning or sticking. Heat olive oil in a deep skillet and add garlic, reduced tomatoes, broth or Vermouth, oregano, pepper flakes, capers, salt and pepper. Sauté 2 minutes. Add shrimp and butter to sauce. Put cooked pasta in ovenproof dish and pour sauce over pasta. Sprinkle with feta cheese to taste and bake 10 minutes (until hot and bubbly). Remove from oven and sprinkle with ouzo or pernod. Serve immediately.

Yield: 4 to 6 servings

Charcoaled Snapper

4	fresh red snapper fillets
2	lemons, halved
2	teaspoons Worcestershire sauce
8	drops hot pepper sauce
	Garlic salt to taste
	Pepper to taste
	Seasoned salt to taste
	Paprika to taste
4	tablespoons chopped chives
½	stick margarine
½	cup fresh lemon juice

Arrange fillets on fish rack. Squeeze juice of one lemon half on each fillet and sprinkle ½ teaspoon of Worcestershire sauce on each. Sprinkle fillets with seasonings. Melt margarine with lemon juice. Grill fillets over low coals, basting with lemon and margarine mixture. Cook 20 to 30 minutes or until fish flakes with a fork.

Yield: 4 servings

BEAR IN MIND: *May substitute bass or flounder fillets.*

Linguine with Seafood

½	cup olive oil	¼	cup chopped garlic
¼	cup chopped shallots	12	fresh shrimp, peeled and
4	teaspoons finely chopped		deveined
	fresh basil	12	scallops
4	teaspoons finely chopped	1	cup diced fresh fish
	fresh oregano	1	cup white wine
4	teaspoons finely choppped	2	sticks unsalted cold butter
	fresh parsley	1	pound linguine, cooked

Pour olive oil in hot sauté pan or skillet. Add shallots, basil, oregano, parsley, garlic, shrimp, scallops and fish. Sauté 3 to 5 minutes. Add white wine and allow liquid to reduce by half. Whisk in cold butter. Toss with linguine.

Yield: 4 servings

BEAR FLAIR: *Fresh oregano sprigs create a lovely garnish for each serving.*

BEAR IN MIND: *This recipe comes from Bud and Alley's Restaurant in Seaside, Florida.*

Linguine with Seafood and Herb Sauce

1	pound linguine	⅓	cup lemon juice
⅓	cup combination of olive oil	1	tablespoon basil
	and vegetable oil (propor-	1	tablespoon parsley
	tioned to taste)	1	tablespoon oregano
1	stick butter	½	teaspoon salt
3	to 4 garlic cloves, minced	½	teaspoon pepper
2	pounds fresh shrimp,	3	tablespoons grated
	peeled and deveined		Parmesan cheese
	(may use 1 pound shrimp		
	and 1 pound crab meat)		

Cook pasta al dente. Drain and set aside. Heat oil and butter in large skillet or ovenproof serving dish. Sauté garlic and shrimp until shrimp just turns pink. Add crabmeat if desired. Add lemon juice, basil, parsley and oregano. Simmer 5 minutes, season to taste. Add pasta, toss gently to blend and heat. Sprinkle with Parmesan cheese.

Yield: 6 to 8 servings

BEAR IN MIND: *If fresh herbs are available, use 3 tablespoons each of basil, parsley and oregano.*

Oysters Pierre

½	pound fresh mushrooms, thinly sliced	3	tablespoons minced parsley
			Dash cayenne pepper
1	stick butter, divided	1	teaspoon salt
3	tablespoons flour	⅓	cup sherry
2	small garlic cloves, minced	4	dozen small oysters, drained
3	tablespoons chopped green onions	½	cup bread crumbs

Preheat oven to 350°. Sauté mushrooms in 2 tablespoons butter and set aside. In large skillet melt 4 tablespoons butter. Add flour and cook on low heat, stirring constantly until lightly browned. Add garlic, onions, parsley and cook 5 minutes. Add cayenne, salt and sherry. Stir in oysters and mushrooms and cook 5 minutes. Spoon into 6 individual baking dishes. Top with bread crumbs and dot with remaining butter. Bake 15 to 20 minutes or until lightly browned.

Yield: 6 servings

BEAR FLAIR: *Serve in oyster shells, adding fresh coriander for garnish.*

Oyster Casserole

3	green onions with tops, chopped	4	tablespoons all-purpose flour
2	sticks butter, divided	1	cup half and half
1	(6-ounce) jar mushrooms	2	tablespoons grated Parmesan cheese
1	quart oysters		Bread crumbs for topping
	Salt and pepper to taste		

Preheat oven to 375°. Grease 2½-quart baking dish. In large skillet, sauté onions in 1 stick butter. Add mushrooms and oysters. Salt and pepper to taste. Cook on low heat 4 minutes. In another saucepan, melt remaining stick of butter, add flour and blend well. Slowly add half and half and cheese. Cook on medium-low heat stirring constantly until mixture thickens. Add sautéed onions, mushrooms and oysters. Pour into baking dish. Sprinkle with bread crumbs. Bake 20 to 30 minutes.

Yield: 8 servings

Scalloped Oysters

1	pint oysters	¾	cup chicken broth
2	cups crushed oyster crackers	¼	teaspoon Worcestershire sauce
1	stick butter, melted Pepper to taste		

Preheat oven to 350°. Grease 1½-quart casserole. Drain oysters, reserving ¼ cup liquor. Combine cracker crumbs and butter. Spread one-third crumbs in casserole. Cover with half the oysters. Pepper lightly. Sprinkle with another one-third crumbs and cover with remaining oysters. Pepper lightly. Combine chicken broth, oyster liquor and Worcestershire sauce and pour over oysters. Top with remaining crumbs. Bake 40 minutes.

Yield: 4 servings

Oysters and Wild Rice Casserole

2	cups uncooked wild rice	1	(10¾-ounce) can cream of celery soup
1	stick butter	1	cup half and half
2	pints small oysters, well-drained	2	tablespoons minced onion
	Salt and pepper to taste	¾	teaspoon thyme

Preheat oven to 300°. Butter a 9x13-inch baking dish. Rinse rice and cook according to package directions until open and soft. Drain well. Slice butter and mix with hot rice until butter has melted. Spread rice evenly in dish. Cover with oysters and sprinkle with salt and pepper. In small saucepan heat soup and half and half. Add onion and thyme. Pour evenly over rice. Bake 45 minutes.

Yield: 10 to 12 servings

Crab 'n' Capers

1	pound crabmeat, cartilage removed	¼	teaspoon freshly ground pepper
¼	cup mayonnaise		Dash cayenne pepper
¼	cup sour cream	1	tablespoon fresh lemon juice
2	tablespoons diced pimiento		
¼	cup capers	1	teaspoon sugar
1	teaspoon Dijon-style mustard	1	cup bread crumbs
		4	tablespoons butter
½	teaspoon salt		

Preheat oven to 375°. Grease 1½-quart casserole or individual ramekins. Put crabmeat in medium bowl. Mix mayonnaise, sour cream, pimiento, capers, mustard, salt, pepper, cayenne pepper, lemon juice and sugar together. Pour on top of crabmeat and mix lightly. Pour into casserole or individual crab shells. Top with buttered bread crumbs and bake 30 minutes.

Yield: 4 servings

BEAR FLAIR: *Edible nasturtium blossoms and leaves add a lot of color and peppery taste.*

BEAR IN MIND: *Plant nasturtium seeds or plants in the spring to enjoy all summer.*

Auntie's Deviled Crab

1	pound lump white crabmeat	2	eggs, beaten
1	pound claw crabmeat		Salt and pepper to taste
	Juice of 1 lemon	1	stick butter, melted
1	tablespoon Worcestershire sauce	4	slices bread, toasted
		1	cup milk
1	tablespoon mayonnaise		Bread crumbs for topping

Preheat oven to 375°. Remove cartilage and shell from crabmeat. Add lemon juice, Worcestershire sauce, mayonnaise, eggs, salt, pepper and melted butter. Break toast into small pieces and pour milk over it to soften. Add bread to crab mixture. Spoon into scallop or clam shells and sprinkle with bread crumbs. Place shells in pan with about ½ inch water. Bake 20 to 30 minutes.

Yield: 8 servings

Deviled Crab à la Helen

¾	stick butter		Hot pepper sauce to taste
3	celery stalks, minced	½	teaspoon salt
½	small bell pepper, minced	½	teaspoon pepper
1	medium onion, minced	2	eggs, beaten
1	pound crabmeat, cartilage removed	2	slices bread, dried and crumbled
1	tablespoon Worcestershire sauce		Dry bread crumbs for topping
	Juice of ½ lemon	3	tablespoons mayonnaise

Preheat oven to 350°. In skillet, melt butter and sauté celery, bell pepper and onion until soft. Mix all ingredients except bread crumbs and mayonnaise. Spoon into 8 individual baking dishes. Sprinkle with bread crumbs and divide mayonnaise evenly over bread crumbs.

Yield: 8 servings

BEAR IN MIND: *This may be put into foil potato bakers, wrapped tightly and frozen.*

Crab Imperial

½	cup medium white sauce, page 164.	1	teaspoon dry mustard
1	egg, separated	¼	teaspoon cayenne pepper
2	tablespoons mayonnaise	1	teaspoon salt
2	teaspoons Old Bay seasoning	1	pound crabmeat, flaked
2	teaspoons Worcestershire sauce	1	egg, slightly beaten
			Bread crumbs for topping
			Butter for topping

Preheat oven to 400°. Grease 1-quart casserole. In medium-size bowl combine white sauce, egg yolk, mayonnaise, Old Bay seasoning, Worcestershire sauce, mustard, cayenne pepper and salt. Mix well. Combine crabmeat and beaten whole egg. Beat egg white stiff, but not dry, and fold into mixture. Pour into casserole. Cover with bread crumbs and dot with butter. Bake 30 minutes.

Yield: 6 servings

BEAR FLAIR: *Create a lemon crown for garnish by cutting zig-zag fashion around the lemon, being sure to cut through to the core each time. Separate halves. Place sprig of parsley in center of each crown.*

Crab Eshcol

3	tablespoons butter	5	tablespoons dry sherry
4	tablespoons flour	1	pound white lump crab-
½	pint whipping cream		meat, cartilage removed
	Salt to taste	¾	cup grated sharp cheddar
	Cayenne pepper to taste		cheese
1	(4-ounce) can sliced mush-		
	rooms, with juice		

Preheat oven to 375°. Grease 1-quart casserole. Melt butter in saucepan. Stir in flour and cook 2 to 3 minutes. Add cream, stirring constantly until thickened. Add salt, pepper, mushrooms, juice and sherry. Remove from heat and add crab. Pour into casserole and sprinkle with grated cheese. Bake until cheese is melted.

Yield: 6 servings

BEAR FLAIR: *Garnish with fresh parsley, sculpted mushrooms and green onion flowers.*

Crabmeat Étouffée

¾	stick margarine	¼	teaspoon white pepper
1	medium onion, chopped	⅛	teaspoon cayenne pepper
½	bell pepper, chopped	1½	tablespoons chopped
2	garlic cloves, pressed		parsley
¼	cup chopped chives	1	(2-ounce) jar chopped
1	tablespoon cornstarch, dis-		pimiento
	solved in ½ cup water	1	pound lump white crab-
1	cup hot water		meat, cartilage removed
½	teaspoon salt	2	cups cooked rice

Melt margarine in skillet. Sauté onion and bell pepper over medium heat. Do not brown. Reduce heat and add garlic and chives. Sauté 3 more minutes. Stir in cornstarch, dissolved in water and continue to stir constantly while it thickens. Add hot water and stir until it becomes medium consistency. Add salt, white pepper, cayenne pepper, parsley and pimiento. Fold in crabmeat gently. Allow to heat through over medium-low heat. Serve over hot rice.

Yield: 4 to 5 servings

BEAR IN MIND: *Use 1 cup milk instead of 1 cup water and add 1 cup shredded cheese when sauce thickens to create Crabmeat au Gratin.*

"Fairfields"

St. Marys County Crab Cakes

1 pound fresh crabmeat (frozen can be used)	½ teaspoon salt
1 egg	¼ teaspoon pepper
1 cup bread crumbs, seasoned with lemon pepper	1 tablespoon minced onion, optional
¼ to ⅓ cup mayonnaise	1 tablespoon minced bell pepper, optional
1 teaspoon dry mustard	Margarine or oil for frying
1 teaspoon Worcestershire sauce	

Clean all shell and cartilage from crabmeat. In medium-size bowl mix egg, bread crumbs, mayonnaise, mustard, Worcestershire sauce, salt and pepper. Mix in onion and bell pepper if desired. Add crabmeat and mix gently, but thoroughly. Shape into 6 cakes. Fry in skillet with just enough oil to prevent sticking, about 5 minutes on each side, until cakes are golden brown.

Yield: 6 crab cakes

BEAR FLAIR: Garnish with fresh parsley and slice of lemon.

Salmon Cheese Casserole

1½ cups milk	1½ cups grated sharp cheddar cheese
2 tablespoons margarine	⅛ teaspoon pepper
1 cup soft bread crumbs	Dash paprika
3 eggs, beaten	1 (16-ounce) can salmon, cartilage removed
2 tablespoons minced parsley	
2 tablespoons minced onion	

Preheat oven to 350°. Grease 1½-quart casserole. Heat milk and margarine in saucepan, until margarine is melted. In medium bowl, stir bread crumbs into eggs. Add hot milk, parsley, onion, cheese, pepper and paprika. Mix until well-blended. Place salmon in casserole. Pour egg mixture over salmon. Set casserole in larger pan of hot water. Bake 1 hour or until "custard" is set. Serve hot.

Yield: 4 to 6 servings

Tuna Oriental

¾ cup chopped celery
¼ cup chopped onion
1 tablespoon butter
1 (6½-ounce) can tuna, drained and flaked
1 (10¾-ounce) can cream of mushroom soup
½ cup milk

1 (4-ounce) can sliced mushrooms, drained
1 (3-ounce) can chow mein noodles, divided
½ cup chopped cashews, water chestnuts or peanuts
Salt and pepper to taste

Preheat oven to 350°. Grease 1½-quart casserole. Sauté celery and onion in butter in skillet until tender. Combine with remaining ingredients using only 1 cup chow mein noodles. Put in casserole. Bake 25 to 30 minutes. Top with remaining noodles and bake an additional 5 minutes.

Yield: 4 servings

Tuna Ring with Cheese Sauce

1 egg
2 (6½-ounce) cans tuna, drained
½ cup chopped onion
½ cup shredded sharp cheddar cheese

¼ cup chopped parsley
1 teaspoon celery salt
¼ teaspoon pepper
2 cups biscuit mix
½ cup cold water

Cheese sauce:
½ stick margarine
¼ cup biscuit mix
¼ teaspoon salt
¼ teaspoon pepper

2 cups milk
1 cup shredded cheddar cheese

Preheat oven to 375°. Beat egg slightly. Set aside 1 tablespoon of the egg. Stir tuna, onion, cheese, parsley, celery, salt and pepper into remaining egg. Stir biscuit mix and water to form a soft dough. Knead 8 times on floured surface. Roll into 10x15-inch rectangle. Spread with tuna mixture. Roll up, beginning with longest side. With sealed edge down, shape into ring on greased baking sheet; pinch ends together. With scissors, make cuts two-thirds of the way through ring at 1-inch intervals. Turn each cut section on its side to show filling. Brush top with reserved egg (may add teaspoon of milk if desired). Bake 25 to 30 minutes. Serve hot with cheese sauce.

To prepare sauce: In medium saucepan, melt margarine over low heat. Blend in biscuit mix, salt and pepper. Cook over low heat, stirring until smooth and bubbly. Remove from heat. Stir in milk. Heat to boiling, stirring constantly. Boil and stir another minute. Stir in cheese until melted.

Yield: 4 to 6 servings

Seafood Casserole

½   cup chopped bell pepper
½   cup chopped onion
½   cup chopped celery
1   stick margarine
⅔   cup all-purpose flour
1   (10¾-ounce) can shrimp soup
½   teaspoon minced garlic
½   teaspoon salt
½   teaspoon paprika
    Dash red pepper
2   cups milk
1   (7-ounce) can crabmeat, cartilage removed

1   (6-ounce) package frozen crabmeat, cartilage removed
1   (12 to 16-ounce) package frozen shrimp
1   (4-ounce) can sliced mushrooms, drained
1   (8-ounce) can sliced water chestnuts, drained
½   cup grated sharp cheddar cheese
2   tablespoons butter, softened
½   cup bread crumbs

Preheat oven to 350°. In large skillet, sauté bell pepper, onion and celery in margarine until tender. Stir in flour and cook 1 minute. Add soup and seasonings. Then stir in milk and continue to stir until thick. Mix crabmeat, shrimp, mushrooms and water chestnuts and put into 2-quart casserole. Pour soup mixture on top. Combine cheese, butter and bread crumbs and sprinkle over casserole. Bake 30 to 35 minutes or until golden brown and bubbly.

Yield: 6 servings

Spicy Bass

½	stick margarine	⅓	cup dry white wine
1	tablespoon flour	1	teaspoon fresh lemon juice
⅓	cup minced bell pepper	1	teaspoon A-1 sauce
⅓	cup minced onion	6	drops hot pepper sauce
⅓	cup minced celery	1	teaspoon Heinz 57 sauce
1	teaspoon dried parsley	1½	pounds bass fillets, cut in
1	garlic clove, minced		2x3-inch pieces
1	(16-ounce) can tomatoes, with liquid	2	cups cooked rice

Melt margarine in large skillet over medium heat. Stir in flour and cook until it browns. Add bell pepper, onion, celery, parsley and garlic. Cook until tender. Cut tomatoes into small pieces. Add with their liquid to skillet. Stir in remaining ingredients except fish and rice. Mix well and simmer uncovered 1 hour, adding water if necessary, stirring occasionally. Place fish in skillet with sauce; cover. Bring to a boil and cook 7 to 10 minutes, or until the fish flakes easily with a fork. Serve over rice.

Yield: 4 servings

BEAR FLAIR: *Julienned lemon rind creates an elegant garnish.*

Steve's Lemon Buttered Bass

10	(½-pound) fresh bass fillets, skinned	¼	cup dried parsley flakes, divided
1	cup lemon juice	¼	cup grated Parmesan cheese, divided
	Salt and pepper to taste		
1	stick butter		

Marinate fillets in lemon juice 30 minutes in refrigerator. Drain, salt and pepper fillets. Melt butter in skillet. Sauté fillets until they turn white. Sprinkle with half of parsley and cheese. Turn and cook until fish flakes with fork. Sprinkle with remaining parsley and cheese.

Yield: 10 servings

BEAR FLAIR: *Using a zester or scoring tool, cut away rind in lengthwise strips, ¼-inch apart, around 2 lemons. Slice lemons crosswise. Slice salad tomatoes. Arrange bibb lettuce on plate with fillets. Place lemon and tomato slices on lettuce.*

BEAR IN MIND: *Cut slits in fillets to speed up marinating and cooking time.*

Microwave Poached Salmon

1½	cups hot water	1	bay leaf, broken in half
⅓	cup dry white wine	1	teaspoon minced onion
2	black peppercorns	4	salmon steaks, ½-inch thick
1	teaspoon lemon juice		

Sauce:

½	cup sour cream	½	teaspoon dried dill weed or
1	teaspoon chopped fresh parsley		2 teaspoons fresh dill weed
1	teaspoon lemon juice		Pinch white pepper

Put hot water, wine, peppercorns, lemon juice, bay leaf and onion in 7x11-inch microwave baking dish. Cook on HIGH 5 minutes or until liquid reaches a boil. Carefully place salmon in hot liquid. Cover with plastic wrap and cook on HIGH 1 minute. Let stand 5 minutes. To prepare sauce, put all ingredients in glass measuring cup and mix well. Microwave until hot. Drain salmon. Pour heated sauce over salmon. Serve immediately.

Yield: 4 servings

Red Snapper à la Charleston

1	(6-pound) red snapper, dressed and slit for stuffing	1	egg, beaten
		1	cup bread crumbs
	Salt and pepper to taste	1	teaspoon chopped parsley
½	pound fresh shrimp, peeled, deveined and cooked	1	stick butter, melted (reserve 2 tablespoons)
½	cup chopped onion	½	cup chopped ripe olives
¼	cup sherry	2	bacon slices, uncooked

Preheat oven to 375°. Salt and pepper fish. For stuffing, combine shrimp, onion, sherry, egg, bread crumbs, parsley and melted butter. Stuff fish with mixture and pour reserved butter over fish. Place olives and bacon on fish. Bake about 30 minutes or until done.

Yield: 6 servings

BEAR FLAIR: *Scoop out 6 lemons and fill with tartar sauce or your favorite sauce.*

BEAR IN MIND: *Pompano or other baking fish may be cooked in this manner. Crabmeat can be substituted for shrimp.*

Lobster Tails Thermidor

6	(8-ounce) packages frozen lobster tails	1	teaspoon salt
4	tablespoons butter	1	cup milk
2	(4-ounce) cans sliced mushrooms, drained	1	cup half and half
		2	egg yolks, slightly beaten
4	tablespoons all-purpose flour	1	tablespoon lemon juice
		2	tablespoons sherry
1	teaspoon dry mustard	½	cup bread crumbs
	Dash ground nutmeg	2	tablespoons melted butter
	Dash ground cayenne pepper	2	tablespoons grated Parmesan cheese

Preheat oven to 400°. Boil lobster tails according to package directions. Let cool, remove meat and chop into large pieces. Set aside. Melt 4 tablespoons butter in saucepan. Add mushrooms and sauté until lightly browned. Blend in flour, mustard, nutmeg, cayenne pepper and salt. Gradually add milk and half and half, stirring constantly. Cook over medium heat until mixture thickens, continuing to stir until mixture comes to a boil.

Whisk small amount of hot mixture into egg yolks. Whisk egg yolks into remaining sauce. Remove from heat, stir in lemon juice, sherry and lobster meat. Place in 6 individual baking dishes. Combine bread crumbs, melted butter and Parmesan cheese and sprinkle over each dish. Bake about 15 minutes or until crumbs are browned.

Yield: 6 servings

 # Sauce Arnaud for Shrimp

6	yolks of hard-cooked eggs	2	tablespoons paprika
2	cups olive oil	½	cup lemon juice
1	cup tarragon vinegar	1	cup creole-style mustard
½	cup Worcestershire sauce		Salt to taste

Put yolks through ricer, strainer or in food processor. Add olive oil and mix well. Next add vinegar, Worcestershire sauce, paprika, lemon juice, mustard and salt. Beat well.

Yield: 4 cups sauce

BEAR FLAIR: *This sauce may be served hot or cold over boiled shrimp.*

BEAR IN MIND: *A spicy brown Dijon-style mustard may be substituted for creole mustard.*

Processor Béarnaise Sauce

2	teaspoons dried tarragon	1	teaspoon salt
5	tablespoons white vinegar, divided		Dash hot pepper sauce
½	teaspoon dry mustard	½	teaspoon Worcestershire sauce
3	green onions, finely chopped	2	cups salad oil
2	large eggs		

Soak tarragon in 2 tablespoons vinegar 5 minutes. Add mustard and green onions. Set aside. Blend eggs, 3 tablespoons vinegar, salt, hot pepper sauce, and Worcestershire sauce in processor. With machine running, slowly add oil until sauce is thick. Turn off machine and add tarragon mixture. Blend 15 seconds.

Yield: 2½ cups sauce

BEAR FLAIR: *Serve with fish. For serving with beef, add chopped and squeezed-dry dill pickle.*

Remoulade Sauce

2	cups mayonnaise	1	teaspoon Worcestershire sauce
½	cup Creole-style mustard	⅛	teaspoon garlic powder
2	tablespoons prepared mustard	2	to 3 dashes hot pepper sauce
1	tablespoon horseradish Juice of ½ lemon		Salt to taste

Mix all ingredients together.

Yield: This recipe will cover 3 pounds shrimp or 1 pound crabmeat.

BEAR FLAIR: *Serve over boiled shrimp or lump crabmeat on lettuce bed.*

Tangy Tartar Sauce

1	cup mayonnaise	2	tablespoons minced onion
1½	teaspoons pickle relish	1	tablespoon minced fresh parsley, optional
2	teaspoons fresh lemon juice		

Mix all ingredients in bowl. Cover and chill to blend flavors.

Yield: About 1 cup sauce

BEAR IN MIND: *Will keep for weeks in refrigerator.*

Pink Homemade Mayonnaise

1	egg		(with tarragon or basil
1	teaspoon salt		flavor)
½	teaspoon paprika	2	cups salad oil
2	tablespoons wine vinegar	2	tablespoons lemon juice

Blend egg, salt, paprika and wine vinegar in food processor with steel blade for a few seconds. Slowly add salad oil alternately with lemon juice (rarely takes entire amount of oil). Blend until thick.

Yield: 2 cups sauce

BEAR FLAIR: This recipe excellent for "frosting" a whole cooked salmon and then decorate with capers, pimientos, olives, or parsley.

Beef, Pork and Game

"BEARING GIFTS"

*TEDDY'S TWIN MEAT LOAVES, page 235 ... place unbaked mixture in 10-inch bundt pan; bake and unmold on round platter. Fill center of meat loaf with braised carrots and surround with mashed potatoes, sprinkled with chopped fresh chives.

*TEDDY'S TWIN MEAT LOAVES, page 235 ... also a super recipe if you need to take a dish and need one for your family as well.

*ITALIAN NOODLE BAKE, page 246 ... easy dish to prepare and give in an aluminum foil no-return pan.

*MAGGIE'S LASAGNE WITH SPINACH, page 245 ... easily adapted to individual or family-size gifts; note the Bear in Mind idea under the recipe.

*SPICY POT ROAST, page 240 ... slice and overlap slices on platter; surround with ROSEMARY RED POTATOES, page ... 149.

*SICILIAN MEAT ROLL, page 242 ... unusual, tasty gift.

*BRAISED PORK ROAST, page 248 ... slice, arrange in center of platter; spoon mashed potatoes around slices, sprinkle with ginger.

*MAKE MINE MINT SAUCE, page 257 ... and any of the other sauces in this section make fantastic gifts; look for unusual bottles and jars to fill with these sauces.

"BEAR ESSENTIALS FOR ENTERTAINING"

*To dress up your Easter ham, or to share with a shut-in, boil eggs, prepare deviled eggs. (Before stuffing, dip egg white sections in warm food colorings; pat dry and fill with stuffing mixture.) Put eggs back together to form whole eggs; place around ham on bed of parsley or curly endive. Pretty and edible.

*Dress up the plain hamburger! Shape hamburger patties around a flattened ball of cheese (use soft cheese, like Roquefort or cottage cheese mixed with chopped chives) or put cooked vegetables in the center of patty. Cook hamburger patties as usual, deglazing the skillet after patties are cooked, using water or wine. Pour sauce over patties and serve.

Teddy's Twin Meat Loaves
best meatloaf you ever tasted!

1½	pounds ground beef	¼	teaspoon dry mustard
½	pound ground pork	1	tablespoon Worcester-
¼	cup finely chopped onion		shire sauce
2	tablespoons finely	4	slices soft bread, without
	chopped celery, optional		crusts and cubed
2	teaspoons salt	½	cup milk
½	teaspoon poultry	2	eggs
	seasoning	1	cup chili sauce, divided
¼	teaspoon pepper		

Preheat oven to 350°. Coat 9x13-inch shallow baking pan with vegetable cooking spray. Mix meats well or have butcher grind them together. Stir in onion, celery, salt, poultry seasoning, pepper, dry mustard and Worcestershire sauce. Soak bread cubes in milk, add eggs and beat with rotary beater. Combine meat and egg mixture. Form 2 loaves and place in pan. With a knife, score the tops of loaves and spread each loaf with ½ cup chili sauce. Pour ½ cup boiling water around loaves. Bake uncovered 1 hour at 350°.

Yield: 8 to 10 servings

BEAR IN MIND: *Good cold for sandwiches the next day.*

Steak à la Norne

2	cube steaks, ½-inch thick	2	tablespoons fresh
½	teaspoon dry mustard		lemon juice
¼	teaspoon salt	½	teaspoon Worcestershire
¼	teaspoon pepper		sauce
3	tablespoons butter	8	fresh mushrooms, sliced
1	teaspoon chopped chives	¼	cup chopped shallots

Sprinkle one side of both steaks with ¼ teaspoon mustard, ⅛ teaspoon salt, and ⅛ teaspoon pepper. Pound with mallet. Repeat on other side with same ingredients. Melt butter in skillet. Add steaks and cook 2 minutes each side on very high heat. Transfer to warm platter. Add chives, lemon juice and Worcestershire sauce to skillet. Bring to a boil. Lower heat. Add mushrooms and shallots and sauté. Spoon sauce over steaks and serve immediately.

Yield: 2 servings

Steak au Poivre

4	tablespoons coarsely cracked black peppercorns	5	tablespoons margarine
4	individual steaks, 1 to 1½ inches thick (tenderloin or fillet)		Salt
		¾	(10½-ounce) can beef broth
		½	pint whipping cream

Sprinkle peppercorns on each side of steaks, pressing them into the meat. Melt butter in a large skillet. Sear steaks in melted margarine 2 to 3 minutes each side. Place a weighted meat press on steaks as they cook to get a nice brown sear. Remove steaks from skillet and place in a covered dish to keep warm. Add broth to skillet and stir to loosen browned particles. Bring to a boil. Allow broth to reduce, stirring frequently until slightly thickened. Gradually add cream, stirring until smooth and well-blended. Reduce heat. Stir until mixture turns a caramel color. Remove from heat. Pour sauce over steaks and serve hot.

Yield: 4 servings

Sautéed Bacon and Calves Liver

6	strips bacon		Seasoned flour to dredge
2	bell peppers, cut into strips	1	tablespoon butter
1	large onion, sliced	1	tablespoon apple cider vinegar
½	pound calves liver, cut into strips ¼ to ½-inch wide and about 1½-inches long		Parsley, optional

Cook bacon and set aside to drain. Remove all but 2 tablespoons bacon fat from pan and reserve. Quickly sauté pepper strips. Drain in colander or sieve and keep warm. Wipe out pan with paper towel and add 2 tablespoons reserved bacon fat to pan. Add onions; sauté until golden brown. Drain in colander or sieve and set aside. Add 2 more tablespoons bacon fat to pan and heat to point where it is almost smoking. Add calves liver which has been dredged in seasoned flour and cook 2 minutes. Drain in colander or sieve. Add 1 tablespoon butter to pan, add liver and toss, add pepper and onions, blending well. Add vinegar and blend. Serve piping hot, garnished with bacon and parsley.

Yield: 2 servings

Fillets with Madeira Mushroom Sauce

6   (1-inch thick) tenderloins

Sauce:

½   pound fresh mushrooms, sliced
1   tablespoon butter
2   tablespoons flour
1   tablespoon minced onion
1   (10½-ounce) can beef broth

¼   cup Madeira wine
¼   cup sherry
1   teaspoon minced parsley
     Salt and pepper to taste

Sauté mushrooms in butter. Sprinkle with flour and onion. Stir in beef broth, Madeira and sherry. Cook, stirring until sauce bubbles and thickens. Add parsley, salt and pepper to taste. Brown fillets to desired darkness. Pour sauce on fillets.

Yield: 6 servings

Bulkogi

2   pounds flank steak (partially frozen to slice easier)
½   cup chopped onion
4   garlic cloves, pressed
5   tablespoons soy sauce
5   tablespoons salad oil
1½   tablespoons sugar

1   tablespoon sesame seeds, crushed
2½   tablespoons black peppercorns, crushed
3   tablespoons dry sherry
3   tablespoons sliced scallions, optional

Trim off any excess fat. Cut steak in half lengthwise. Slice each half, across the grain, in very thin slices, about ¼-inch thick. In small bowl combine onion, garlic, soy sauce, oil, sugar, sesame seeds, pepper and sherry; mix well. Arrange steak slices in shallow glass baking dish. Pour marinade over steak, coating well. Cover and chill about 2 hours. In heavy skillet or wok, brushed lightly with oil, pan-broil steak over high heat, searing quickly 1 minute. Do not overcook. Arrange on platter. Sprinkle with scallions.

Yield: 6 servings

Sukiyaki

1½ pounds sirloin steak, about 2 inches thick

1 medium sweet onion, thinly sliced

2 bell peppers, cut in thin strips

3 celery stalks, cut diagonally

½ pound mushrooms, sliced

2 bunches scallions, trimmed and cut in 2-inch pieces

1 pound spinach, stems removed

2 (7-ounce) cans bamboo shoots, drained and sliced

1 (10½-ounce) can beef broth

½ cup soy sauce

3 tablespoons sugar

Trim fat from meat and reserve some of the larger pieces of fat. With sharp knife, cut steak across the grain into ⅛-inch thick slices (if steak is partially frozen, it will slice easier), slices may be cut in half if too long. Prepare vegetables and arrange on tray with meat. Combine broth, soy sauce and sugar in bowl. In wok, or very large skillet, heat trimmed fat pieces over medium-high heat until melted. Remove fat pieces. Add beef slices and cook, stirring until lightly browned. Add onion, bell peppers and celery. Add half the broth mixture. Cook quickly, stirring often, about 5 minutes; add more broth as needed. Stir in mushrooms and scallions, cook 1 minute. Add spinach and bamboo shoots, cook 1 minute. Serve while hot.

Yield: 4 to 6 servings

BEAR IN MIND: *This is great when served over cooked rice, accompanied by fresh fruit compote.*

Beef Roulades

3   pounds round steak about
    ¼-inch thick
    (cut into 6 pieces about
    4x6 inches)
¾   pound ground pork
1   teaspoon poultry
    seasoning
¼   teaspoon salt
½   teaspoon garlic salt
2   tablespoons finely
    chopped onion
¼   cup soft white bread
    crumbs

6   bacon slices
1½ pounds small white onions
    (or canned onions)
⅓   cup all-purpose flour
1   tablespoon meat extract
    paste (if available)
1   (10½-ounce) can beef
    bouillon
2½ cups red burgundy wine
1½ pounds mushrooms, sliced
1   bay leaf

Preheat oven to 350°. Combine ground pork, poultry seasoning, salt, garlic salt, chopped onion and bread crumbs, mix well. Place ¼ cup pork mixture on each beef slice. Roll up from short side, wrap slice of bacon around each and tie up like a package with string. Brown on all sides in hot butter in Dutch oven. Remove and set aside. Add white onions and brown. (If you use canned onions, don't cook as long.) Remove Dutch oven from heat. Stir in ⅓ cup flour and meat extract paste and gradually stir in bouillon and burgundy. Return to heat and bring to a boil stirring constantly. Add roulades with sliced mushrooms and bay leaf. Cover and bake 2 hours. If sauce is too thick, thin with additional wine. To serve: Remove string, place on platter, surround with onions and sprinkle with parsley. Serve sauce separately.

Yield: 6 servings

BEAR IN MIND: *If Dutch oven isn't oven-proof transfer roulades to an 8-inch square baking dish.*

Beef Bourguignonne

5	pounds chuck or shoulder roast, about 2 inches thick	3	large garlic cloves, minced
10	slices bacon, cooked crisp and crumbled, reserve drippings	1	large bay leaf
		12	small whole onions (may use canned)
	Salt and pepper to taste	8	medium carrots, sliced
2	(10½-ounce) cans beef broth	1	pound fresh mushrooms, sliced or 2 (4-ounce) cans sliced mushrooms, drained
2¼	cups water	3	tablespoons flour
1	cup dry red wine	¼	cup water

Trim fat from roast and cut into 1½-inch cubes. In large heavy pan, brown roast cubes in bacon drippings, pour off fat. Add bacon, sprinkle of salt and pepper, beef broth, 2¼ cups water, wine, garlic and bay leaf. Simmer one hour, stirring occasionally. Add onions, carrots and mushrooms and simmer an additional hour or until tender. Remove bay leaf. Blend ¼ cup water with flour. Add to meat and cook and stir until thickened. Serve over rice.

Yield: 8 servings

BEAR IN MIND: *This can be made the day before and reheated or frozen for use at a later time.*

Spicy Pot Roast

3	pounds boneless chuck roast	1½	tablespoons Worcestershire sauce
¼	cup oil	2½	tablespoons soy sauce
1½	teaspoons salt	1	teaspoon rosemary
¼	cup wine vinegar	¾	teaspoon garlic powder
¼	cup ketchup	½	teaspoon dry mustard

In saucepan, brown roast on all sides in heated oil. Sprinkle with salt. Combine wine vinegar, ketchup, Worcestershire sauce, soy sauce, rosemary, garlic powder and dry mustard and pour over meat. Cover and simmer 2 hours. Serve sauce over meat.

Yield: 8 servings

Lean Beef Pomodori

1	pound lean sirloin beef, thinly sliced	1	(10¾-ounce) can cheddar cheese soup
2	medium garlic cloves, pressed	¾	cup beef broth
2	tablespoons oil	1½	teaspoons salt
1	cup sliced onions	½	teaspoon lemon pepper
⅓	cup dry red wine	1	pound zucchini, thinly sliced
1	(15-ounce) can herb tomato sauce	6	cups cooked rice

Cut beef in 1-inch strips. In large skillet brown beef and garlic in oil. Add onions and cook 2 minutes longer. Blend in wine, tomato sauce, soup, broth, salt and lemon pepper. Cover and simmer about 30 minutes. Stir in zucchini, replace cover and continue cooking 20 minutes longer. Serve over beds of fluffy rice.

Yield: 6 servings

Spiced Corned Beef

5	pounds corned beef brisket	1	teaspoon celery seed
¼	cup vinegar	6	whole cloves
½	cup water	¼	teaspoon ginger
2	tablespoons molasses	¼	teaspoon dry mustard
2	bay leaves		
1	teaspoon freshly ground pepper		

Place corned beef in a shallow pan. Combine ingredients and pour over corned beef. Refrigerate overnight, turning once. Place corned beef in deep saucepan and add just enough water to cover. Bring to a boil, reduce heat, cover and simmer 3½ to 4 hours or until meat is tender.

Yield: 2 servings per pound

BEAR FLAIR: *Shred 1 (2-pound) cabbage into ¼-inch strips. Sauté in ¾ stick unsalted butter and sprinkle with 1 tablespoon caraway seeds and 1 tablespoon vinegar. Serve with Spiced Corn Beef.*

After Opera Special

½	pound beef, chopped in small cubes (any tender cut)	½	cup dry white wine
2	tablespoons butter	1	tablespoon grated Parmesan cheese
1	(16-ounce) can artichoke hearts, thinly sliced		English muffins or toast points
1	pint sour cream		Paprika to garnish

Brown beef in butter. Stir in artichoke hearts, sour cream, white wine and Parmesan cheese. Cook until well-blended and heated thoroughly. Serve on English muffins or toast points. Sprinkle with paprika.

Yield: 4 servings

BEAR IN MIND: *Good as a late night supper or appetizer.*

Sicilian Meat Roll
unusual combo and presentation

2	eggs, beaten	¼	teaspoon pepper
¾	cup soft bread crumbs	1	small garlic clove, pressed
½	cup tomato juice	2	pounds lean ground beef
2	tablespoons chopped parsley	8	thin slices boiled ham
½	teaspoon oregano	1½	cups shredded Mozzarella cheese
¼	teaspoon salt	3	slices Mozzarella cheese

Preheat oven to 350°. Oil 9x13-inch baking dish. Combine eggs, bread crumbs, tomato juice, parsley, oregano, salt, pepper and garlic; stir in beef. Mix well. On tin foil, pat meat to a 10x12-inch rectangle. Arrange ham slices on top and sprinkle with shredded cheese. Start with long end and roll up meat. Place roll, seam side down, in baking dish. Bake 1 hour 45 minutes. Place cheese slices on top of meat loaf last 5 minutes of cooking.

Yield: 8 servings

BEAR IN MIND: *This freezes well.*

Potatoes in Beef Jackets

12	small potatoes	¼	teaspoon pepper
1	pound ground beef	2	cups tomato juice
1	egg	1	large onion, chopped
1½	teaspoons salt	½	pound mushrooms, sliced

Preheat oven to 350°. Grease a 9x13-inch baking dish. Boil potatoes in large saucepan until almost tender. Remove skins. Mix beef, egg, salt and pepper. Cover each potato with beef mixture, forming a jacket. Press well. Place "jackets" in dish. Pour tomato juice over "jackets" and add chopped onion and mushrooms. Bake 20 minutes or until browned.

Yield: 6 servings

Pasta Amatrice Style

2	tablespoons mild olive oil		Salt and freshly ground pepper to taste
1	tablespoon butter		
2	garlic cloves, pressed	¼	cup whipping cream
1	cup finely chopped onion	¼	cup vodka
4	ounces Prosciutto or slab bacon, cut into ¼-inch cubes	1	pound bucatini, rotini or any other short, thick, round pasta
1	pound fresh ripe plum tomatoes, peeled, seeded and chopped (about 1½ cups)		Freshly grated Parmesan cheese to garnish

Heat oil and butter in heavy skillet over medium-high heat. When foam subsides, add garlic and sauté until golden brown, about 1 to 2 minutes. Add onion and Prosciutto to oil. Sauté, stirring occasionally, until onion begins to turn golden, about 5 minutes. Add fresh tomatoes with juices; heat to boiling. Reduce heat to low; simmer until juice is reduced and tomatoes are thick and dense, but not puréed. This takes about 15 to 20 minutes. Season to taste with salt and pepper. Add whipping cream and vodka. Heat, but do not boil. Add mixture to hot cooked pasta. Toss gently and serve with Parmesan cheese.

Yield: 4 servings

BEAR IN MIND: *1 (14-ounce) can Italian plum tomatoes, with juice reserved, may be substituted for fresh tomatoes.*

Manicotti

Filling:

¼	cup chopped onion
1	large garlic clove, pressed
2	tablespoons olive oil
1	(10-ounce) package frozen chopped spinach, thawed
1	pound ground sirloin
1	(16-ounce) carton ricotta cheese
2	eggs, beaten
½	teaspoon salt
¼	teaspoon pepper
½	cup grated Parmesan cheese
½	teaspoon oregano
14	to 16 manicotti shells

Tomato sauce:

3½	cups tomato purée
1½	teaspoons salt
¼	teaspoon pepper
¾	teaspoon oregano
1	teaspoon sugar, optional
¾	teaspoon basil

White sauce:

1	stick butter
¼	cup flour
1	(12-ounce) can evaporated milk
½	cup water
1	teaspoon salt
⅛	teaspoon white pepper
	Dash nutmeg

In large skillet, sauté onion and garlic in oil. Stir in spinach and cook until most of the moisture evaporates. Remove mixture to large bowl. Lightly brown sirloin in same pan. Drain. Add sirloin, ricotta, eggs, salt, pepper, Parmesan cheese and oregano to spinach mixture. Mix well. Cook manicotti only halfway. Fill shells with about ⅓ cup of mixture. Set aside.

To prepare tomato sauce: Combine tomato purée, salt, pepper, oregano, sugar and basil. Simmer 15 minutes. Pour 1 cup tomato sauce on bottom of each of 2 (3-quart) shallow baking dishes. Place manicotti on top side by side. Set aside.

To prepare white sauce: Melt butter and stir in flour. Add milk and water. Stir constantly over medium heat until thick. Do not boil. Remove from heat and add salt, pepper and nutmeg. Divide white sauce into 2 parts. Divide remaining tomato sauce into 2 parts. Pour white sauce over each dish of stuffed shells. Then top with tomato sauce. Sprinkle with Parmesan cheese. Bake in 350° oven 35 to 40 minutes or until heated through.

Yield: 8 to 12 servings

Maggie's Lasagne with Spinach

1	pound lean ground beef	1	teaspoon marjoram
¼	pound ground hot sausage	1	cup dry burgundy
1	large onion, chopped	1	tablespoon sugar
2	to 3 garlic cloves, minced	1	egg, beaten
2	(16-ounce) cans tomatoes	1	(16-ounce) container
1	(8-ounce) can tomato		ricotta cheese
	sauce	6	lasagne noodles, cooked
1	(6-ounce) can tomato	1	(8-ounce) package frozen
	paste		chopped spinach, cooked
1	teaspoon salt		and squeezed dry
¼	to ½ teaspoon cayenne	8	ounces Mozzarella cheese,
	pepper		sliced or shredded
2	teaspoons oregano	1	cup grated Parmesan
2	teaspoons basil		cheese

In skillet, sauté meats, onion and garlic. Add tomatoes, spices, burgundy and sugar. Simmer 1 hour or until thickened. In separate bowl, mix egg and ricotta cheese. In 9x13-inch dish, spread 1 cup sauce. Then alternate layers of noodles, sauce, ricotta, spinach, Mozzarella and Parmesan, ending with sauce, Mozzarella and Parmesan. Bake in 350° oven 40 to 50 minutes until lightly browned and bubbly. Allow to stand 15 minutes, slice into squares and serve.

Yield: 8 servings

BEAR IN MIND: *Wrap leftover squares in double aluminum foil and freeze. Pull individual packets when needed and bake in 350° oven 45 minutes. Instant, easy, delicious!*

Italian Noodle Bake

2 tablespoons butter	2 teaspoons brown sugar
1 pound ground chuck	4 large ripe tomatoes,
½ cup diced onion	peeled and sliced
½ cup diced celery	1 (8-ounce) package
1 garlic clove, minced	medium-wide noodles
½ cup sliced mushrooms	6 green onions, chopped
1 teaspoon salt	3 ounces cream cheese
Dash pepper	½ pint sour cream
1 (16-ounce) jar spaghetti	1 cup shredded cheddar
sauce	cheese

Preheat oven to 350°. Melt butter in skillet and brown meat. Add onion, celery, garlic, mushrooms, salt and pepper. Simmer 10 minutes. Add sauce, sugar and tomatoes. Continue to simmer over low heat. Prepare noodles according to directions on package. Drain. Blend green onions, cream cheese and sour cream in blender. Toss this with noodles. Place a third of noodles in 3-quart casserole. Top with a third of meat mixture. Alternate until all noodles and meat are used. Top with cheddar cheese. Bake 20 minutes.

Yield: 6 to 8 servings

BEAR IN MIND: *A delicious quick dish that can be prepared ahead.*

Mustard Ham with Broccoli

½ stick margarine	¼ cup lemon juice
2 tablespoons Dijon-style	8 ounces smoked ham,
mustard	cut in julienne strips
½ pint whipping cream	Boiling salted water
⅛ teaspoon salt	6 cups broccoli flowerets
½ teaspoon pepper	

Melt margarine in heavy saucepan over medium heat. Stir in mustard, cream, salt and pepper. Add lemon juice and stir until hot. Add ham and heat about 3 minutes. Cook broccoli in boiling salted water 4 minutes. Drain. Arrange broccoli on plates. Spoon ham mixture over broccoli.

Yield: 4 servings

Veal Marsala

½ pound fresh mushrooms, sliced
3 tablespoons butter
1 garlic clove
2 pounds veal cutlets

Salt and pepper to taste
All-purpose flour to dredge
½ stick butter
¾ cup Marsala wine
¾ cup beef broth

Sauté mushrooms in butter. Cut off end of garlic clove and rub opened garlic over veal. Lightly sprinkle veal with salt and pepper and dredge each piece in flour. Melt butter in a heavy skillet, allowing butter to get sizzling hot, but not brown. Add veal (do not overlap pieces) and cook until lightly browned (no longer than 2 minutes on each side). Remove meat and place on hot platter. Scrape skillet to loosen pan drippings and add wine and broth to hot skillet, stirring vigorously. Cook until broth and wine are reduced by half in volume. Pour over meat. Serve immediately.

Yield: 8 servings

BEAR FLAIR: *To overlapping cutlets on platter, add sculpted mushrooms and tomato roses.*

Wild Rice and Sausage

1 cup uncooked wild rice or 1 (6-ounce) box long grain and wild rice
½ pound pork sausage
1 medium onion, chopped
1 medium bell pepper, chopped

½ cup chopped celery
1 (10¾-ounce) can cream of mushroom soup
1 (10¾-ounce) can cream of chicken soup
1 (4-ounce) can sliced mushrooms

Preheat oven to 325°. Grease 3-quart casserole. Cook rice as directed on package until tender. Brown sausage in skillet. Add onions, bell pepper and celery and cook until limp. Add rice, mushroom soup, chicken soup and mushrooms. Mix well and pour into casserole. Cover and bake 1 hour.

Yield: 8 to 10 servings

BEAR IN MIND:
(1) Great for a covered dish supper or a cold winter night.
(2) Can also be put into two 1½-quart casseroles, so one may be frozen for later use.

Onion Biscuit Ring with Ham Madeira

2   cans (10 biscuits each) refrigerated buttermilk or country-style biscuits
½   stick margarine, melted
1   cup chopped onion, divided
2   tablespoons margarine
1   pound ham, cut into ½-inch cubes
8   ounces fresh mushrooms, sliced
¼   cup Madeira wine
2   tablespoons all-purpose flour
1   (13-ounce) can evaporated milk
½   teaspoon prepared mustard
2   tablespoons chopped pimiento

Preheat oven to 375°. Grease a 9-inch ring mold pan. Separate biscuit dough into 20 biscuits. Combine melted margarine and ½ cup onion. Dip each biscuit into onion mixture; place biscuits on edge 1 inch apart in prepared ring mold pan. Bake 18 to 20 minutes or until golden brown. Turn ring onto platter. In 10-inch frying pan, melt 2 tablespoons margarine and sauté ham, mushrooms and ½ cup onions. Add wine; cook over medium heat until most of liquid has evaporated. Sprinkle flour over ham mixture. Stir in milk; cook and stir until sauce is smooth and thickened. Stir in mustard and pimiento. Spoon into center of warm biscuit ring.

Yield: 5 to 6 servings

Braised Pork Roast

1   (4-pound) boneless pork roast
½   teaspoon salt
½   teaspoon pepper
½   cup grape jelly
½   cup water
½   cup cider vinegar
1¼   teaspoon ginger
2   onions, thinly sliced
1   large bay leaf
1   tablespoon cornstarch
⅓   cup water

Salt and pepper roast. Brown in large pot, starting with fat side down. Drain fat. Mix jelly, water, vinegar and ginger together and pour over roast. Add onions and bay leaf. Cover and cook on low heat 1½ to 2 hours, basting occasionally. Add extra water if needed. Remove meat from gravy and slice. Mix cornstarch with water and stir into gravy. Continue cooking until gravy is thickened. Discard bay leaf. Serve gravy over meat.

Yield: 8 servings

Stuffed Pork Chops

6	(1-inch thick) pork chops	2	cups herb-seasoned stuffing mix
½	stick margarine	1	tablespoon chopped parsley
1	medium onion, chopped	4	to 6 tablespoons sour cream
1	(4½-ounce) can sliced mushrooms		

Preheat oven to 350°. Slice pocket in each of pork chops. Melt margarine in skillet. Sauté onions, add mushrooms and cook 2 minutes. Stir in stuffing and parsley. Add sour cream last. Stuff chops with this mixture and secure with a wooden toothpick. Put a small amount of water in a 9x13-inch pan. Place chops in pan and bake covered 30 minutes. Remove cover and bake an additional 30 minutes.

Yield: 6 servings

Fruit Topped Baked Pork Chops

4	(1-inch thick) loin chops	½	teaspoon dry mustard
¼	cup oil	½	teaspoon salt
1	cup chopped dates	¼	teaspoon pepper
2	tart apples, cored and halved	¼	cup chili sauce
1	tablespoon light brown sugar, firmly packed	2	tablespoons cider vinegar
		½	cup chopped onion

Preheat oven to 350°. In a skillet over low heat, brown chops in oil on both sides. Place in 2-quart baking dish. Place ¼ cup dates on each chop. Top with apple. Combine brown sugar, mustard, salt, pepper, chili sauce, cider vinegar and onions. Pour over apple. Cover with foil. Bake 45 minutes. Remove foil. Bake 15 minutes longer, basting 2 to 3 times.

Yield: 4 servings

Simply Delicious Pork Chops
wonderfully easy

6	(¾-inch thick) pork chops	1	tablespoon Worcestershire sauce
2	tablespoons oil		
2	tablespoons ketchup	1	tablespoon soy sauce
1	tablespoon lemon juice		

Preheat oven to 350°. Arrange chops in a single layer in baking dish. In small bowl, mix oil, ketchup, lemon juice, Worcestershire sauce and soy sauce using a wire whisk or fork. Spread half of mixture over chops. Bake uncovered 30 minutes. Turn chops and spread with remaining sauce. Bake uncovered 30 minutes.

Yield: 4 servings

Ragout de Pork au Vin Blanc

3	tablespoons oil	1	bay leaf
2	pounds boneless pork shoulder, cut into 1½-inch cubes	½	teaspoon rosemary
		¼	teaspoon thyme
		½	teaspoon salt
1	cup chopped onions	¼	teaspoon pepper
1	garlic clove, pressed	2	cups carrots, cut in ¼-inch slices
3	tablespoons all-purpose flour	2	tablespoons butter
3	tablespoons water	1	pound fresh mushrooms, sliced
1	(10½-ounce) can chicken broth		Chopped fresh parsley to garnish
1¼	cups dry white wine, divided		

In a large saucepan, heat oil. Brown half of the pork, remove and brown remaining pork. Remove from pan. Sauté onions and garlic in pan drippings until golden. Add flour which has been dissolved in water and stir for 1 minute. Stir in chicken broth, 1 cup of wine, bay leaf, rosemary, thyme, salt and pepper. Cook and stir until it boils and thickens. Stir in browned pork. Simmer covered 1 hour, stirring once. Stir in carrots and simmer, covered, 30 minutes longer. Add water if needed. Meanwhile in a large skillet, melt butter, add mushrooms and sauté until golden. Add to sauce pot with remaining ¼ cup wine. Stir gently. Simmer covered 3 minutes longer. Sprinkle with parsley.

Yield: 6 servings

General Hints on Game

Do not pull the breast out of birds. It is quicker, but birds will not be as tender and juicy when cooked.

Game birds with darker meat can be served rare or medium. Birds with white meat should be well-done.

When freezing cleaned birds, submerge them in water.

Birds should be at room temperature before cooking.

When frying quail or dove it is best to use a heavy pan with a tight-fitting lid.

For a quick venison dish men will love, fry ½ to ¾-inch thick loin steaks as you would birds. Be careful not to overcook.

Ground venison can be used along with or in place of ground beef in any recipe.

Doves should be picked. The last joint of the wing and last joint of the leg with foot can be cut off. Quail can be picked or skinned. The last joint of the leg with foot can be cut off.

Soak game birds in refrigerator in slightly salty water to draw out the blood.

Be certain to remove any feathers imbedded by shot.

The quicker any game is dressed and refrigerated, the better it will be.

To skin a rabbit, lift skin on back and make a 1 to 2-inch cut crossways. Insert fingers in cut and pull in opposite directions. Skin will come off easily.

It is considerably harder to pluck water fowl than to clean upland game birds, but it is worth the effort.

George's Marinated Grilled Duck

2	garlic cloves, minced	1	teaspoon salt
1	(10-ounce) bottle soy sauce	½	teaspoon pepper
1	(750-milliliter) bottle burgundy wine	4	ducks, quartered

Combine garlic with soy sauce, wine, salt and pepper. Pour over ducks and marinate 12 hours in refrigerator. Remove legs and quarter. Parboil for 30 minutes. Return to marinade 3 hours. Place on grill over hot coals, skin side up. Turn over every 10 minutes, brushing marinade over all. Cook as you would beef.

Yield: 8 servings

Roast Duck with Orange Sauce

2 ducks (about 3 pounds each)	1 medium tart apple, peeled, cored and sliced
2 teaspoons salt	¾ cup orange juice
¼ teaspoon pepper	1 tablespoon cornstarch
2 tablespoons butter	2 tablespoons cold water
1 small onion, sliced	

Sprinkle ducks with salt and pepper. Melt butter in roasting pan. Brown ducks in butter on all sides. Add onion and apple. Add juice and bring to a boil. Reduce heat to simmering, cover and cook on low 2 hours. Remove duck and chunks of apple and onion. Mix cornstarch and water together. Add to gravy and cook on low heat until thickened. Serve gravy over duck.

Yield: 4 servings

BEAR FLAIR: *Score 2 navel oranges and slice. Cut each slice in half and arrange around serving platter, alternating with slices of green Granny Smith apple.*

Wild Duck in Soy Marinade

2 wild ducks, quartered	¼ cup shortening or bacon drippings
1 (13½-ounce) can pineapple chunks	1 (3-ounce) can mushrooms, drained
½ cup soy sauce	
1 teaspoon ginger	

Marinate ducks overnight in mixture of pineapple, soy sauce and ginger. Preheat oven to 350°. Wipe meat; brown in fat. Place in shallow casserole; pour on marinade and mushrooms. Bake, covered, 1½ hours or until tender (add water, if necessary).

Yield: 4 servings

Duckling Pâté

1	(3-pound) duck, quartered (use 2 if small)	1	(12-ounce) can chopped black olives
3	cups water	¼	teaspoon hot pepper sauce
2	teaspoons salt	1	teaspoon salt
10	peppercorns	1	teaspoon grated onion
1	bay leaf	12	ounces cream cheese, softened
4	cloves		
1	teaspoon Worcester-shire sauce	1	(8 to 12-ounce) package liver pâté
½	cup sour cream	¼	cup brandy

Stew duck and giblets in water with salt, peppercorns, bay leaf and cloves until tender. Let cool in broth ½ hour. Pour off broth and let fat rise. Skim off fat, reserving ¾ cup fat. (If using wild duck, there may not be much fat.) Discard skin. Using steel blade of food processor, process meat and giblets until finely ground. Put ground duck into large bowl and add remaining ingredients. Blend well with fingers. Add enough of reserved fat to bind the pâté mixture. Pack into small serving bowl. Pour remaining fat on top to seal. Chill before serving. Can be made a few days ahead. Do not freeze.

Yield: 20 to 25 servings

BEAR IN MIND: *If you don't care for the flavor of liver pâté, you can omit it. It makes only a subtle difference in taste.*

Dove and Gravy

12	dove breasts	⅛	teaspoon pepper
1	(0.87-ounce) package chicken gravy mix	2	tablespoons margarine
¼	teaspoon salt	½	cup water

Preheat oven to 350°. Line pan with foil using enough to wrap doves completely. Place doves in pan. Sprinkle with gravy mix, salt and pepper. Dot with margarine. Drizzle water over doves. Seal foil tightly. Bake 1 hour.

Yield: 6 servings

Mushroom and Dove Turnovers

Pastry for turnovers:

1	(8-ounce) package cream cheese, softened
2	sticks butter, softened

2¼	cups flour
1	teaspoon salt

Mushroom and dove filling:

4	doves
3	tablespoons butter
⅔	cup finely chopped onion
½	pound mushrooms, finely chopped
¼	teaspoon thyme

½	teaspoon salt
	Freshly ground black pepper to taste
2	tablespoons all-purpose flour
¼	cup sour cream

To prepare pastry: Blend cream cheese and butter. Add flour and salt and work with fingers or pastry blender until smooth. Chill well 4 hours or overnight.

To prepare filling: Boil doves in medium saucepan until tender. Cool slightly and remove meat from bones. In skillet, heat butter, add onion and brown lightly. Add mushrooms and cook, stirring often, about 3 minutes. Add thyme, salt and pepper and sprinkle with flour. Stir in dove meat and sour cream and cook gently until thickened.

Preheat oven to 450°. Remove dough from refrigerator and roll it to ⅛-inch thickness on lightly floured surface and cut into rounds with 3-inch biscuit cutter. Place a teaspoon of mushroom and dove filling on each and fold the dough over the filling. Press the edges together with a fork. Prick top crusts to allow steam to escape. (May be frozen on cookie sheet, then placed in plastic bag.) Bake 15 minutes.

Yield: 2 dozen tarts

BEAR IN MIND: *Can be made into larger turnovers for an entrée.*

Doves Chasseur

16	doves	⅔	cup white wine
	Salt and pepper to taste	1	(12-ounce) can sliced
	Flour to dredge		mushrooms
8	bacon slices	2	tablespoons butter
⅛	teaspoon hot pepper	1	teaspoon lemon juice
	sauce		Chopped parsley for
4	tablespoons Worcester-		garnish
	shire sauce		

Dry, salt and pepper doves well, inside and out. Dust lightly with flour. In Dutch oven, cook bacon until crisp. Drain and reserve drippings; set bacon aside. Brown doves on all sides in hot bacon grease. Add hot pepper sauce, Worcestershire sauce and wine. Turn breast-side down, cover and cook on low heat 20 minutes. Stir and turn doves breast-side up. Cover and continue cooking 20 minutes. Add more wine if necessary. While doves are cooking, sauté mushrooms lightly in butter and lemon juice. Add mushrooms to doves for last 15 minutes of cooking. Before serving, crumble bacon over doves. Garnish with chopped parsley.

Yield: 8 servings

Lynn's Roasted Goose

1	(8 to 10-pound) goose	Garlic salt to taste
	Salt and freshly ground	
	pepper to taste	

One to two days before serving, wash goose. Salt and pepper inside and out. Rub garlic salt inside and out, then slip in plastic bag and leave 2 days if possible (at least 24 hours) in refrigerator.

When ready to cook, preheat oven to 350°. Remove goose from bag and place in baking pan. Roast uncovered, breast side up. Turn after 1½ hours. Baste with fat in pan and prick with fork to release more fat. Cook until bird is brown all over and the wing pulls away easily from the body.

Yield: 8 to 10 servings

Grilled Venison Roast

10	to 14-pound venison roast	1	teaspoon salt
1	cup oil	2	teaspoons lemon pepper
1	cup vinegar		seasoning
½	cup water	2	teaspoons Worcester-
1	medium onion, chopped		shire sauce
½	teaspoon pepper		

One day before serving, wash roast and place in oblong baking pan. Combine remaining ingredients in medium saucepan and boil until onion is done (looks clear). Pour this mixture over roast, cover and refrigerate overnight. When ready to cook, preheat charcoal grill to high temperature. Place roast on rack and close lid. (Put coals to one end of grill and place roast on opposite end.) Close air vents partially to reduce cooking temperature slightly. Cook 4 to 6 hours or until tests done with meat thermometer.

Yield: 15 to 20 servings

BEAR IN MIND: *You can cook an entire hind-quarter in this manner if it isn't too big.*

Venison Loin Steaks

8	(1 to 1½-inch thick) loin steaks	8	teaspoons margarine Worcestershire sauce
8	bacon slices		to taste

Wrap steaks in bacon slices and place in oblong metal cake pan. Put a pat of margarine on each steak and sprinkle with Worcestershire sauce. Place pan on gas grill over low heat. Cook until bacon begins to sizzle. Close lid and cook 30 to 45 minutes more. Take steaks out of pan and sear over fire. Return steaks to juices in pan until done.

Yield: 8 servings

BEAR IN MIND: *This recipe won the wild game cook-off in Americus.*

"Lazy" Plum Sauce

1 cup plum jam	¼ teaspoon ground ginger
1 tablespoon cider vinegar	(more, if desired)
½ teaspoon allspice	

Combine all ingredients in small saucepan. Bring to a boil over medium-low heat, stirring constantly. Remove from heat and cool. Place in jar and cover. Refrigerate.

Yield: About 1 cup sauce

Make Mine Mint Sauce

¼ cup minced fresh mint leaves	1 teaspoon sugar
¼ cup red wine vinegar	¼ cup water

Combine the minced mint, vinegar, sugar and water. Stir until sugar dissolves. Serve at room temperature.

Yield: ½ cup sauce

BEAR FLAIR: *Serve with lamb, curries or venison.*

Barbecue Sauce for Pork

1 cup strong black coffee	¼ cup lemon juice
1½ cups Worcestershire sauce	2 tablespoons sugar
1 cup ketchup	1 teaspoon red pepper
1 stick butter	

In medium saucepan combine all ingredients. Cook over low heat 20 minutes, stirring occasionally.

Yield: 4 ½ cups sauce

BEAR FLAIR: *Enough sauce for 6 to 8 pork chops or a 6 to 8-pound pork roast.*

Chili Sauce

3	heaping quarts cut up tomatoes, drained	4	bell peppers, chopped
1	quart vinegar	3	hot peppers, chopped
1	quart sugar	1	teaspoon salt
1	quart chopped onions	1	teaspoon celery seed

Mix all ingredients in 8-quart saucepan. Cook slowly 2 hours on simmering heat. Pour into hot, sterilized jars and wipe jar rims. Adjust lids.

Yield: 6 pints

Cajun Barbecue Sauce

1	(1-pound) box light brown sugar	2	(32-ounce) bottles ketchup
1	(6-ounce) jar prepared mustard	½	(12-ounce) bottle Louisiana Hot Sauce
1	(15-ounce) bottle Worcestershire sauce		

Mix brown sugar and mustard until well blended. Add remaining ingredients.

Yield: About ½ gallon sauce

BEAR IN MIND: *This is great with chicken, ribs, anything you grill. Divide in decorative jars, give as gifts.*

Mango Chutney Sauce

1	cup mango chutney	2	tablespoons cornstarch
2	cups cream sherry		

Chop larger chunks of chutney until even consistency. Combine ingredients in small saucepan. Cook over medium heat, stirring constantly until sauce thickens and clears.

Yield: 2½ cups sauce

BEAR FLAIR: *Use this as a glaze for browning ham and the rest to serve at the table.*

Raisin Cider Sauce

¼	cup brown sugar, firmly packed	8	whole cloves or 1 teaspoon powdered cloves
1½	tablespoons cornstarch	1	(2-inch) cinnamon stick or 1 teaspoon ground cinnamon
⅛	teaspoon salt		
1	cup apple cider	1	tablespoon butter
¼	cup raisins		

Combine sugar, cornstarch and salt in small saucepan. Stir in apple cider, raisins, cloves and cinnamon. Cook over medium heat, stirring constantly until thickened. Takes about 10 minutes. Add butter. Remove whole spices if they are used instead of powdered spices. Serve hot with ham or pork dishes.

Yield: About 1 cup sauce

Teriyaki Sauce

½	cup light brown sugar, firmly packed	2	garlic cloves, pressed
		1	cup sherry
¼	teaspoon ground ginger	½	cup soy sauce

Mix all ingredients together. Pour over meat that is to be marinated.

Yield: 2 cups sauce

Horseradish Sauce

1	tablespoon prepared mustard	3	tablespoons lemon juice
		½	teaspoon salt
3	tablespoons prepared horseradish	1	cup sour cream

Mix all ingredients together, cover and refrigerate.

Yield: 1½ cups

BEAR IN MIND:

(1) Great for roast beef sandwiches or as dip for rumaki.

(2) Omit horseradish, add 1 tablespoon fresh finely snipped dill weed, ¼ teaspoon pepper, 2 tablespoons finely snipped chives and ¾ cup coarsely chopped cucumber. This is good for shrimp mousse.

Lemony Dill Sauce for Grilled Meats

3	tablespoons mayonnaise	2	teaspoons snipped fresh
2	tablespoons Dijon-style		dill weed or ½ teaspoon
	mustard		dried dill weed
2	tablespoons lemon juice		

In small bowl stir together mayonnaise, mustard, lemon juice and dill weed. Brush sauce on one side of meat 1 minute before removing from grill. Serve remaining sauce on the side.

Yield: ½ cup sauce, enough for 4 pork chops

BEAR IN MIND: *To grill pork loin chops: Choose chops that are 1½ inches thick. Place chops on an uncovered grill, directly over medium coals for 25 minutes. Turn and grill for 20 to 25 minutes or until no pink remains. Test by cutting in center of chop.*

Ginger Pear Chips

24	cups sliced and peeled pears	4	ounces preserved ginger
8	cups sugar	4	lemons

Core and peel pears. Slice very thinly. Put into large stock pot. Add sugar and ginger. Let stand overnight. Cut lemons into small pieces, removing seeds. Add to pears. Bring to a boil. Reduce heat to medium and boil slowly 3 hours or until thick. Pour into 6 hot, sterilized pint jars. Wipe jar rims. Adjust lids.

Yield: 6 pints

Sweets

"BEARING GIFTS"

*MINIATURE FRUIT CAKES, page 295 or LANE CAKE, page 180 ... bake in miniature muffin tins; garnish with a piped whipped cream "star" and present in a Christmas tin.

*GINGER BEARS, page 307 ... for Christmas gifts, these can't be beat, using the Bear Flair under the recipe.

*MARY'S CHOCOLATE CHIP COOKIES, page 310 ... stack cookies in a covered freeze-dried potato chip can; put a pretty bow on lid.

*LEMON CUSTARD IN MERINGUE CUPS, page 266 ... prepare meringue shells, put in pretty tin. Present as a gift, including a jar of the filling or fresh fruit. Tie with a ribbon and a fresh lemon.

*CHOCOLATE FUDGE SAUCE, page 313, or CARAMEL SAUCE, page 314 ... pour into a glass apothecary jar, add bow and copy of the recipe. Wonderful for teachers' gifts or Christmas Bazaars.

*CHRISTMAS STRAWBERRY DELIGHTS, page 312, are beautiful garnishes, but equally beautiful gifts. Mound strawberries in a small bowl or basket lined with green tissue.

*CRYSTALLIZED VIOLETS, page 265 ... arrange in a lovely crystal or silver bowl, cover with clear wrap and tie with silver ribbon. Elegant! Wonderful as a hostess gift. These are great for garnishing trays or topping whipped cream dollops.

*FRUIT GO-ROUND, page 264 ... give with the pan. Especially nice in the summer when a variety of fruits are abundant.

*TOASTED ALMOND TRUFFLES, page 311, and MACADAMIA NUT TRUF-FLES, page 312 ... place in brandy snifters, cover and decorate with a fancy bow — a most welcomed gift!

*Our best mailing cookies: CHILDREN CAN BEARLY WAIT COOKIES, page 308; LEMON CARAWAY COOKIES, page 308, and BEAR BITES, page 309; place in airtight container in large box; cover bottom of box with popcorn (or for extra fun use "Cracker Jacks" instead of popcorn). Place cookie tin in center. Cover with more popcorn or Jacks. They arrive virtually intact.

"BEAR ESSENTIALS FOR ENTERTAINING"

*For a child's party centerpiece, place BEAR BITES, page 309 and TOASTED ALMOND TRUFFLES, page 311 in a cloth-lined toy such as a sand pail, dump truck or wheelbarrow.

*Fruits such as strawberries, kiwi, banana and fresh cherries with stems are beautiful dipped in chocolate, white or dark. A combination is pretty. Dip whole slices of banana or strawberries and cherries. Dip only half of a slice of kiwi or orange for a neat effect. Lovely as a garnish for cakes or cookie trays.

*To make chocolate leaves, melt ¼ cup semi-sweet chocolate chips and 1 teaspoon shortening, in double boiler over simmering heat, stirring until smooth. Brush onto underside of well-washed and dried leaves. Chill when finished brushing with chocolate. Use camellia, lemon or ivy leaves; the thicker leaves give better results.

*Dust pans for chocolate cake with cocoa instead of flour; keeps "white lumps" away!

*To make chocolate curls, chocolate square should be at room temperature. Carefully pull a vegetable peeler across the broad, flat side of the square. Keep curls chilled until ready to use.

Almond Cheesecake Supreme
heavenly flavor

Crust:

1 cup graham cracker crumbs

½ cup ground almonds, toasted

½ stick butter, melted

2 tablespoons sugar

1 tablespoon almond-flavored liqueur

Cake:

½ (8-ounce) can almond paste, crumbled

½ cup sugar

2 tablespoons all-purpose flour

⅓ cup almond-flavored liqueur

3 (8-ounce) packages cream cheese, softened

4 eggs

Topping:

1 cup sour cream

3 tablespoons almond-flavored liqueur

2 tablespoons sugar

¼ cup sliced unblanched almonds

Preheat oven to 350°. Butter 9-inch springform pan.

For crust: Combine graham cracker crumbs, ground almonds, butter, sugar and liqueur in small bowl. Mix well. Press crumb mixture in bottom and 1½ inches up sides of springform pan. Refrigerate.

For cheesecake: Beat almond paste, sugar and flour in large mixing bowl on low speed until smooth. Beat in liqueur gradually until well-blended. Add cream cheese a third at a time, beating well after each addition. Add eggs one at a time, beating well after each. Pour into crust and bake 50 minutes.

For topping: Combine sour cream, liqueur and sugar in small bowl. Remove cheesecake from oven and spread sour cream mixture evenly over top. Return to oven and bake 25 minutes more or until topping is set. Cool in pan on wire rack 1 hour. Refrigerate at least 6 hours or overnight. Remove sides of pan. Garnish with sliced almonds.

Yield: 16 servings

BEAR IN MIND: *Partially freeze cheesecake before cutting for prettier slices.*

Chocolate Mousse

¾	cup whole milk (do not substitute lowfat or skim milk)	2	eggs
		2	tablespoons orange-flavored liqueur
1	(6-ounce) package semi-sweet chocolate chips	3	tablespoons hot strong coffee

In saucepan, scald milk. Put chocolate chips, eggs and liqueur in blender. Pour coffee and milk over the ingredients. Blend on low a few seconds, then on high 2 minutes. Pour into 4 sherbet/champagne glasses. Chill several hours.

Yield: 4 servings

BEAR IN MIND: *This recipe cannot be doubled, because blender would not be able to whip enough air into liquid.*

Fruit-Go-Round

Crust:

2	sticks butter, softened	1½	cups all-purpose flour
¼	cup brown sugar, firmly packed	¼	cup chopped nuts

Filling:

1	(8-ounce) package cream cheese, softened	1	teaspoon vanilla extract
2	cups powdered sugar	1	(9-ounce) container frozen whipped topping, thawed

Topping:
(Fresh or canned fruit of your choice.)

1	kiwi, peeled and thinly sliced crosswise, then cut circles in half	½	cup halved seedless grapes
		½	cup sliced peaches
6	to 8 large strawberries, sliced lengthwise	½	cup blueberries, optional
			Fresh mint sprigs for garnish

Glaze:

4	tablespoons water or 2 tablespoons water and 2 tablespoons orange-flavored liqueur	1	cup apricot preserves

For crust: Preheat oven to 350°. Lightly grease 12-inch pizza pan. In mixing bowl, cream butter, sugar, flour and nuts. Pat mixture evenly in pan, being sure to include sides of pan. Bake 10 to 15 minutes. Cool completely.

For filling: Beat cream cheese, powdered sugar and vanilla until fluffy. Fold in whipped topping. Spread over cooled crust. Chill. (Can chill up to a day in advance.)

For topping: Arrange fruit over filling in concentric circles, alternating fruit for color and textural interest. With the suggested amounts of fruit, begin with kiwi half circles at outer edge. Then a circle of strawberries, slightly overlapping each other. Next a circle of grape halves, followed by "pinwheel" of peaches. In the center of pan put a whole strawberry or fan-cut strawberry. Add blueberries to fill empty areas.

For glaze: In small saucepan heat water and preserves. Cool slightly. Brush glaze over all fruit. This helps keep fruit from darkening and gives a lovely sheen. Chill.

Yield: 12 to 15 servings

BEAR FLAIR: *Tuck in a few mint sprigs at serving time.*

BEAR IN MIND: *This can be shaped into individual pizzas for special occasions. Amounts, types of fruit selected and method of cutting fruit lends this recipe a lot of creative freedom.*

Crystallized Violets

| 3 | to 4 dozen violets with
1 to 2-inch stems | 1 | egg white |
| | | ½ | cup sugar |

Pick violets just before beginning. Wash by dipping into water and gently pat dry on paper towel. With fork or small whisk, beat egg white until foamy. Using your finger or a brush, lightly and evenly moisten with egg white the upper and underneath portions of each petal. Lightly sprinkle both sides with sugar. Place on paper towel. Continue with the remaining flowers. Put in refrigerator uncovered to dry until brittle, usually 3 to 4 days.

Yield: 3 to 4 dozen violets

BEAR FLAIR: *Use as a garnish for whipped cream dollops or as a candy trim for pudding or custard or other desserts.*

BEAR IN MIND: *Violets will keep 4 to 6 weeks or longer in refrigerator. You can also crystallize roses, johnny-jumpups, sage or mint leaves.*

Lemon Custard in Meringue Cups

Meringue:

3	egg whites	1	teaspoon vanilla extract
⅛	teaspoon salt	¾	cup sugar
½	teaspoon vinegar		

Lemon Custard:

1	cup sugar	1½	cups boiling water
4	tablespoons cornstarch	1	cup Raspberry Sauce
3	egg yolks		(recipe on page 312)
	Juice of 1 large lemon	½	cup sliced almonds,
	(or 2 small)		toasted
½	teaspoon grated lemon rind		

For meringues: Preheat oven to 300°. Prepare cookie sheets with brown paper, lightly oiled. Put egg whites, salt, vinegar and vanilla in mixing bowl and mix on medium speed until soft peaks form. Add sugar slowly and continue beating until stiff peaks form. Spoon into 6 mounds on cookie sheet. Shape into nests or cups. Bake 45 minutes. Do not open oven while meringues dry in oven 3 hours or overnight.

For custard: Combine sugar, cornstarch, egg yolks, lemon juice and rind in saucepan. Add boiling water and bring mixture to a boil, stirring constantly. Boil 1 minute. Cool. Spoon into meringues and serve immediately.

Yield: 6 servings

BEAR FLAIR: *Top with raspberry sauce and toasted sliced almonds or a blueberry glaze, or top with dollops of whipped cream and Crystallized Violets (refer to page 265).*

BEAR IN MIND: *Be sure not to open the oven door for at least 3 hours after baking. Refrigerate custard and store meringues in an airtight container if not to be served right away. Meringues will get soggy if custard is put in too soon.*

Red Wine Strawberry Mousse

1	envelope unflavored gelatin	3	egg whites
½	cup red wine	¼	cup sugar
1	(10-ounce) package frozen strawberries in syrup, thawed	½	pint whipping cream, whipped
⅛	teaspoon salt		Fresh strawberries and whipped cream for garnish

In medium saucepan, sprinkle gelatin over wine. Place over low heat; stir constantly until gelatin dissolves, about 3 minutes. Remove from heat and stir in strawberries and salt. Chill, stirring occasionally, until mixture mounds slightly when dropped from a spoon. Beat egg whites until soft peaks form. Gradually beat in sugar until stiff peaks form. Fold in gelatin mixture and then fold in whipped cream. Spoon mixture into 8 sherbet glasses. Chill until set.

Yield: 6 to 8 servings

BEAR FLAIR: *Put a dollop of whipped cream on each serving topped by a fresh strawberry.*

Strawberries Tiffany

2	pints strawberries	1	cup sour cream
2	tablespoons sugar	2	tablespoons vanilla sugar (see directions below)
2	ounces orange-flavored liqueur or crème de banana		

Wash and stem strawberries. Save 6 to 8 whole strawberries for garnish. Cut remaining strawberries into quarters. Add sugar and liqueur and chill 2 to 5 hours. Mix sour cream and vanilla sugar. Spoon strawberries into serving bowls and top with sour cream mixture. Garnish with whole strawberries.

For vanilla sugar: Split 1 vanilla bean. Scrape insides well and add to ½ cup sugar. Allow flavor to be absorbed at least 1 day in covered container. Will keep indefinitely.

Yield: 6 to 8 servings

Chocolate Raspberry Ring

1 **cup sugar**	2 **tablespoons orange-**
1¼ **cups semi-sweet**	**flavored liqueur**
chocolate chips	1 **teaspoon vanilla**
½ **cup boiling water**	**extract**
4 **large eggs**	2 **sticks unsalted butter, at**
⅛ **teaspoon salt**	**room temperature, divided**

Raspberry Cream:

1 **pint whipping cream**	4 **tablespoons red raspberry**
4 **tablespoons sugar**	**jam**
4 **tablespoons vanilla extract**	

Preheat oven to 350°. Butter 5-cup ring mold. Put sugar and chocolate chips in food processor. Add boiling water and process until chocolate is smooth. Add eggs, salt, liqueur and vanilla. Process until well-blended, stopping machine to scrape down sides. Add butter, a third at a time, processing briefly but thoroughly. Transfer mixture into mold. Place mold into large baking pan and fill pan with 2 inches of hot water. Bake 40 minutes. Remove mold from water and let cool 1 hour on a wire rack. Cover and chill at least 3 hours or up to 4 days. Unmold on platter and spoon raspberry cream in center of dessert ring.

For Raspberry Cream:
In mixing bowl, whip all ingredients until soft peaks form.

Yield: 12 servings

BEAR FLAIR: *A lovely party dessert. Garnish lavishly with piped whipped cream and fresh fruit.*

BEAR IN MIND: *To unmold easily, dip mold quickly into very warm water as you would for unmolding gelatin.*

Chocolate Yogurt Cheesecake

Crust:

1   cup chocolate wafer crumbs (about 20 wafers)

½   stick butter, melted

Cake:

2   (8-ounce) packages cream cheese, softened
1   cup sugar
3   eggs, at room temperature

1½   teaspoons vanilla extract
6   ounces semi-sweet chocolate, melted and cooled
1   cup plain yogurt

Chocolate Glaze:

3   ounces semi-sweet chocolate
2   tablespoons butter

1   tablespoon light corn syrup
½   teaspoon vanilla extract

Preheat oven to 300°.

For crust: Mix crumbs with butter until blended. Press firmly into bottom of 8-inch springform pan. Chill.

For cake: Beat cream cheese and sugar until smooth. Beat in eggs and vanilla. Stir in chocolate and yogurt. Blend well. Pour into crust. Place pan of water on bottom rack of oven. Place cheesecake on middle rack. Bake 1 hour and 20 minutes or until edges pull away slightly. Turn off oven and let cake cool in oven with door ajar. Run thin blade between cake and sides of pan.

For glaze: Melt glaze ingredients in saucepan over medium heat. Remove from heat and cool slightly. Pour over cheese cake. Chill.

Yield: 16 servings

BEAR FLAIR: *This cake is unbearably rich, so serve small portions. Add a fresh pink rose for garnish.*

Lemon-Glazed Cheesecake

Crust:

2 cups graham cracker crumbs	6 tablespoons butter, melted
	2 tablespoons sugar

Cake:

3 (8-ounce) packages cream cheese, softened	¼ cup fresh lemon juice
¾ cup sugar	2 teaspoons grated lemon rind
3 eggs	2 teaspoons vanilla extract

Topping:

2 cups sour cream	1 teaspoon vanilla extract
3 tablespoons sugar	

Glaze:

½ cup sugar	⅓ cup fresh lemon juice
1½ tablespoons cornstarch	1 egg yolk
¼ teaspoon salt	1 tablespoon butter
¾ cup water	1 teaspoon grated lemon rind

Preheat oven to 350°. Butter 9-inch springform pan.

For crust: Combine graham crumbs, melted butter and sugar. Press evenly onto bottom and sides of pan. Bake 5 minutes. Cool.

For cake: Beat cream cheese until soft. Add sugar blending well. Add eggs one at a time, mixing well after each. Mix in lemon juice, rind and vanilla. Pour into pan and bake 35 minutes. While cake is baking combine ingredients for topping. Remove cake from oven and gently spread sour cream topping over cake. Return to oven and bake 12 minutes longer. Cool on rack 30 minutes.

For glaze: In saucepan mix sugar, cornstarch and salt. Add water, lemon juice and egg yolk, stirring to blend. Cook over low heat, stirring constantly, until mixture comes to a slow boil and thickens. Add butter and rind. Cool slightly. Spread glaze evenly over cheesecake. Chill several hours or overnight before removing sides of pan.

Yield: 16 servings

Praline Cheesecake

Crust:

1   cup graham cracker crumbs

3   tablespoons sugar

3   tablespoons margarine, melted

Cake:

3   (8-ounce) packages cream cheese, softened

1¼ cups dark brown sugar, firmly packed

2   tablespoons all-purpose flour

3   eggs

1½ teaspoons vanilla extract

½   cup finely chopped pecans

Topping:

¼   cup maple syrup

Pecan halves, optional

Preheat oven to 350°.

For crust: Combine graham crumbs, sugar and margarine. Press into bottom of 9-inch springform pan. Bake 10 minutes.

For cake: Combine cream cheese, sugar and flour, beating with mixer at medium speed until well-blended. Add eggs one at a time, beating well after each. Add vanilla and chopped pecans. Pour into pan. Bake 50 to 55 minutes. Cool and loosen cake from sides of pan. Chill. Brush with maple syrup and garnish with pecan halves if desired.

Yield: 16 servings

BEAR IN MIND: *To keep cheesecake from cracking while baking put pan of water on bottom rack of oven.*

Banana Split Supreme

2 cups graham cracker crumbs	1 (12-ounce) container frozen whipped topping, thawed
3 sticks margarine, divided	½ cup chocolate syrup
6 bananas, sliced	Maraschino cherries to garnish
2 cups powdered sugar	Chopped nuts to garnish
2 eggs	
1 teaspoon vanilla extract	
1 (20-ounce) can crushed pineapple, drained	

Combine cracker crumbs and one stick melted margarine until mixed and line 9x13-inch pan. Cover crumb mixture with sliced bananas. Beat powdered sugar, eggs, vanilla and two sticks margarine until well-mixed (mixture will be stiff). Spread mixture over bananas. Spread drained pineapple over creamed mixture and cover with whipped topping. Drizzle chocolate syrup over whipped topping and garnish with cherries and chopped nuts. Chill.

Yield: 16 servings

BEAR IN MIND: *Try filling two 9-inch graham cracker pie crusts.*

Outa Sight Dessert

1½ cups all-purpose flour	1 (21-ounce) can lemon pie filling (or any flavor)
1½ cups chopped pecans or almonds	1 (20-ounce) can crushed pineapple, well-drained
1½ sticks margarine	1 (9-ounce) container frozen whipped topping, thawed
1 (14-ounce) can sweetened condensed milk	

Preheat oven to 350°. Mix flour, nuts and margarine with pastry blender. Pat into 9x13-inch pan. Bake 15 minutes. Cool completely. Mix remaining ingredients in large bowl. Pour over baked crust. Chill overnight.

Yield: 12 to 18 servings

BEAR FLAIR: *Garnish with lemon slices or Crystallized Violets (refer to page 265). If using strawberry pie filling, for garnish, cut fresh whole strawberries into fan shapes by slicing almost all the way through at stem end and all the way through pointed end.*

Chocolate Peppermint Delight

1½ cups vanilla wafer
    crumbs, divided
1¼ sticks margarine
2   ounces unsweetened
    chocolate
2   eggs, separated
2   cups powdered sugar
1   teaspoon vanilla extract

½   cup chopped pecans
    (or more)
½   gallon peppermint
    ice cream, softened to
    room temperature
    Whipped cream to garnish
    Crushed peppermint candy
    to garnish

Cover bottom of ungreased 9x13-inch baking pan with 1 cup crumbs.
Melt margarine and chocolate together; set aside. Beat egg yolks and add
powdered sugar, chocolate mixture and vanilla, beating until smooth.
Beat egg whites until stiff and fold into chocolate mixture. Add pecans.
Spread over crumbs in pan. Spread softened ice cream on top. Freeze,
then sprinkle on remaining crumbs. Top with whipped cream and crushed
peppermint candy. Store in freezer.

Yield: 10 to 12 servings

BEAR IN MIND: *A refreshing warm weather dessert ready in the freezer.
If you have trouble finding peppermint ice cream, use vanilla ice cream
and 10 ounces ground peppermint candy combined in food processor.
Or use the Easy Peppermint Ice Cream recipe in this section.*

Fudge Coffee Ice Cream Bars

2½ cups crushed vanilla
    wafers, divided
3   ounces unsweetened
    chocolate
1   stick margarine

2   cups powdered sugar
4   eggs, separated
1   cup coarsely chopped
    pecans
½   gallon coffee ice cream

Line 9x13-inch pan with 1¾ cups crumbs. Melt chocolate and margarine.
Stir in sugar; set aside. Beat egg yolks and stir into chocolate mixture.
Beat egg whites stiff and fold into chocolate mixture. Pour over crumbs.
Top with pecans. Freeze solid (overnight). Soften ice cream. Spread over
chocolate layer and top with remaining crumbs. Cover with foil and
freeze. To serve, cut in 2½ x 2 ¼-inch bars.

Yield: 20 servings

BEAR IN MIND: *May freeze as long as 6 months.*

Bisque Tortoni Mold

⅓ cup water	2½ teaspoons almond extract, divided
1 cup sugar	2 cups whipping cream
4 egg whites, room temperature	1 teaspoon vanilla extract
⅛ teaspoon salt	Whipped cream to garnish
¾ cup whole blanched almonds, divided	Fresh Bing cherries to garnish

Preheat oven to 350°. Combine water with sugar in 1-quart saucepan. Cook over low heat, stirring until sugar is dissolved. Boil over medium heat uncovered and without stirring to 236° (use candy thermometer). Meanwhile, beat egg whites with salt until stiff peaks form. Pour hot syrup in thin stream over egg whites, beating constantly until mixture forms very stiff peaks. Cover and chill 30 minutes.

Place almonds in shallow pan and bake about 10 minutes until toasted. Grind almonds finely in blender or processor. Reserve ¼ cup ground almonds for garnish. Add 2 teaspoons almond extract to remaining almonds; set aside.

In medium bowl, beat whipping cream with ½ teaspoon almond extract and vanilla until stiff. With wire whisk or rubber spatula fold cream mixture into egg whites. Add almond mixture and thoroughly combine. Spoon into 1½-quart mold or bowl. Cover with foil. Freeze until firm or overnight.

To unmold, run small spatula around edge of mold. Dip quickly into hot water. Invert on serving dish. Sprinkle with reserved ground almonds. Return to freezer until serving.

Yield: 8 to 10 servings

BEAR FLAIR: *Pipe whipped cream around outer edge. Add Bing cherries as desired.*

BEAR IN MIND: *This can be made several days ahead. Just wrap mold in freezer wrap.*

Frozen Tarts

1 (8-ounce) package cream cheese	1 teaspoon vanilla extract
1 cup powdered sugar	2½ cups frozen whipped topping, thawed

Blend all ingredients except whipped topping in food processor. Fold in whipped topping. Place in paper liners in muffin tins and freeze.

Yield: 12 servings

Frozen Champagne Cream in Chocolate Cups

Chocolate cups:

1 (6-ounce) package semi-sweet chocolate chips	8 fluted paper cupcake liners

Champagne cream:

¾ cup champagne, divided	5 egg yolks
½ cup sugar	1½ cups whipping cream

To prepare chocolate cups: Partially melt chocolate in top of double boiler over hot, not boiling water. When chocolate is about half-melted, remove from heat and let stand to melt completely. Dip small brush into chocolate and "paint" inside of cupcake liners. Build up sides thickly or cups will break when paper is removed. Invert on baking sheet and chill until hardened. Carefully peel off paper. Keep cool.

To prepare champagne cream: Combine ½ cup champagne with sugar in small saucepan and bring to boil over medium-high heat. Continue boiling without stirring until syrup registers 236° (soft ball stage) on candy thermometer. Beat egg yolks in large bowl until light and lemon-colored. When syrup has reached 236° add to beaten yolks in a steady stream, beating constantly until mixture is thick and creamy, about 10 minutes. Gradually blend in remaining champagne. Chill until mixture is thick, but not stiff. Whip cream in chilled bowl until stiff. Fold into champagne mixture. Cover bowl and freeze overnight. When ready to serve, spoon champagne cream into chocolate cups. Serve immediately!

Yield: 8 servings

BEAR FLAIR: *A bit of trouble, but worth it for a special occasion. Garnish with Crystallized Violets, page 265.*

BEAR IN MIND: *Purchased chocolate cups may be used instead of making your own.*

Mango Sorbet

A beautiful and delicious dish!

2	large ripe mangoes, peeled and cut into 2-inch chunks
¼	cup water
¼	cup orange juice
3	tablespoons fresh lemon juice
1	teaspoon grated lemon rind
⅓	cup sugar
2	kiwi, peeled
	Mint sprigs or lemon balm sprigs for garnish

Process mango chunks until smooth, using pulse method at first. Add water, orange juice, lemon juice, rind and sugar. Process until well-blended, about 30 seconds. Pour mixture into shallow tray or pan. Cover. Freeze until solid, overnight. Remove mango mixture from freezer. Break into small pieces and process half the mixture at a time until smooth. Place mixture in freezer container and freeze at least 12 hours. When ready to serve, slice kiwi. Place 1 slice in bottom of serving dish. Add a scoop of sorbet. Garnish with mint or lemon balm sprig.

Yield: 4 to 6 servings

BEAR IN MIND:
   (1) Papaya (or most any fruit) can be substituted for mango.
   (2) Sorbet needs to be at room temperature about 20 minutes before serving.

 Orange Ice

1	cup sugar
1	cup water
½	cup corn syrup
2	cups fresh orange juice
	Juice of 2 lemons
2	egg whites
	Whipped cream and orange slices for garnish

Boil sugar and water 5 minutes. Add corn syrup and juices. Mix well, put in container and freeze until hard. Remove and beat egg whites and frozen ice until fluffy. Serve immediately, topped with whipped cream and orange slices.

Yield: Approximately ½ gallon

 **Easy Peppermint Ice Cream**

8	ounces peppermint stick candy	2	cups milk
		1	pint whipping cream

Crush candy and soak 12 hours in milk. Add cream. Freeze mixture in covered container. Serve with hot Chocolate Fudge Sauce, page 313, if desired.

Yield: 1½ quarts

BEAR IN MIND: *Use this recipe when making Chocolate Peppermint Delight, page 273.*

Apples Amaretty

9	firm cooking apples, peeled and cored	1	teaspoon cinnamon
⅓	cup almond-flavored liqueur	½	teaspoon nutmeg
		½	teaspoon salt
½	cup granulated sugar	1½	sticks cold butter
1½	cups all-purpose flour	1½	cups chopped pecans, toasted
1½	cups brown sugar, firmly packed		Whipped cream to garnish

Preheat oven to 375°. Slice apples and place in 9x13-inch baking dish. Sprinkle with liqueur and granulated sugar. In separate bowl mix flour, brown sugar, cinnamon, nutmeg, salt and butter until crumb-like texture. Sprinkle crumb topping over apples. Sprinkle pecans over crumb topping. Bake 50 minutes.

Yield: 14 servings

BEAR FLAIR: *Good served warm with whipped cream or ice cream.*

BEAR IN MIND: *Brandy may be substituted for almond-flavored liqueur.*

Chinese Almond Torte

2	eggs	2	teaspoons almond extract
1½	cups sugar	½	cup slivered almonds
¼	cup all-purpose flour, sifted	1	medium apple,
2½	teaspoons baking powder		finely chopped
¼	teaspoon salt		

Preheat oven to 350°. Lightly grease and flour 8-inch square pan. Beat eggs until light and fluffy. Gradually add sugar and beat until thick and lemon-colored. Sift together flour, baking powder and salt. Add egg mixture to flour mixture. Add almond extract, nuts and apple, folding gently. Pour batter into pan. Bake 25 to 30 minutes.

Yield: 4 to 6 servings

Date and Nut Pudding

1	cup finely chopped dates, coated with flour	1	teaspoon baking powder
1	cup chopped nuts	3	eggs, separated
¾	cup sugar	1	teaspoon vanilla extract
¼	teaspoon salt		Whipped cream and sherry for garnish
5	tablespoons all-purpose flour		

Preheat oven to 275°. Grease and flour 9-inch square pan. In large mixing bowl, combine dates, nuts, sugar and salt. Add flour and baking powder. Beat egg yolks in separate bowl. Stir into date mixture and add vanilla. Mix lightly with fork. Beat egg whites until stiff. Fold into date mixture. Pour into pan. Bake 1 hour.

Yield: 6 to 8 servings

BEAR FLAIR: *Flavor whipped cream with sherry to taste. Dollop on each serving.*

BEAR IN MIND: *A super holiday dessert. A variation of traditional plum pudding.*

Chocolate Éclairs

Cream Puff Pastry:

½ cup water
½ stick butter

½ cup all-purpose flour
2 eggs

Custard Filling:

⅓ cup plus 1 tablespoon sugar
¼ cup plus 1 tablespoon all-purpose flour

Dash salt
1½ cups milk
2 egg yolks, beaten
1½ teaspoons vanilla extract

Frosting:

½ ounce unsweetened chocolate
1 teaspoon butter

½ cup powdered sugar
1 tablespoon boiling water

For pastry: Preheat oven to 400°. In saucepan, heat water and butter until butter melts. Quickly stir in flour over low heat until it forms a ball (about 1 minute). Remove from heat, cool slightly, beat in eggs one at a time. Beat until smooth. Shape into 6 "fingers" about 4 inches long and 1-inch wide. Bake 45 to 50 minutes or until puffed, golden brown and "dry". Cool. Cut off tops, scoop out filaments of soft dough. Fill with custard, replace top and frost.

For custard filling: Mix sugar, flour and salt. Stir in milk. Cook in saucepan over medium heat, stirring until it boils. Boil 1 minute. Remove from heat. Stir half this mixture into beaten eggs. Then blend egg mixture into remaining hot mixture. Bring to a boil stirring constantly, until mixture thickens. Cool and stir in vanilla. Fill éclairs.

For frosting: Melt chocolate and butter in double boiler. Remove from heat. Blend in sugar and water. Beat only until smooth, not stiff. Drizzle over éclairs.

Yield: 6 servings

BEAR IN MIND:

(1) Unbaked pastry may be piped into round shapes for cream puffs.
(2) Can also substitute vanilla pudding mix for the custard recipe.
(3) Cooked pastry shells are wonderful filled with sweetened whipped cream or ice cream and garnished with fresh strawberries.

Kolacky

Pastry:

2 packages dry yeast
1 tablespoon granulated sugar
1 cup lukewarm milk
2 sticks butter
3 tablespoons powdered sugar

¼ tablespoon grated lemon rind
½ teaspoon salt
   Pinch mace
6 eggs, separated
4 cups sifted all-purpose flour, divided

Prune filling:

1¾ cups prunes
½ cup sugar
1 tablespoon lemon juice

1 tablespoon grated lemon rind

Apricot filling:

1¾ cups chopped dried apricots
½ cup sugar
1 tablespoon orange juice

1 tablespoon grated orange rind

Cheese filling:

16 ounces dried cottage cheese
2 egg yolks
½ teaspoon salt

1 teaspoon grated lemon rind
1 cup powdered sugar
4 tablespoons butter
½ cup raisins

For pastry: Grease cookie sheet. Dissolve yeast and granulated sugar in milk. Set aside. Cream butter and powdered sugar. Add lemon rind, salt and mace. Beat in egg yolks, one at a time. Stir 1½ cups flour into yeast mixture and beat into creamed mixture. Beat egg whites slightly. Add to batter. Stir in remaining flour. Put batter into greased bowl. Cover. Let dough rise in warm place until doubled in bulk. Gently punch down and roll out on floured surface to ¼-inch thickness. Cut with 2-inch cookie cutter, dipped in flour each time. Place on cookie sheet. Let rise until doubled in size. Preheat oven to 350°. Press three finger tips into each "tart" to make indentations for fillings. Bake 10 minutes. (Do not allow them to brown.) Fill tarts with prune, apricot or cheese filling.

For prune filling: Cook prunes in small amount of water, about 30 minutes or until tender. Cool and drain. Remove pits and chop fine. Add sugar, lemon juice and rind. Blend well. Fill tarts.

For apricot filling: Cook apricots in small amount of water. Cool and drain. Add sugar, orange juice and rind. Blend well. Fill tarts.

For cheese filling: Combine dried cottage cheese (for directions on how to "dry" cheese, see Cheese Blintzes, page 61), egg yolks, salt, lemon rind, sugar and butter. Beat well. Add raisins. Fill tarts.

Yield: 9 to 10 dozen

BEAR IN MIND: *May use canned filling of your choice.*

Filled Butterhorns

Pastry:

2	cups all-purpose flour	2	tablespoons warm water
1½	teaspoons granulated sugar	¼	cup sour cream, heated and cooled
½	teaspoon salt	2	egg yolks
1	stick butter		Powdered sugar
1	package dry yeast		

Filling:

2	egg whites	¼	teaspoon almond extract
½	cup sugar	½	cup finely chopped pecans
¼	teaspoon vanilla extract		

For pastry: Mix flour, sugar and salt. Cut in butter with pastry blender or 2 knives. Sprinkle yeast on water in small bowl. Let stand a few minutes, stir to dissolve. Blend sour cream with egg yolks, add yeast and mix. Stir into flour mixture and blend well. Cover and chill at least 3 hours, but not more than 24 hours. Remove from refrigerator and let stand until soft enough to handle. Preheat oven to 375°. Divide dough into 4 equal parts. Shape one section at a time into a ball, roll out on surface sprinkled with powdered sugar. Roll out from center to form an 8-inch circle. Cut each circle into 8 wedges. Cover each wedge not quite to edges with filling. Roll up from curved edge to point. Put on baking sheet, point side up. Bake 15 to 20 minutes. Cool and store in airtight container.

For filling: May be prepared while dough is coming to room temperature. Beat egg whites until stiff peaks are formed. Gradually add sugar and the extracts. Fold in chopped nuts.

Yield: 32 butterhorns

BEAR FLAIR: *Good with vanilla ice cream and Raspberry Sauce, page 312.*

BEAR IN MIND: *Almonds may be used instead of pecans.*

🐾 Plum Pudding

1	cup raisins	¼	cup chopped lemon rind
½	cup currants	¼	cup chopped citron
1½	cups water	½	cup chopped peeled apple
1	cup ground suet	2½	tablespoons chopped crystallized ginger
1½	cups finely-crumbled dry bread crumbs	¼	cup chopped dried figs
¾	cup all-purpose flour	¼	cup chopped blanched almonds
⅔	cup sugar		Juice and rind of 1 orange
¾	teaspoon cinnamon		Juice and rind of ½ lemon
½	teaspoon nutmeg	2	cups brandy, divided
½	teaspoon salt	6	eggs, beaten
¼	teaspoon cloves	8	to 10 sugar cubes, soaked in lemon extract, for garnish
¼	teaspoon mace		
¼	cup chopped preserved orange rind		

Steam raisins and currants in 1½ cups boiling water until plump, drain well. In large bowl, mix suet, bread crumbs, flour, sugar, cinnamon, nutmeg, salt, cloves, mace, orange rind, lemon rind, citron, apple, ginger, figs and almonds, then add juices and 1 cup brandy. Blend well. Cover bowl and refrigerate 6 to 8 days. Each day add 2 tablespoons brandy and toss mixture.

On the day pudding is to be served, stir eggs into batter and pack firmly into 2 buttered (7-cup) molds. Cover molds tightly and steam in water bath 5 hours. When ready to serve, place on platter, surrounding base with Hard Sauce. Place sugar cubes soaked in lemon extract on top and ignite.

Yield: 12 to 18 servings

🐾 Hard Sauce

1	stick butter		Pinch salt
1½	cups powdered sugar	2	tablespoons brandy

Cream butter and sugar until light and fluffy. Add salt and brandy. Serve over plum pudding. Store remainder in refrigerator.

Yield: 2 cups

Perfect Pie Pastry

If you can't make pie pastry, you need this recipe!

4	cups all-purpose flour	½	cup water
1	tablespoon sugar	1	tablespoon vinegar
2	teaspoons salt	1	egg
1¾	cups shortening		

Combine flour, sugar and salt in large bowl. Add shortening. Mix well with 2 knives until crumbly. May be mixed in food processor. In small bowl, beat together water, vinegar and egg. Combine the two mixtures, stirring with a fork until all ingredients are moistened. Divide dough into 5 portions. Shape each portion into flat round patty with hands. Wrap each patty in plastic wrap and chill at least 1 hour before rolling out. May also freeze wrapped dough patty at this point for later use.

Yield: 5 pie crusts

BEAR IN MIND: *To avoid sogginess on bottom pie crust, prick with a fork and brush with egg white.*

Judy's Apple Kuchen

2	cups all-purpose flour	1	teaspoon cinnamon
¼	teaspoon salt	¾	cup sugar
¼	teaspoon baking powder	2	egg yolks
1	stick margarine	1	cup sour cream
3	tablespoons sugar		
1	(20-ounce) can pie sliced apples		

Preheat oven to 400°. Mix flour, salt, baking powder, margarine and sugar. Press into bottom and two-thirds of the way up sides of 9-inch baking dish. Top with apples. Mix cinnamon and sugar. Sprinkle over apples. Bake 15 minutes at 400°. Remove from oven. Lower oven temperature to 350°. Mix together egg yolks and sour cream. Pour over apples. Bake 40 minutes.

Yield: 6 to 9 servings

BEAR IN MIND: *Add grated cheese to taste to crust of any apple pie.*

Blueberry Torte

1	(8-ounce) package cream cheese, softened	¾	cup water
2	eggs	½	cup sugar
1	cup sugar	3	tablespoons cornstarch
1	(9 or 10-inch) graham cracker crust	2	cups blueberries

Preheat oven to 375°. Beat cream cheese with eggs and sugar until smooth. Pour into crust and bake 20 to 25 minutes. Mix water, sugar and cornstarch in saucepan. Cook over low heat until thickened. Add blueberries, heating through. Cool. Pour on top of cream cheese mixture. Chill.

Yield: 8 servings

BEAR IN MIND: *Frozen blueberries may be used as well as fresh.*

Brownie Tarts

1	stick butter, softened	2	tablespoons butter
1	(3-ounce) package cream cheese	2	eggs, beaten
1	cup all-purpose flour	⅔	cup sugar
4	ounces semi-sweet chocolate	½	teaspoon vanilla extract
			Pinch salt
		½	cup chopped pecans

Preheat oven to 350°. Spray miniature muffin tins with vegetable spray.

Cream butter in large bowl with cream cheese until light and fluffy. Add flour and continue mixing until well-blended. (Butter, cream cheese and flour may be blended in food processor.) Process until dough forms a ball. Wrap and refrigerate a few hours.

Melt chocolate and butter in double boiler. Remove from heat. Add eggs, sugar, vanilla and salt. Mix well and set aside. Press a rounded teaspoonful of dough into bottom and sides of miniature muffin tins. Sprinkle nuts on pastry in each cup. Spoon in chocolate mixture. Bake 30 minutes. Remove from pans. Cool.

Yield: 32 tarts

Chocolate Meringue Pie

1	cup sugar	½	teaspoon vanilla extract
⅓	cup all-purpose flour	1	teaspoon butter
⅓	cup cocoa	1	(9-inch) pastry shell,
	Dash salt		baked
2	egg yolks	4	egg whites
2	cups milk	6	to 8 tablespoons sugar

Preheat oven to 350°. Sift together sugar, flour, cocoa and salt. Set aside. Beat egg yolks. Combine beaten egg yolks and milk. Cook sugar, flour, cocoa mixture in top of double boiler. Gradually add egg and milk to mixture. Stir constantly until thickened. Remove from heat and add vanilla and butter. Let cool. Pour mixture into baked pastry shell. Beat 4 egg whites, gradually adding 6 to 8 teaspoons sugar. Beat until stiff peaks form. Spread meringue on top of chocolate mixture and seal edges. Bake 15 minutes or until a delicate brown.

Yield: 6 to 8 servings

French Silk Tarts

1	stick plus 2 tablespoons butter, softened	3	eggs
		12	(3-inch) pastry shells,
2	tablespoons oil		baked or individual
1	cup sugar		graham cracker shells
6	tablespoons cocoa		Whipped cream, optional
1½	teaspoons vanilla extract		Chopped pecans or
¼	teaspoon almond extract		almonds, optional

Combine butter, oil and sugar. Cream until light and fluffy. Add cocoa, then flavorings. Add eggs, one at a time, beating 5 minutes after adding each egg. Chill mixture 1 to 2 hours. Spoon into tart shells. Top with whipped cream. Add nuts if desired.

Yield: 12 tarts

Grapefruit Meringue Pie

6	tablespoons cornstarch	1½	teaspoons grated grapefruit rind
1½	cups sugar		
¼	teaspoon salt	1	tablespoon butter
½	cup cold water	1	(8 or 9-inch) pastry shell, baked
2	cups fresh grapefruit juice (about 3 medium grapefruit)		
		3	egg whites
		¼	teaspoon cream of tartar
3	egg yolks	6	tablespoons sugar

Preheat oven to 350°. Mix cornstarch, sugar and salt in large saucepan. Stir in water and grapefruit juice. Cook over medium heat, stirring constantly, until mixture comes to a boil. Cook 5 minutes, stirring constantly. Remove from heat. In small bowl, beat egg yolks until well-mixed. Gradually stir into yolks a small amount of hot grapefruit mixture. Then stir egg yolks into remaining hot mixture and cook another 2 minutes, stirring constantly. Stir in grapefruit rind and butter. Cool 10 minutes. Turn into pastry shell.

Beat egg whites with cream of tartar until frothy. Gradually beat in sugar 1 tablespoon at a time. Beat until stiff enough to hold sharp points. Spoon over grapefruit filling in pastry shell and spread so that it touches edges of crust. Bake 12 to 15 minutes, until lightly browned.

Yield: 6 to 8 servings

 # Lemon Pie

2	tablespoons cornstarch		Rind of 2 lemons
1½	cups sugar, divided	⅔	cup cold water
	Pinch salt	1	(9-inch) pastry shell, unbaked
2	whole eggs		
4	eggs, separated	¼	teaspoon cream of tartar
½	cup lemon juice		

Preheat oven to 450°. Mix cornstarch, 1 cup sugar and salt together. Beat well 2 whole eggs and 4 yolks; add to the sugar and cornstarch mixture. Add lemon juice, lemon rinds and water. Stir well. Pour in unbaked pastry shell; bake 10 to 12 minutes. Reduce heat to 300° and bake until pie is set about 20 to 25 minutes. Whip 4 egg whites with salt until foamy, add cream of tartar and beat until blended. Beat in remaining sugar gradually, beating until stiff. Spread meringue over pie and bake 20 minutes.

Yield: 6 to 8 servings

Kiwi Lime Pie

¾ cup sugar
⅓ cup all-purpose flour
⅛ teaspoon salt
1¾ cups milk
3   eggs, beaten
½ stick butter
2   teaspoons grated lime rind
¼ cup lime juice
1   cup lemon yogurt

2   to 3 drops green food coloring
1   (8 or 9-inch) pastry shell, baked
½ pint whipping cream, whipped
2   to 3 kiwi, peeled and sliced
1   to 2 limes, sliced

Combine sugar, flour and salt in medium saucepan. Stir in milk, cooking until thickened and bubbly. Reduce heat; cook and stir 2 minutes more. Remove from heat. Stir 1 cup of hot mixture into eggs. Pour egg mixture into saucepan; cook and stir until thickened. Cook and stir 2 minutes more. Do not boil. Remove from heat. Stir in butter, lime rind and juice. Fold in yogurt. Tint with food coloring. Cover with clear plastic wrap. Cool. Spread lime filling into baked shell. Chill overnight. Pipe whipped cream in a circle on top of pie. Alternate slices of kiwi and lime in the whipped cream circle. Keep chilled until serving.

Yield: 6 to 8 servings

Out of this World Pie

1   (20-ounce) can tart cherries (packed in water)
2   (8½-ounce) cans crushed pineapple
1   cup sugar
⅓ cup all-purpose flour
1   (3-ounce) package orange-flavored gelatin

1   teaspoon vanilla extract
1   cup chopped nuts
9   bananas, sliced
3   graham cracker crusts
    Whipping cream for garnish, optional

Drain cherries and pineapple. Reserve juice. In saucepan, combine fruit juices, sugar and flour. Boil until thickened. Add gelatin. Stir until dissolved. Cool. Add vanilla, nuts, bananas, cherries and pineapple. Pour into crusts. Chill or freeze. May be served with whipped cream dollops as garnish.

Yield: 3 pies (1 to eat, 1 to give, 1 to freeze)

BEAR FLAIR: *Add a crystallized violet to whipped cream dollops for special occasions. See page 265.*

Soda Cracker Peach Pie

3	egg whites	½	pint whipping cream
1	cup sugar	1	(16-ounce) can sliced
12	saltine crackers, crushed		peaches, drained,
¼	teaspoon baking powder		or 2 cups fresh peaches,
1	teaspoon vanilla extract		sweetened to taste
1	cup chopped pecans		

Preheat oven to 350°. Coat 9-inch pie plate with cooking spray. Beat egg whites until soft peaks form. Add sugar 1 tablespoon at a time, beating after each addition. Beat until stiff peaks form. Add cracker crumbs, baking powder, vanilla and pecans. Spread in bottom and up sides of pie pan. Bake 30 minutes. Cool. Whip cream. Alternate layers of whipped cream and peaches in pastry shell. Chill 1 to 2 hours.

Yield: 6 to 8 servings

BEAR IN MIND: *This soda cracker "crust" can be the basis for a multitude of fruit fillings.*

Peanut Butter Pie

1	(8-ounce) package cream cheese, softened	¾	cup powdered sugar
1	(9-ounce) container frozen whipped topping	1	(9-inch) graham cracker crust
¾	cup crunchy-style peanut butter		Whipped topping and crushed peanuts for garnish

Thoroughly mix all ingredients. Spoon into graham cracker crust. Chill. Top each slice with whipped topping and crushed peanuts.

Yield: 6 to 8 servings

Coffee Pecan Pie

1 egg, separated, room temperature	¼ cup boiling water
¼ teaspoon salt	2 cups miniature marshmallows
¼ cup sugar	1 teaspoon almond extract
1½ cups finely chopped pecans	1 pint whipping cream, divided
1 tablespoon instant coffee	Grated chocolate, optional

Preheat oven to 400°. Grease 8-inch pie plate. Combine egg white and salt; beat until stiff but not dry. Gradually beat in sugar, then fold in pecans. Spread into pie plate and prick with fork. Bake 12 minutes, then cool. In saucepan, dissolve coffee in boiling water, add marshmallows. Place over medium heat until marshmallows melt. Beat egg yolk; slowly add marshmallow mixture, beating constantly until mixture begins to set. Stir in almond extract. Whip ½ pint whipping cream and fold into filling. Spoon mixture over crust. Chill. Whip remaining cream. Spread over top of chilled pie. Garnish with grated chocolate if desired.

Yield: 6 to 8 servings

BEAR IN MIND: *This is better if made a day ahead.*

Date Pecan Pie

3 egg whites	½ cup chopped dates
1 cup sugar	1 teaspoon vanilla extract
½ cup graham cracker crumbs	Whipped cream or frozen whipped topping
1 cup chopped pecans	

Preheat oven to 350°. Butter 9-inch glass pie plate. Beat egg whites until stiff, gradually adding sugar while beating. Fold in graham cracker crumbs, then pecans, then dates and vanilla. Spread mixture evenly into pie plate and bake 30 minutes. Serve warm with whipped topping.

Yield: 6 to 8 servings

Sour Cream Pecan Pie

4	eggs, separated
2	cups sugar
2	cups sour cream
½	cup all-purpose flour
½	teaspoon lemon extract
¼	teaspoon salt

½	cup brown sugar, firmly packed, then sifted
2	cups chopped pecans
2	(9-inch) pastry shells, baked

Preheat oven to 325°. In top of double boiler, combine egg yolks, sugar, sour cream, flour, lemon extract and salt. Cook over simmering water until thickened, stirring with whisk. Spoon mixture into baked pastry shells. Beat egg whites, until frothy, then add brown sugar gradually. Stir in nuts. Spread over pie filling. Bake until light brown, about 15 minutes.

Yield: 12 to 16 servings

BEAR FLAIR: *For a simple garnish, sprinkle finely chopped pecans on top of "meringue" around the circumference of pie, before baking.*

French Strawberry Pie

1	(3-ounce) package cream cheese
3	tablespoons half and half
1	(9-inch) pastry shell, baked
1	quart strawberries, divided

1	cup sugar
2	tablespoons cornstarch
2	drops lemon juice
½	pint whipped cream, sweetened, for garnish

Blend cream cheese and half and half until soft. Spread this mixture over cooled pastry shell. Wash and hull berries. Select half of the best ones, slicing the larger ones in half and set aside. Add sugar to remaining strawberries and let stand until juicy. Mash sugared strawberries thoroughly and mix with cornstarch. Add lemon juice. Cook until mixture is thick and transparent, stirring constantly. Cool and pour half over cream cheese. Arrange remaining berries on this and pour remaining half of filling over berries; chill overnight. Serve topped with whipped cream.

Yield: 6 servings

BEAR IN MIND: *The longer this is refrigerated, the better.*

Surprise Pie

1	(14-ounce) can sweetened condensed milk	½	pint whipping cream, whipped and sweetened or 1 (8-ounce) carton frozen whipped topping
1	graham cracker crust		
2	firm bananas, not too ripe		
1	cup chopped pecans		

Place unopened can of sweetened condensed milk, with label removed, in large pan filled with water to cover can. Cook on medium to medium-low heat (simmer) 3 hours, making sure can is always submerged under water. (Do not cover pan with lid.) Let can cool before opening. Line crust with banana slices. Mix nuts with can of cooked milk and pour over bananas, chill and top with sweetened whipped cream. Keep chilled.

Yield: 6 to 8 servings

BEAR IN MIND: *You must be sure water is kept at a simmering boil to be sure the condensed milk will caramelize. Check water level every 20 minutes to be sure can is covered with water.*

Luscious Ice Cream Pie

½	cup butter, melted	½	pint whipping cream
7	ounces flaked coconut	¼	cup powdered sugar
2	tablespoons all-purpose flour		Chocolate curls to garnish
½	cup chopped pecans	½	to ⅔ cup almond-flavored liqueur
½	gallon chocolate ice cream, softened		

Preheat oven to 375°. Combine butter, coconut, flour and pecans. Mix well and press on bottom and sides of 10-inch pie plate. Bake 10 to 12 minutes. Cool. Spoon softened ice cream into pie shell and freeze until firm. Beat whipping cream until slightly thickened. Add sugar, gradually beating until soft peaks form. Spread over frozen pie. Top with chocolate curls. Pour 1 tablespoon almond-flavored liqueur over each serving.

Yield: 6 to 8 servings

BEAR FLAIR: *To make chocolate curls, use vegetable peeler to shave off room temperature chocolate into "curls". Chill. Garnish pie.*

BEAR IN MIND: *Substitute coffee ice cream and coffee-flavored liqueur.*

Chocoholic Cake

Cake:

2 cups sugar	2 teaspoons vanilla extract
½ cup cocoa	2 eggs
1½ cups butter-flavored shortening	2 cups self-rising flour
	1½ cups milk

Frosting:

¾ cup butter-flavored shortening	1 teaspoon rum extract
6 tablespoons cocoa	½ teaspoon maple extract
1 egg white	½ teaspoon salt
1 teaspoon vanilla extract	1 (1-pound) box powdered sugar

For cake: Preheat oven to 350°. Grease and flour 4 (9-inch) cake pans. In mixing bowl combine sugar, cocoa and shortening. Cream well. Stir in vanilla. Beat in eggs, one at a time. Beat until light and fluffy. Add alternately flour and milk, blending well. Divide batter equally between pans and bake 30 to 35 minutes. Cool 10 minutes in pans. Remove. Let cool completely.

For frosting: Combine shortening and cocoa. Whip in egg white. Add extracts and salt. Add powdered sugar, beating until light and fluffy. May need to add tablespoon or two of milk to make spreadable. Frost cake.

Yield: 10 to 12 servings

BEAR IN MIND:
(1) Butter or margarine may be used instead of shortening if desired.
(2) For a different touch, smooth frosting on top and using any shape stencil or paper doily, sift powdered sugar over. Remove stencil. This is also pretty on cheesecakes or light-colored frosted cakes using cocoa.

Hot Fudge Cake

Cake:

1½ cups sugar	1 teaspoon salt
½ cup shortening	1½ cups buttermilk
2 eggs	1 teaspoon vanilla extract
2 cups cake flour	½ to ¾ gallon vanilla
⅔ cup cocoa	ice cream
1½ teaspoons baking soda	

Fudge Sauce:

1 (14½-ounce) can evaporated milk	1 teaspoon vanilla extract
2 cups sugar	½ teaspoon salt
4 ounces unsweetened chocolate	Whipped cream and maraschino cherries to garnish
½ stick butter	

For cake: Preheat oven to 350°. Grease and flour 9x13-inch pan. Cream sugar and shortening. Add eggs. Beat well. Sift flour, cocoa, soda and salt together and add to creamed mixture, alternately with buttermilk. Stir in vanilla. Bake 35 to 40 minutes or until done. Let cool and slice in half lengthwise (making 4½ x 13-inch halves). Spread vanilla ice cream on bottom layer. (May cut ice cream in 1-inch slices for ease in layering.) Cover with cake layer. Wrap tightly with plastic wrap. Overwrap with aluminum foil. Freeze.

For fudge sauce: Heat milk and sugar to rolling boil, stirring constantly. Boil and stir one minute. Add chocolate, stirring until melted. Beat over heat until smooth. (If sauce looks slightly curdled, continue to beat until smooth.) Remove from heat, blend in butter, vanilla and salt. This may be made a few days ahead and reheated in double boiler before serving. Serve fudge sauce warm over squares of cake filled with ice cream. Top with whipped cream and cherry.

Yield: 10 to 15 servings

BEAR IN MIND: *Dust pans for chocolate cakes with cocoa instead of flour and avoid "white lumps".*

Cream of Coconut Cake

3	cups sugar	1	(3½-ounce) can flaked
4	sticks margarine		coconut
9	eggs	1	(15½-ounce) can cream of
1	teaspoon vanilla extract		coconut
1	teaspoon almond extract		Powdered sugar for
3	cups all-purpose flour		garnish

Preheat oven to 350°. Grease and flour 10-inch tube pan. Cream sugar and margarine until fluffy. Add eggs, one at a time, beating well after each. Add vanilla and almond extract. Add flour gradually. Beat until batter is creamy. Add flaked coconut and mix well. Pour into pan. Bake 1 hour or until cake tests done. Remove from oven and while cake is still hot, spoon on a third of cream of coconut. Invert cake on plate and spoon remaining cream of coconut on sides and top. When cake is cool, sift powdered sugar on top.

Yield: 12 to 15 servings

Beary Special Pound Cake

3	sticks margarine, softened	6	eggs
1	(8-ounce) package cream	3	cups all-purpose flour
	cheese, softened		Dash salt
3	cups sugar	1½	teaspoons vanilla extract

Preheat oven to 325°. Coat 10-inch tube pan with cooking spray. Cream margarine and cream cheese. Add sugar gradually to mixture. Add eggs one at a time, beating well after each. Stir in flour and salt. Then add vanilla. Pour batter into pan. Bake 1½ hours.

Yield: 10 to 12 servings

BEAR FLAIR: *Slice cake in thirds, horizontally. Sweeten 1 pint whipped cream with 1 cup powdered sugar. Spread between layers. Place 1 cup sliced strawberries on each layer. For the finishing touch, glaze 12 to 16 whole strawberries with apricot preserves and cognac or brandy. Place hull side down on top of cake.*

BEAR IN MIND: *May be baked in 9x13-inch pan, 1 hour and 10 minutes.*

Miniature Fruit Cakes

1 cup sugar	1 (8-ounce) package candied
1 cup self-rising flour	cherries, chopped
1½ (8-ounce) packages	4 cups chopped pecans
dates, chopped	3 eggs

Preheat oven to 300°. Grease (do not flour) miniature muffin tins. Blend sugar and flour, add dates, cherries, and pecans. Beat eggs until foamy. Add eggs to sugar mixture. Pour batter into muffin tins. Use 1 tablespoon batter for each muffin. Do not pack down. Bake 10 to 20 minutes or until golden brown. Cool before removing from tins.

Yield: 5 to 7 dozen miniature cakes

***BEAR IN MIND:** This would make a bear-ly resistable Christmas gift packed in decorative tins or baskets.*

Individual Lemon Cheese Cakes

Cake:

6 tablespoons ice water	1½ cups all-purpose flour
1½ cups sugar	1½ teaspoons vanilla extract
6 eggs, separated	¾ teaspoon salt

Filling:

Juice and rind of 3 lemons	½ stick butter
1 cup sugar	Powdered sugar to dust
3 eggs, beaten	

Cake: Preheat oven to 325°. Grease 2 (7x11-inch) baking pans. Line with waxed paper. Combine water, sugar and egg yolks. Beat 10 minutes. Stir in flour, vanilla and salt. Fold in stiffly beaten egg whites. Bake 20 to 30 minutes or until done. When cool, split cakes lengthwise. Cut each layer into 12 squares. Spread filling between layers. Dust with powdered sugar.

For filling: Grate lemon rind. In top of double boiler mix juice from lemons, sugar and eggs. Cook and stir over boiling water until thick. Add butter and grated rind. Cool and spread between cake layers.

Yield: 1 dozen miniature cakes

Italian Cream Cake

a hint of orange

Cake:

2	sticks butter, softened	1	teaspoon vanilla extract
2	cups sugar	1	teaspoon orange-flavored liqueur
5	eggs, separated		
2	cups cake flour	1	(6-ounce) package flaked coconut
1	teaspoon baking soda		
1	cup buttermilk	1	cup finely chopped nuts

Frosting:

½	stick butter	1	teaspoon vanilla extract
2	(8-ounce) packages cream cheese, softened	1	teaspoon orange-flavored liqueur
1½	(1-pound) boxes powdered sugar, sifted	1	cup chopped nuts

For cake: Preheat oven to 350°. Grease 3 (9-inch) cake pans. Line with waxed paper. Grease again and flour. For best results, all ingredients should be at room temperature. In mixing bowl, cream butter and sugar. Add egg yolks, one at a time, beating well after each. Combine flour and baking soda. Add alternately with buttermilk to creamed mixture, beginning and ending with flour. Stir in flavorings, coconut and nuts. In separate bowl, beat egg whites until stiff, but not dry. Fold in batter. Pour into pans. Bake 20 to 25 minutes. Cool 10 minutes in pan and turn out onto wire racks. Cool completely before frosting.

For frosting: Cream butter and cream cheese. Add sugar, flavorings and nuts. Frost cake.

Yield: 16 to 20 servings

Pecan Torte

Cake:

2¼ cups cake flour
1½ cups brown sugar, firmly packed
1   cup milk
1½ sticks butter, softened

3   eggs
2   teaspoons baking powder
1½ teaspoons vanilla extract
¼   teaspoon salt
1   cup finely chopped pecans

Whipped cream filling:

½   pint whipped cream
2   tablespoons powdered sugar

Browned butter glaze:

2   tablespoons butter
1   cup powdered sugar, sifted

1   teaspoon vanilla extract
1   to 2 tablespoons hot water

For cake: Preheat oven to 350°. Grease and flour 3 (8 to 9-inch) cake pans. Beat flour, brown sugar, milk, butter, eggs, baking powder, vanilla and salt in large mixing bowl on low speed 30 seconds, scraping bowl constantly. Beat on high speed 3 minutes, scraping bowl occasionally. Stir in finely chopped pecans. Divide batter evenly among pans, spread evenly. (Batter will be thick and appear curdled.) Bake 20 to 25 minutes or until wooden pick inserted in center comes out clean. Cool 10 minutes; remove from pans. Cool completely. Fill layers with whipped cream filling. Spread browned butter glaze over top of cake. Garnish with pecan halves. Refrigerate torte until serving time. Refrigerate any remaining torte.

For filling: Beat whipping cream and powdered sugar in chilled bowl until stiff. Refrigerate until ready to assemble layers.

For glaze: Heat butter in saucepan over medium heat until delicate brown. Stir in powdered sugar and vanilla. Beat in water 1 tablespoon at a time, until desired consistency.

Yield: 16 to 20 servings

Sweet Potato Nut Roll

Filling:

1	cup powdered sugar, sifted	2	(3-ounce) packages cream cheese, softened
½	stick butter, softened	½	teaspoon vanilla extract

Cake:

3	eggs	½	teaspoon salt
1	cup sugar	1	teaspoon ginger
⅔	cup cooked and mashed sweet potatoes	2	teaspoons cinnamon
		½	teaspoon nutmeg
1	teaspoon lemon juice	1	cup chopped pecans
¾	cup all-purpose flour		Powdered sugar to dust
1	teaspoon baking powder		

Preheat oven to 350°. Grease and flour (10½ x 15½-inch) jelly roll pan. Combine all filling ingredients and beat until smooth. Set aside.

For cake: Beat eggs five minutes. Stir in sugar, sweet potatoes and lemon juice. Combine flour, baking powder, salt, and spices and fold into sweet potato mixture. Pour into pan. Sprinkle with nuts and bake 15 minutes. Sprinkle powdered sugar on clean dish towel and invert cake on towel. Roll immediately beginning with narrow edge. Cool. Unroll and spread on filling. Reroll and chill. Sprinkle top with powdered sugar before serving.

Yield: 12 servings.

BEAR IN MIND: *For a change, add a dash of rum to filling.*

Nutty-Orange Date Cake

Cake:

½ cup shortening	1 teaspoon baking powder
1 stick margarine	½ teaspoon salt
2 cups sugar	1⅓ cups buttermilk
4 eggs	1 cup chopped nuts
4 cups cake flour, divided	1 (8-ounce) package
1 teaspoon baking soda	chopped dates

Glaze:

2 cups sugar	2 teaspoons grated
1 cup orange juice	orange rind

For cake: Preheat oven to 300°. Grease and flour 10-inch tube pan. Cream shortening, margarine and sugar until light. Add eggs, one at a time, beating well after each egg. Combine 3½ cups flour, baking soda, baking powder and salt. Add alternately with buttermilk to creamed mixture, beginning and ending with flour. Using the remaining flour, dredge dates and nuts. Stir into batter. Pour into pan. Bake 1½ hours.

For glaze: Mix sugar and orange juice in saucepan. Bring to a rolling boil. Add rind. Pour over cake while still warm. Cool in pan.

Yield: 12 to 15 servings

BEAR IN MIND: *Flour or dredge dates, nuts or candied fruit before adding to cake batter, and they won't sink to the bottom.*

My Favorite Caramel Frosting

3 cups sugar, divided	Pinch salt
¾ cup evaporated milk	1 stick butter, cut in pieces
1 egg, beaten	1 teaspoon vanilla extract

Sprinkle ½ cup sugar in heavy saucepan. Place over medium heat, stirring constantly, until sugar melts and syrup is light golden brown. In separate bowl, combine remaining sugar, milk, egg and salt. Mix well. Stir in butter. Stir butter mixture into hot caramelized sugar. (The mixture will tend to lump, becoming smooth with further cooking.) Cook over medium heat, stirring frequently, until a candy thermometer reaches 230° (about 15 to 20 minutes). Cool 5 minutes. Add vanilla. Beat to almost spreading consistency and spread immediately on cooled cake.

Yield: Enough to cover 1 (2-layer) cake

Fabulous Cocoa Frosting

5	cups sugar	2	cups milk
½	cup cocoa	2	sticks butter
3	tablespoons all-purpose flour	1	teaspoon vanilla extract

In large saucepan, blend sugar, cocoa and flour. Add milk and cook on medium heat to a gentle boil so frosting reaches soft ball stage (233°). Remove from heat. Add butter and vanilla. Cook until butter melts. Remove from heat and cool to lukewarm. Beat until spreading consistency.

Yield: Frosting for one large cake

BEAR IN MIND: *Divide in half for beating so it will be easier to spread.*

Chocolate Marshmallow Frosting

wonderful frosting for brownies

2	ounces unsweetened chocolate	1	teaspoon vanilla extract
1	stick butter	2	cups miniature marshmallows
1½	cups powdered sugar	1	cup chopped pecans or walnuts
1	egg		

Melt chocolate and butter in top of double boiler. Cool. Combine sugar, egg, vanilla and chocolate mixture in bowl. Beat with electric mixer until smooth. Stir in marshmallows and nuts.

Yield: Enough to frost 1 (9x13-inch) cake

Pineapple Filling

1	(20-ounce) can crushed pineapple, undrained	1	tablespoon lemon juice Lemon rind to taste
1½	cups sugar	½	stick butter
¼	cup cornstarch		

Mix pineapple, sugar and cornstarch in medium-size saucepan. Add lemon juice and rind. Boil until thick. Add butter and cool slightly before frosting.

Yield: Enough to frost a 2-layer cake

Seven Minute Frosting

1½ cups sugar	2 teaspoons light corn syrup
3 egg whites	¼ teaspoon salt
5 tablespoons water	1 teaspoon vanilla extract

Combine sugar and egg whites in top of double boiler. Add water, corn syrup, salt and vanilla. Stir until blended. Place over boiling water. Beat with electric mixer until soft peaks form (7 minutes). Frost cake as soon as frosting is ready. Frosting will begin to harden quickly.

Yield: Enough frosting for a 2-layer cake

BEAR FLAIR: *This is especially good for coconut cake or lemon cheese cake.*

BEAR IN MIND: *Using a pastry bag and star cake decorating tip, pipe onto miniature Lane Cakes, page 301, for a Christmas open house.*

Butterscotch Cheesecake Bars

1 (12-ounce) package butterscotch morsels	1 (8-ounce) package cream cheese, softened
5½ tablespoons butter	1 (14-ounce) can sweetened condensed milk
2 cups graham cracker crumbs	1 teaspoon vanilla extract
1 cup chopped nuts	1 egg

Preheat oven to 350° (325° for glass dish). Grease 9x13-inch baking dish. In medium saucepan melt morsels and butter. Stir in crumbs and nuts. Press half the mixture firmly into bottom of baking dish. In large mixing bowl, beat cheese until fluffy; beat in condensed milk, vanilla and egg. Mix well. Pour over crumb mixture and top with remaining crumb mixture. Bake 25 to 30 minutes or until toothpick inserted in center comes out clean. Cool to room temperature. Chill before cutting into bars. Refrigerate leftovers.

Yield: 24 bars

Perfect Pecan Pastries

2 cups all-purpose flour	2 sticks butter, softened
¾ cup powdered sugar	

Topping:

½ cup brown sugar, firmly packed	1 stick plus 3 tablespoons butter, melted
3 tablespoons whipping cream	3½ cups coarsely chopped pecans
½ cup honey	

Preheat oven to 350°. Grease 9x12-inch baking pan. Sift flour and sugar and cut in butter until crumbly. Pat into pan. Bake 20 minutes until edges are light brown. Remove and set aside.

For topping: Combine sugar, cream, honey and butter. Stir in pecans. Coat completely. Spread over prepared crust. Return to oven and bake 25 minutes. Cool completely.

Yield: 24 squares

Czech Cookies

2 sticks butter, melted	2 cups chopped pecans
1 cup sugar	1 (16-ounce) jar apricot preserves
2 egg yolks	
2 cups all-purpose flour	

Preheat oven to 325°. Cream butter and sugar in bowl. Add egg yolks. Mix well. Add flour. Blend well. Fold in nuts. Pat half the batter on bottom of 8x11-inch baking pan. Spread with preserves. Pat remaining batter on top. Bake 35 to 40 minutes. Cool before cutting into squares.

Yield: 2 dozen squares

BEAR IN MIND: *This is better when mixed "by hand", rather than with electric mixer. To pat batter on top of preserves, divide into 6 portions and pat each flat. Overlap squares slightly, making sure to seal edges.*

Date-Nut Meringue Squares

4	egg whites	1	cup sugar
⅛	teaspoon salt	1	cup chopped dates
½	teaspoon vanilla extract	1	cup chopped nuts, toasted
½	teaspoon almond extract		

Preheat oven to 350°. Grease 8x12-inch pan. Beat egg whites, salt, vanilla and almond flavoring until stiff. Gradually add sugar. Fold in dates and nuts. Gently spread in pan. Bake 35 minutes or until golden. Cool and cut in squares.

Yield: 1½ dozen squares

BEAR IN MIND: *Use greased knife to slice to minimize crumbling.*

Rum-Butter Frosted Brownies

Brownies:

2	sticks butter	2	teaspoons vanilla extract
4	ounces unsweetened chocolate	1	cup all-purpose flour, sifted
4	eggs	¼	teaspoon salt
2	cups sugar	1½	cups chopped pecans

Rum-butter cream:

1	stick butter, softened	3	to 4 tablespoons rum
1	(1-pound) box powdered sugar	6	ounces unsweetened chocolate

For brownies: Preheat oven to 350°. Grease 9x13-inch baking pan. Melt butter and chocolate in medium saucepan over low heat. Cool. Beat eggs until fluffy. Gradually add sugar until mixture is thick. Stir in chocolate mixture and vanilla. Fold in flour and salt until smooth. Stir in nuts. Spread evenly in pan and bake 30 minutes or until shiny and firm on top. Cool completely.

For rum-butter cream: Blend butter with half of sugar. Beat in remaining sugar alternately with 3 to 4 tablespoons rum until spreading consistency. Spread over cooled brownies. Melt chocolate over low heat. Spread evenly over rum-butter cream to glaze. Let stand until firm and cut into squares.

Yield: 2 dozen squares

Mint Brownies

Brownie Layer:

1	stick butter, softened
1	cup sugar
4	eggs
1	cup all-purpose flour

½	teaspoon salt
1	(16-ounce) can chocolate syrup
1	teaspoon vanilla extract

Mint cream frosting:

½	stick butter, softened
2	cups powdered sugar, sifted

1	teaspoon peppermint extract
1	to 2 teaspoons milk

Chocolate glaze:

3	ounces semi-sweet chocolate chips

2	tablespoons butter
1	teaspoon vanilla extract

For brownies: Preheat oven to 350°. Grease and flour 9x13-inch baking pan. Cream butter; gradually add sugar, beating until light and fluffy. Add eggs, one at a time, beating well after each addition. Combine flour and salt; add to creamed mixture alternately with chocolate syrup, beginning and ending with flour mixture. Stir in vanilla. Pour batter into pan. Bake 25 to 28 minutes. Cool completely. (Brownies will shrink from sides of pan while cooling.)

For mint frosting: Cream butter; gradually add powdered sugar and then peppermint extract. Add 1 to 2 teaspoons of milk, and continue beating, to thin frosting to a spreadable consistency. Spread evenly over cooled brownies. Chill about 1 hour.

For chocolate glaze: Melt chocolate chips and butter in saucepan over low heat. Stir in vanilla. Drizzle glaze over mint frosting. Cover and chill until firm. Cut into bite-size pieces.

Yield: 5 dozen 1-inch squares

BEAR IN MIND: *Substitute crème de menthe for peppermint extract or add a drop of green food coloring to mint frosting for a "Christmas touch".*

Mocha Bars

Bars:

2 sticks butter	½ teaspoon salt
1 cup brown sugar, firmly packed	1 (6-ounce) package semi-sweet chocolate chips
1 tablespoon instant coffee	½ cup chopped pecans
2¼ cups all-purpose flour	
½ teaspoon baking powder	

Glaze:

½ (1-pound) box powdered sugar	1 tablespoon butter
	Evaporated milk to glaze

For bars: Preheat oven to 350°. Grease 9x13-inch baking dish. Cream butter and sugar. Add coffee, flour, baking powder and salt. Press into pan. Top with chocolate chips and pecans. Press into mixture. Bake 25 minutes.

For glaze: In saucepan over low heat mix together powdered sugar, butter and enough milk to make a glaze. Glaze while warm.

Yield: 2 dozen bars

Southern Toffee Shortbread

2 sticks butter, divided	1 (14-ounce) can sweetened condensed milk
6 tablespoons sugar, divided	
1 cup all-purpose flour	4 ounces semi-sweet chocolate
1 teaspoon baking powder	
1 tablespoon light corn syrup	

Preheat oven to 350°. Cream together 1 stick butter and 2 tablespoons sugar. Fold in flour and baking powder. Spread mixture in 9x9-inch pan and bake 25 minutes. Shortbread will be pale tan in color. Cool. In heavy saucepan, add remaining butter, remaining sugar, corn syrup and condensed milk and boil slowly until mixture coats wooden spoon, about 15 minutes. Spread mixture over shortbread and allow to cool. Melt chocolate and spread evenly over all. Cool completely. Cut in squares.

Yield: 2 dozen squares

Fudge Crispy Bars

1	(12-ounce) package milk chocolate chips	1	cup powdered sugar
1	stick butter	4	cups oven-toasted rice cereal
½	cup light corn syrup	½	cup chopped almonds, toasted
2	teaspoons vanilla extract		

Butter 9x13-inch pan. In medium saucepan, combine chips, butter and corn syrup. Stir over low heat until melted. Remove from heat and add vanilla extract and sugar. Stir in cereal and almonds and mix until well coated. Spread in pan. Chill until firm. Cut in squares. Store in refrigerator.

Yield: 2 dozen squares

Christmas Cookies

2¼	cups sifted all-purpose flour	2	eggs
1	teaspoon baking soda	1	(12-ounce) package semi-sweet chocolate chips
1	teaspoon salt	1	cup chopped pecans
2	sticks butter, softened	1	(10-ounce) can coconut
¾	cup granulated sugar	20	candied red cherries, chopped
¾	cup dark brown sugar, firmly packed	20	candied green cherries, chopped
1	teaspoon vanilla extract		
½	teaspoon water		

Preheat oven to 375°. Grease cookie sheets. Sift together flour, baking soda and salt and set aside. Cream together butter, sugars, vanilla and water. Beat eggs into butter mixture. Add flour mixture and mix thoroughly. Stir in chocolate chips, pecans, coconut and cherries. Drop dough by ½ teaspoonful onto cookie sheet. Bake 5 to 7 minutes. Remove from cookie sheet and cool on racks.

Yield: 10 dozen cookies

BEAR IN MIND: *This freezes well!*

Ginger Bears

1	cup shortening	2	to 3 teaspoons ginger
1	cup sugar	1	teaspoon cinnamon
1	cup molasses	1	teaspoon ground cloves
1	egg		Raisins, cinnamon-flavored
2	tablespoons vinegar		candies or any other small
5	cups all-purpose flour		decorative candies for
1½	teaspoons baking soda		garnish
½	teaspoon salt		

In mixing bowl, cream shortening and sugar, beating until light and fluffy. Add molasses, egg and vinegar; mix well. Combine flour, soda, salt, ginger, cinnamon and cloves; mix well. Gradually add flour mixture to molasses mixture, stirring well. Shape dough into a ball. Knead until smooth. Chill overnight.

Preheat oven to 375°. Divide dough in half. Place one portion in refrigerator. Roll half of dough to ⅛ to ¼-inch thickness on lightly floured surface. Cut with 3½-inch bear-shaped cookie cutter, and place on ungreased cookie sheets. Press raisins or other candies into dough for eyes, nose, mouth and buttons. Remove remaining dough and repeat process. Bake 6 to 7 minutes or until edges start to brown. Remove from pan, cool on wire racks.

Yield: 5 dozen (3½-inch) ginger bears

BEAR FLAIR: *Bear's "topcoat" may be frosted and sprinkled with finely chopped crystallized ginger.*

Gooey

5	large eggs	⅔	cup all-purpose flour
2½	cups sugar	3	tablespoons cocoa
2	sticks butter, softened	1¼	cups chopped pecans
2	teaspoons vanilla extract		

Preheat oven to 300°. Grease 12x14-inch baking pan. Beat eggs. Add sugar and beat 10 minutes. Add butter and vanilla. Sift together flour and cocoa and add to creamed mixture. Add nuts and mix by hand. Pour into baking pan and place it in a larger pan of water and bake 1 hour. Cut in squares.

Yield: 12 to 14 servings

BEAR FLAIR: *Any bear would love a scoop of ice cream on these!*

Children Can Bearly Wait Cookies

1	stick butter	3	cups oatmeal
½	cup milk	½	cup peanut butter
2	cups sugar	1	teaspoon vanilla extract
½	cup cocoa		

In saucepan, combine butter, milk, sugar and cocoa. Bring to a boil and boil 1 minute. Remove from heat. Add oatmeal, peanut butter and vanilla. Mix well. Drop by teaspoonfuls onto waxed paper. Cool and eat!

Yield: 3 dozen cookies

Lemon Caraway Cookies

different and not too sweet

1	stick butter, slightly softened		Grated rind of ½ lemon
1	cup sugar	2¼	tablespoons lemon juice
1	egg	2⅓	cups all-purpose flour
1⅛	teaspoons caraway seed	½	teaspoon baking powder
		½	teaspoon salt

Cream butter and sugar. Add egg and continue beating until light. Add caraway seed, lemon rind and lemon juice. Mix well. Combine flour, baking powder and salt. Stir into creamed mixture. Shape into a roll about 2 inches in diameter. Wrap in wax paper and chill 1 hour. Remove from refrigerator and roll lightly on counter so that cookies will be round when cut. Chill several more hours or overnight. Preheat oven to 375°. Grease cookie sheet. With sharp knife, cut dough in slices about ⅛-inch thick. Place on cookie sheet. Bake about 10 minutes. Cool on racks. Store in airtight container.

Yield: 6 dozen cookies

BEAR FLAIR: *Good with ice cream or fresh fruit.*

Bear Bites

2	egg whites	1	teaspoon vanilla extract
⅛	teaspoon cream of tartar	1	(6-ounce) package semi-
½	teaspoon salt		sweet chocolate chips
¾	cup sugar	¼	cup chopped pecans

Preheat oven to 350°. Line cookie sheet with brown paper. Beat egg whites, cream of tartar and salt until stiff. Slowly beat in sugar. Add vanilla, chocolate chips and pecans. Place teaspoon-size dollops on prepared cookie sheets. Bake until light brown, about 20 minutes.

Yield: 4 dozen cookies

BEAR IN MIND: *Avoid making these on a rainy day.*

Crunchy Oatmeal Cookies

1	cup granulated sugar	1	teaspoon baking soda
1	cup brown sugar,	½	teaspoon cinnamon
	firmly packed	¼	teaspoon nutmeg
2	sticks butter	2	cups oatmeal
2	eggs	2	cups flaked coconut
2	cups all-purpose flour	1	cup chopped pecans
⅛	teaspoon salt	2	teaspoons vanilla extract
1	teaspoon baking powder		

Preheat oven to 300°. Cream sugars and butter. Add eggs and beat well. Sift together flour, salt, baking powder, baking soda, cinnamon and nutmeg. Add to creamed mixture and mix well. Stir in oatmeal, coconut, pecans and vanilla. Roll into 1-inch balls and place on ungreased cookie sheet. Bake until light brown, 10 to 12 minutes.

Yield: 6 dozen cookies

Mary's Chocolate Chip Cookies

very crisp and delicious

2	sticks butter, softened	1	teaspoon salt
1	cup oil	2	eggs, beaten, room
1	cup granulated sugar		temperature
1	cup powdered sugar, sifted	1	teaspoon vanilla extract
4	cups all-purpose flour	1	(12-ounce) package
1	teaspoon baking powder		chocolate chips
1	teaspoon baking soda	½	cup chopped nuts, optional

Preheat oven to 350°. In mixing bowl, combine butter, oil and sugars. Cream well. In another bowl, mix flour, baking powder, soda and salt. Add to creamed mixture alternately with eggs. Stir in vanilla, chocolate chips and nuts. Drop by scant teaspoonfuls onto ungreased cookie sheet. Bake 10 to 12 minutes. Cool a few minutes on cookie sheet. Remove cookies to cooling rack. Store under lock and key!

Yield: 13 to 14 dozen (2-inch) cookies

Wanda's Wonderful Toffee Chips

	Enough graham crackers to line jelly roll pan	1	(12-ounce) package semi-sweet chocolate chips
2	sticks butter		Heath bits or toasted
1	cup light brown sugar, firmly packed		almonds to sprinkle

Preheat oven to 400°. Line 10x15-inch jelly roll pan with foil. Place crackers in single layer on bottom of pan. In medium saucepan, melt butter and sugar. Boil exactly 3 minutes. Pour mixture over crackers and bake exactly 5 minutes. Remove from oven and while hot sprinkle with chocolate chips. When chips are melted, spread chocolate evenly over top with buttered spatula. Sprinkle with Heath bits or toasted almonds. Cool to room temperature. Chill several hours. Break into pieces and store in tightly-sealed container in refrigerator.

Yield: About 3 dozen broken pieces

Cracker Surprise

1   (18-ounce) jar creamy or
    crunchy-style peanut
    butter
1   (1-pound) box butter-
    flavored crackers

1   (16-ounce) package vanilla
    confectionary coating

Spread peanut butter between 2 crackers, making a sandwich. Melt vanilla coating on 70% power in microwave, stirring every three minutes, until smooth. Dip sandwiches in coating and allow to dry on waxed paper. Must store in airtight container.

Yield: Approximately 36 crackers

BEAR IN MIND: *Try other flavors of confectionary coating (Melt 'n' Mold).*

Toasted Almond Truffles

½   cup evaporated milk
¼   cup sugar
1   (12-ounce) package milk
    chocolate chips

½   to 1 teaspoon almond
    extract
1   cup finely chopped
    almonds, toasted

In small heavy saucepan, mix evaporated milk and sugar. Cook over medium heat, stirring constantly, until mixture comes to a full boil. Boil 3 minutes longer, stirring constantly. Remove from heat and stir in chocolate chips and almond extract. Mix until chips are completely melted and mixture is smooth. Chill 45 minutes. Shape into balls about 1 inch in size. Roll in chopped, toasted almonds. Chill until ready to serve.

Yield: 2½ to 3 dozen truffles

BEAR IN MIND: *Try other extract flavorings such as coconut or mint for a different taste.*

Macadamia Nut Truffles

a delicious taste treat

1	(12-ounce) package semi-sweet chocolate chips	⅛	teaspoon salt
¾	(14-ounce) can sweetened condensed milk	1	teaspoon vanilla extract
		40	macadamia nuts
			Cocoa to roll truffles

In saucepan, over low heat, melt chips. Remove from heat. Add milk, salt and vanilla. Chill 45 minutes. Wrap each nut in enough chocolate to form 1-inch ball. Roll in cocoa. Chill until ready to serve.

Yield: 40 truffles

Christmas Strawberry Delights

4	(3-ounce) packages straw-berry-flavored gelatin	1	cup sweetened condensed milk
2	cups finely ground almonds		Red and green sugar crystals to dredge
2	cups flaked coconut		

Blend all ingredients well. Cover and chill overnight. When mixture is at room temperature, mold into strawberry shapes. Roll in red sugar crystals. Dip stem end in green sugar crystals. Dye almond slivers for stems. Insert stems. Store in airtight container in refrigerator.

Yield: 6 to 8 dozen

Raspberry Sauce

1	(10-ounce) package frozen raspberries, thawed	2	tablespoons sugar
		1	tablespoon cornstarch

Press thawed raspberries through a sieve to remove seeds, reserving juice. In small saucepan, combine sugar and cornstarch; stir well. Gradually add raspberries and their juice to sugar mixture. Bring to a boil over medium heat, stirring constantly. Cook 2 minutes. Put sauce in covered container and chill.

Yield: About 1 cup sauce

BEAR FLAIR: *Serve over ice cream, cake, trifle or Lemon Custard in Meringue Shells, page 266.*

Pineapple Sauce Terrific

1	cup unsweetened pineapple juice	3	tablespoons butter
½	cup sugar		Grated rind of 1 lemon
2	tablespoons cornstarch		Grated rind of ½ orange
			Juice of 1 lemon

In top of double boiler, combine pineapple juice, sugar and cornstarch. Stir constantly until it thickens. Add butter, rinds and lemon juice. Stir until smooth and thick.

Yield: About 1 cup sauce

BEAR FLAIR: *Serve hot over gingerbread, pound cake or muffins.*

BEAR IN MIND: *This can be cooked in microwave, using 1-quart measuring cup. Cook on MEDIUM-HIGH about 5 minutes, whisking after each minute. Quick and easy!*

Chocolate Fudge Sauce

3	ounces unsweetened chocolate	¾	cup evaporated milk
1	egg, well-beaten	1	teaspoon vanilla extract
1	cup sugar	½	cup chopped pecans, optional

In top of double boiler melt chocolate over hot water. Combine well-beaten egg, sugar and milk in small bowl. Add to melted chocolate and cook about 20 minutes, stirring with whisk. Remove from heat and stir in vanilla; add pecans if desired. Cool before serving. May be refrigerated and reheated in double boiler to serve hot.

Yield: 2 cups

BEAR FLAIR: *Great over ice cream or as a dip for strawberries.*

BEAR IN MIND: *Easy to do in microwave, if you're in a hurry. Melt chocolate in 1-quart measuring cup on LOW 1 to 2 minutes. Add combined egg, milk and sugar. Cook on MEDIUM about 4 minutes, stirring with whisk after each minute. Stir in vanilla.*

Saucy Apple Sensation

4	Golden Delicious apples, divided	½	teaspoon vanilla extract
1	cup apple juice	½	pint whipping cream
	Juice of 1 lemon	½	cup orange juice
1½	teaspoons sugar	1½	tablespoons orange-flavored liqueur
1	cinnamon stick		

Peel, core and quarter 3 apples. Put apples, apple juice, lemon juice, sugar and cinnamon in 3-quart saucepan. Cover and cook on medium heat until apples are soft (about 15 minutes). Cool and add vanilla. Put in covered container and refrigerate 12 to 24 hours. Discard cinnamon stick. Purée in blender. Add whipping cream and orange juice. Grate the remaining apple (unpeeled) and stir into sauce along with liqueur.

Yield: 5 cups

BEAR FLAIR: *Serve cold over hot apple muffins or Fruit Rage Coffeecake, page 85. Is also great over gingerbread.*

BEAR IN MIND: *For a refreshing summer dessert, serve in champagne glasses. Put a dollop of sour cream, dusted with freshly grated nutmeg. Can also add mint leaf.*

Caramel Sauce

1	(1-pound) box brown sugar	1	tablespoon butter
2	egg yolks	1	teaspoon vanilla extract
½	pint whipping cream	½	teaspoon salt

In medium saucepan, cook brown sugar, egg yolks and cream until creamy. Add butter, vanilla and salt. Stir until smooth. Serve warm over ice cream, gingerbread or a pound cake.

Yield: About 1½ cups sauce

Grin And Bear It

GRIN AND BEAR IT!
When Guests Catch You Bare-Handed

*Have an "ace" up your sleeve by keeping a few bare necessities in your pantry, refrigerator or freezer.

Pantry: canned crab, salmon, shrimp or tuna, artichokes, water chestnuts, bean sprouts, biscuit mix, capers, pimiento, garlic, canned mushrooms, olive oil, pasta, rice, Worcestershire, hot pepper sauce, soy sauce, molasses, pudding mixes, confectioners' sugar, jellies and preserves, crackers

Refrigerator: cream cheese, olives, prepared horseradish, mustard, bacon, celery, lemons, mayonnaise, parsley

Freezer: berries, ground meat, ice cream, nuts, Parmesan or cheddar cheese, pie shells, phyllo dough, shrimp, chicken stock, vegetables

*Mix ¼ cup melted butter, 2 tablespoons Worcestershire sauce, ¾ teaspoon seasoned salt, ½ teaspoon garlic powder, ¼ teaspoon cayenne or red pepper, and 24-ounce jar mixed nuts or pecans. Cook in covered 3-quart microwave dish on HIGH for 3½ minutes. Stir and cook another 3½ minutes. Stir and spread on paper-lined surface to cool. Store in tightly covered container.

*Wrap whole water chestnuts with ⅓ bacon strip. Bake in 350⁰ oven, 15 minutes. Remove and drain drippings. Combine ¼ cup granulated sugar, ¼ cup brown sugar and ½ cup ketchup. Pour over bacon/chestnuts. Bake another 15 minutes. Serve hot.

*Place thinly sliced onions on Melba rounds, cover generously with mayonnaise, then Parmesan cheese. Bake or broil. Serve hot.

*Spread a softened 8-ounce package cream cheese with hot pepper jelly and surround with crackers or bread triangles.

*Spread thinly sliced ham with cream cheese spread, add a well-drained asparagus spear to each slice. Roll up tightly and slice at ½-inch intervals.

*Create a quick spread, using a 4½-ounce can of shrimp with 6 ounces of cream cheese, 1 tablespoon green onions, ¼ teaspoon hot pepper sauce and 1 tablespoon lemon juice. Use on crackers or make finger sandwiches.

*Stack bologna slices with a flavored cream cheese spread or a cheddar cheese spread; spreading on each slice, forming a "stack" of bologna about an inch or so high. Cut into wedges.

*Chop a 2½-ounce package of smoked, pressed turkey, ham or beef and 3 green onions (with tops) and combine with 1 cup mayonnaise. Chill to blend flavors. Serve with triscuits or vegetable sticks.

*Core a large dill pickle, drain well and fill with Old English cheese spread. Chill (or put in freezer a few minutes) and slice ¼-inch thick.

*Whip ½ cup whipping cream and mix with 2 to 3 tablespoons caviar and 1 to 2 tablespoons chopped onion and garnish with slices of hard-cooked eggs and crackers.

*Combine 1 cup jellied cranberry sauce, 1 teaspoon grated onion, ¼ cup finely chopped celery and 1 cup coarse saltine cracker crumbs. Blend well and spread 1 tablespoon on each of 12 slices boiled ham. Roll up tightly. Chill and slice each roll into thirds.

*Sausage balls made from 1 pound cheddar cheese, 1 pound ground hot sausage and 2 to 3 cups biscuit mix. Bake 1-inch balls in 300⁰ oven, 25 minutes.

*Add a small slice of Monterey Jack cheese with jalapeño peppers to a tostado and broil or heat in microwave until hot and cheese is melted.

*Combine equal portions chilled gingerale and white grape juice or apple cider. Add a sprig of mint.

*Whip up a quiche, using a frozen pie shell and ingredients and leftovers you have on hand.

*Carrot salad can be quickly prepared in food processor or blender.

*Pasta salads can be hot or cold and are quick as a flash to prepare.

*Mold hot, cooked rice to which you've stirred in chopped fresh parsley and finely diced cooked carrots. Unmold in a casserole in which you have baked any of our poultry recipes, using a sauce. Sauce doubles as gravy for rice.

*Make cream puff pastry in entrée size instead of miniature size. Freeze and they are ready to be filled with a multitude of salads or creamed dishes.

*Make a spinach ring soufflé by combining a 10-ounce package frozen spinach (thawed and squeezed dry), 3 well-beaten eggs, ½ cup mayonnaise, 2 tablespoons finely minced green onions, 1 tablespoon prepared horseradish and ½ teaspoon salt and bake in an oiled ring mold at 350⁰, 30 to 40 minutes. Turn out onto platter and fill with braised carrots.

*Make a fruit rice curry mix using: 1 cup uncooked regular rice, 1 tablespoon instant minced onion, 2 teaspoons curry powder, 2 beef bouillon cubes, crushed (or use the instant granules), ½ teaspoon salt, ¼ cup mixed dried fruits (chopped), 2 tablespoons golden raisins, and ¼ cup blanched slivered almonds. Combine ingredients and store in airtight container. Makes 2 cups mix. When the unexpected happens, prepare rice using 2½ cups water and 2 tablespoons butter.

*Many of our recipes are fast and use ingredients you probably have on hand: Fancy Franks, Marvelous Mustard Sauce, or Artichokes and Chilies Dip, just to mention a few.

318

GRIN AND BEAR IT!
When You Can't Bear The Results

*Wilted cucumbers? Pare and slice thinly using a vegetable peeler. Place in layers in bowl, salting each layer. Place a weighted plate over cucumbers. Cover and refrigerate 3 to 6 hours. Drain and toss with sour cream or yogurt and garnish with chopped dill, parsley or basil.

*Over-whipped cream that has started to turn to butter? Keep going and actually make butter by putting it in food processor, add ½ cup ice and process until you have watery butter. Drain thoroughly and use. Makes delicious tasting butter!

*Whipping cream past expiration date? Try adding ⅛ teaspon baking soda for each cup of whipping cream before you start to whip. This should prevent curdling.

*The soup's too salty? Add a sliced raw potato and cook a few minutes, remove the potato.

*If you've overcooked your vegetables? Puree and use as side dish or use as a thickener for soup or gravy or use as topping for casserole.

*For vegetables that are dull in color, garnish with toasted pine nuts or almonds; or sprinkle with grated cheese or browned bread crumbs.

*Is the sauce or gravy lumpy? Process in blender until smooth.

*Is the sauce too thick? Add a little more liquid gradually, stirring constantly.

*Is the sauce too thin? Add 2 beaten egg yolks to which a small amount of the hot sauce has been added and cook another 2 minutes.

*If an egg-based sauce begins to separate, add a tablespoon of ice water and whisk vigorously.

*If the gravy is too salty, add a little brown sugar or vinegar.

*If the rice is overcooked and gummy? Use it in soups, combine with ground beef in casseroles, use in a custard, or add to an omelet.

*Is the pasta overcooked? Throw it away; there's very little to salvage.

*If the meat is too rare? Slice and return to oven to complete cooking.

*If meat is too well done? Slice and serve with sauce or grind up for hash or chop and saute with vegetables.

*If gelatin is stubborn in unmolding? Loosen gelatin with a knife around the edges and hold mold in hot water (up to rim) for 10 seconds. Invert onto serving plate.

*To avoid trouble, be sure gelatin is completely dissolved before continuing with recipe. Measure all liquids carefully.

*Fresh pineapples, figs, mangos and papayas have an emzyme that prevents gelatin from setting; use only canned forms of these fruits when making congealed dishes.

*Is the edge of pie crust burned? Remove burned portion. Pipe whipped cream over the "damage". Next time place a strip of aluminum foil around the edge of crust to prevent the problem. Remove foil during the last 15 minutes of baking to brown the edge.

*If cake is too soggy? Slice and toast.

*If cake is too dry? Soak with rum, brandy or a good syrup; or cut cake into cubes and serve with chocolate fondue; or make an English trifle; or mix with pudding and top with meringue.

*If cake looks pitiful? Cover the sides and top with icing and/or fruit; or cut into squares and top each serving with whipped cream.

*Avoid getting caught in a bear trap!

—Don't make candy on a hot, humid day. Room should be 60⁰ to 68⁰F and cooking area needs to be free of drafts and hot vapors of other foods.

—Jams and jellies don't jell well on rainy or very humid days.

—Yeast breads are also affected by high humidity. Avoid drafts for rising times. Temperature of room needs to be between 75⁰ and 80⁰F.

—Damp, humid weather affects meringues also, causing them to be soggy. Keep in airtight containers.

—Croissants should be made only on dry, cold days. Warmth will cause butter to melt and dough will be greasy.

—Crème fraîche needs to be prepared in a warm room.

—Homemade mayonnaise is heading for disaster if made during a thunderstorm. Make sure the bowl is warm and thoroughly dry.

—Avoid overbeating, inaccurate measuring or oven temperature too low to prevent cake from too heavy texture.

—Chill bowl and beaters before whipping cream; and be sure there is no trace of fat or egg yolk in the bowl.

—Remove muffins and bread from pans as soon as they come out of the oven; standing in hot pans will cause them to become soggy.

—Remember that eggs separate best when cold, yet they whip better when at room temperature.

GRIN AND BEAR IT!
When Your Cupboard Is Bare

Arrowroot (1 tablespoon) = 2 tablespoons all-purpose flour mixed with 1 tablespoon cornstarch

Cornstarch (1 tablespoon) = 2 tablespoons all-purpose flour

Baking powder (1 teaspoon) = ¼ teaspoon baking soda mixed with ½ teaspoon cream of tartar

Buttermilk (1 cup) = 1 tablespoon vinegar or lemon juice combined with whole milk to measure 1 cup OR 1 cup plain yogurt OR 1¾ teaspoons cream of tartar and enough milk to measure 1 cup

Chili sauce = 1 cup tomato sauce mixed with ½ cup sugar and 1 tablespoon vinegar

Corn syrup (1 cup) = ¾ cup sugar plus ¼ cup water

Cream
  (light, 1 cup) = 3 tablespoons butter and ⅞ cup milk

  (half and half, 1 cup) = 1½ tablespoons butter and ⅞ cup milk

  (whipping, 1 cup) = 5 tablespoons butter and ¾ cup milk

  (sour, 1 cup) = 3 tablespoons butter and ⅞ cup sour milk OR 1 tablespoon lemon juice plus enough evaporated milk to make 1 cup OR 1 cup cottage cheese, ¼ cup buttermilk and ½ teaspoon lemon juice

Sweetened condensed milk (1 cup) = 1⅓ cups nonfat dry milk powder mixed with ½ cup sugar, 3 tablespoons butter and ½ cup boiling water

Ginger (1 tablespoon, fresh) = ⅛ teaspoon powdered ginger

Horseradish (1 tablespoon, fresh) = 2 tablespoons prepared horseradish

Mace (1 teaspoon) = 1 teaspoon nutmeg

Mustard (1 tablespoon, prepared)	=	1 teaspoon dry mustard
Mushrooms (½ pound, fresh)	=	6-ounce can mushrooms
(3 ounces, dried)	=	1 pound fresh mushrooms
Onion (1 small or ¼ cup, chopped)	=	1 tablespoon instant minced (dehydrated)
Saccharin (¼ grain)	=	1 teaspoon sugar
Artificial sweetener (⅛ teaspoon liquid)	=	1 teaspoon sugar
Tapioca (1 tablespoon, quick-cooking)	=	1 tablespoon flour
Tomato juice (1 cup)	=	½ cup tomato sauce plus ½ cup water
Tomatoes (1 cup, packed)	=	½ cup tomato sauce
Tomato sauce (2 cups)	=	¾ cup tomato paste plus 1 cup water
1 (10¾-ounce) can tomato soup	=	1 cup tomato sauce plus ¼ cup water
1 (10¾-ounce) can cream soup	=	1½ cups thick white sauce
Garlic (1 small clove)	=	⅛ teaspoon garlic powder
Herbs (1 tablespoon, fresh chopped	=	1 teaspoon dried or ¼ teaspoon powdered
Lemon (1 medium)	=	1 to 3 tablespoon juice
	=	1 to 1½ teaspoons grated rind
(1 teaspoon lemon juice)	=	½ teaspoon vinegar
(1 teaspoon grated rind)	=	½ teaspoon lemon extract
Cake flour (1 cup)	=	⅞ cup all-purpose flour
Self-rising flour (1 cup)	=	1 cup all-purpose flour plus 1 teaspoon baking powder and ½ teaspoon salt
Unsweetened chocolate (1 ounce)	=	3 tablespoons cocoa plus 1 tablespoon butter or margarine OR 3 tablespoons carob powder plus 2 tablespoons water
Unsweetened chocolate (1 ounce plus 4 teaspoons sugar)	=	1⅔ ounces semisweet chocolate
Cheddar cheese (4 ounces)	=	1 cup shredded cheese

INDEX

328

Unbearably Good!
Junior Service League of Americus
P.O. Box 92
Americus, GA 31709

Please send me _____ copies of **Unbearably Good!** at $14.95 (plus $2.00 postage and handling) per book. (Georgia residents add 6% sales tax.)

Enclosed is my check or money order for $ _____

Name _____

Address _____

City _____ State _____ Zip _____

Unbearably Good!
Junior Service League of Americus
P.O. Box 92
Americus, GA 31709

Please send me _____ copies of **Unbearably Good!** at $14.95 (plus $2.00 postage and handling) per book. (Georgia residents add 6% sales tax.)

Enclosed is my check or money order for $ _____

Name _____

Address _____

City _____ State _____ Zip _____

Unbearably Good!
Junior Service League of Americus
P.O. Box 92
Americus, GA 31709

Please send me _____ copies of **Unbearably Good!** at $14.95 (plus $2.00 postage and handling) per book. (Georgia residents add 6% sales tax.)

Enclosed is my check or money order for $ _____

Name _____

Address _____

City _____ State _____ Zip _____

-- --

Unbearably Good!
Junior Service League of Americus
P.O. Box 92
Americus, GA 31709

Please send me _____ copies of **Unbearably Good!** at $14.95
(plus $2.00 postage and handling) per book. (Georgia residents add 6%
sales tax.)

Enclosed is my check or money order for $ _____

Name _____

Address _____

City _____ State _____ Zip _____

-- --

Unbearably Good!
Junior Service League of Americus
P.O. Box 92
Americus, GA 31709

Please send me _____ copies of **Unbearably Good!** at $14.95
(plus $2.00 postage and handling) per book. (Georgia residents add 6%
sales tax.)

Enclosed is my check or money order for $ _____

Name _____

Address _____

City _____ State _____ Zip _____

-- --

Unbearably Good!
Junior Service League of Americus
P.O. Box 92
Americus, GA 31709

Please send me _____ copies of **Unbearably Good!** at $14.95
(plus $2.00 postage and handling) per book. (Georgia residents add 6%
sales tax.)

Enclosed is my check or money order for $ _____

Name _____

Address _____

City _____ State _____ Zip _____

-- --

BARE PAGE

BARE PAGE